In *The Indie Producer's Handbook: Creative Producing from A to Z,* Myrl Schreibman has undertaken a doubly daunting task. The first is to define the producer's role in the seemingly paradoxical context of a popular art form where the very best films are uniquely personal visions realized in fully collaborative ways. Oil and water must be made to mix. The second challenge is achieving success in the arena of independent film production where the freedom to create without boundaries inevitably hits the wall of limited resources.

To help producers navigate these complexities Schreibman provides down-to-earth pragmatic advice that draws on his long experience as an independent filmmaker and film school educator. He provides us with both specific information that can be used for day-to-day problem solving and wise counsel on the producer's mission that can serve to chart a life-long career.

Most importantly, we gain an appreciation of how a creative producer must be an adroit juggler of multiple roles—at once a financial provider, resource manager, social engineer and above all, an obsessed visionary.

—Robert Rosen, Dean, UCLA School of
Theater Film and Television

THE INDIE PRODUCER'S HANDBOOK

CREATIVE PRODUCING
FROM A TO Z

BY MYRL A. SCHREIBMAN

ifilm publishing

THE INDIE PRODUCER'S HANDBOOK
Creative Producing from A to Z
Copyright © 2001 Myrl A. Schreibman

LONE EAGLE PUBLISHING COMPANY, LLC™
1024 N. Orange Dr.
Hollywood, CA 90038
Phone 323.308.3400 or 800.815.0503
A division of IFILM® Corporation, www.ifilmpro.com

Cover design by Lindsay Albert
Creative direction by Sean Alatorre
Book design by Carla Green
Photo of the author courtesy of John Josepho

Printed in the United States of America
10 9 8 7 6 5 4 3 2 1

Library of Congress Cataloging-in-Publication Data

Schreibman, Myrl A.
    The indie producers handbook : creative producing from A-Z /
    Myrl A. Schreibman.
        p. cm.
    Includes index.
    ISBN 1-58065-037-6
      1. Motion pictures--Production and direction. 2. Low budget motion
    pictures. I. Title.

    PN1995.9.P7 S345 2001
    791.43'0232--dc21   2001029485

Select references:
Film Production: The Complete Uncensored Guide to Independent Filmmaking, Greg Merritt, Lone Eagle Publishing, L.L.C., 1998.
The Practical Art of Motion Picture Sound, David Lewis Yewdall, M.P.S.E., Focal Press, 1999.
The Industry Labor Guide, 2000 Edition, Entertainment Publishers Inc.
The Directors Guild of America Basic Agreement, 1987.
The Directors Guild of America Freelance Live and Tape Television Agreement of 1993.
The Screen Actors Guild Codified Basic Agreement of 1989 for Independent Producers.

Some definitions used in the Producer's Vocabulary are courtesy of *Filmmaker's Dictionary, 2nd Edition*; copyright Ralph A. Singleton and Lone Eagle Publishing, 2000.

Some of the information contained herein relating to issues of specific guild or union contracts are an interpretive summary. The reader should review the final contracts of all guild and union agreements for precise interpretations of the particulars of each contract.

Distributed to the trade by National Book Network, 800-462-6420

IFILM and Lone Eagle Publishing Company are registered trademarks.

CONTENTS

CHAPTER 9: THE COMPLETION PERIOD

CHAPTER 10: ADMINISTRATION

CHAPTER 11: PUTTING IT ALL TOGETHER

CHAPTER 12: PRODUCING

EPILOGUE

ACKNOWLEDGMENTS

My deepest appreciation and warmest friendship is extended to all the wonderful people who helped make this book a reality: my teaching assistant (and now a director in his own right) Jason Moore, for convincing me to write this book for student filmmakers everywhere; Gil Cates, Lew Hunter and Bob Rosen for their generous words and thoughts included in the book; Adrian Morales for keeping me healthy during its writing; Robert Fiveson for his long-standing friendship; Debbie Allen, Kelly Asbury, Steve Benson, Roger Burlage, John Caldwell, John Coffey, Alex Cox, Del Crooks, Tom Denove, Len Ephraim, Stu Fox, Gyula Gazdag, Eugene Robert Glazer, Bob Gordon, Carla Green, David Haber, Lewis Horwitz, Rawn Hutchinson, John Josepho, Steve Kaminski, Madeline Kozlowski, Sandra Lawton, Joe Lisuzzo, Jeff Margolis, William McDonald, Maggie Murphy, Nancylee Myatt, Nancy Richardson, Chip and David Selby, Lennie Shapiro, Johnny Simmons, Abby Singer, Penelope Spheeris, Herb Stein, Steven M. Stein of Ratner & Prestia, Martin Terrones, Truman Van Dyke, Jamie Wooten and David Lewis Yewdall, for their comments and contributions; Will Gotay, Delia Salvi and Patsy Lake for their endless support and affection; my son, Petty Officer 2nd Class Eyan Schreibman USN, for his love and his belief in me; and most of all: my students, who took reams of notes in my producing classes and who—after they went to work in the business—came back to tell me that they utilized what they had learned. I also thank the hundreds of people I have worked with and met in the industry over the years who have instilled the knowledge and wisdom that only experiences and relationships can teach. And a very special appreciation to the holy trinity: my publisher, Jeff Black, whose energy and wisdom have been invaluable; Norman Hollyn, who pushed for clarity with his notes on the original manuscript; and of course my editor, Lauren Rossini, whose stern, gentle compassion nurtured the life of the book. Finally, to the many others who have so freely given, I thank you.

FOREWORD

Myrl Schreibman knows the business of film production. More important-ly, he knows the business of film. In his new book, *The Indie Producer's Handbook: Creative Producing from A to Z,* Myrl describes the details of all the varied elements that go into the usually chaotic and always surprising activities that result in a motion picture film.

In detailing the producer's role of bringing these disparate and sometimes conflicting elements together, Myrl analyses each person's responsibility and how these individual jobs translate into developing a clear and focused film "vision."

There is a great deal to be said about the usually ignored concern for developing a constructive and positive mood on the set. Myrl Schreibman believes that everyone working on a film can be creative. Indeed it is the har-nessing of each individual's creative drive and support that contributes to a fine film achievement.

Congratulations to Myrl for focusing us all on the creativity in each one of us. That is indeed the 'business' of a great producer.

—Gilbert Cates

INTRODUCTION

by Lew Hunter, author of *Lew Hunter's Screenwriting 434*

I want you, and all around you, to read this book because it is the best @#&%#@ book written about PRODUCING. Why? Because Myrl Schreibman is a current real life Producer.

On my knees I begged Myrl to call his book *SEX, ACTION, VIOLENCE: The Creative Independent Producers Handbook.* I have produced over 100 hours of film and entertainment and I know darn well that our daily existence is fraught with sex, violence and action. "Sex" not as it relates to the story but as it corresponds to the blasted director desperately hustling everyone on the set so he can get a performance with them privately later that night, while you the producer are trying desperately to get the director to do the last shot before the company looses the light. "Action" because as a creative producer you're always trying to hustle up some kind of future screen action so your house payments can be met and your child can go to Harvard. Finally of course, the "violence" you're going to inflict on the writer who wrote the line *"and the Indians took the town."* It just happens to be a line you can't get out of the screenplay because some suited studio executive loves the line and/or the Indians.

I can go on forever about how producers who, on an hourly basis, must deal with sex, action and violence in an incomprehensible compendium of circumstances before and behind the camera. Myrl knows them very well. Many industry war stories are not only just that but also very real because the buck stops with you, the producer, even when there are network, studio, or finance people to answer to and a director and an entire production company that waits for your guidance. There are sets of eyes that look to you for a nod, a headshake or a scream. And this book will keep you from doing the latter less often.

I first met Myrl when he showed up to my dailies of *Fallen Angel* at Columbia Television. Myrl was under contract to the studio as a producer and director at the time and I asked him with open eyes why he was at my dailies so often. He said that the buzz on the lot was that the picture was going great and he was there to see and learn and to gather more producing knowledge and wisdom. I think he looked at me as if I was a refugee from some cuckoo's nest because I knew of his producing credentials at dealing with "mushugannah" people, specifically actors and directors (he was a director himself!), in movies, television and the theater.

Hollywood is choked with actors who never act, directors who never direct, writers who never write and producers who never produce. Myrl Schreibman has produced, is producing and will produce. He hangs his producing hat all over the industry. He also is even more unique in that he totally belies the George Bernard Shaw line "those who can do, and those who can't teach." Myrl is a man who has taught, is teaching and will teach. He also continues to learn by teaching and by producing or directing. In my twenty-one years as a UCLA Professor concurrently with my writing and producing career, I've come to believe that we should always be stretching for the brass ring of knowledge. Particularly if you are the teacher. Myrl's FTV 247 course, "Producing the Independent Feature" is the mainspring of the MFA graduate Producers Program at UCLA, his own alma mater. He teaches versions of this course in various seminars, the UCLA Professional Producers Program, and the UCLA Extension Program. It is attended not only by business affairs and suit executives from every major studio in Hollywood, but also independent producers from throughout the world. All gaining the knowledge that he has to offer.

This book will show you that you, the producer, are the person for all seasons. You need to know about casting, editing, directing, day out of days, call sheets, the spread, the cameras and their crew, set dressing, costumes, acting, budgets, scripts, pre-production, post-production, promotion (and the list goes on) . . . but only a little. Yes, you must know a little about a lot. World-class scholars on any single producing component are not needed or wanted! When I started producing my own scripts it was with the 1981 highly successful television movie *Fallen Angel*, and I asked advice from three of Hollywood's finest producers. They each gave me exactly the same wisdom. They told me, "ask whomever comes to you with a problem, what they would do with the problem. Why? Because—hopefully—you hired the best person available to do the job. When they give you an answer, and if your common sense agrees, tell them you will get back to them in a half-hour. Then call us. We'll tell you what to say!" Well, I never made the call. It sounds simple but it's not. The "but it's not" is what this extraordinary book is about.

Just look at the table of contents. It's all there. Everything you need to know as a producer and didn't know enough to ask. "Above-the-line," "below-the-line," Myrl didn't blow a thing. Why? Because Myrl is a master producer and teacher. Hands on, experiential, illustrative with some of his award winning productions.

I am not writing this introduction to tell you how great the book is because it's in your hands and you'll either buy it to learn, or you've already bought it and you *will* learn! Boy and girl, man and woman—you will learn. You will need to read the book more than once to see the many concepts and nuances of producing that only years of experience can teach. I can only promise you that you will go back to this book again and again for long or short films, narrative or documentary, film or video. So don't give it away. No, do give it away—then go buy another so Myrl can send his son to Harvard!

PROLOGUE

A PRODUCER: He or she who makes things happen! A word that is used quite loosely in the film and video industry. The producer is the one who is able to obtain the creative ingredients to prompt a project to go, or the person who is able to raise the funding to give the project a green light but who then turns it over to another producer who *makes* it happen. Producers are looked at as the enemy by craftsmen who work on a project and are often disdained by actors who bring the soul of a project to life. They are scorned by film school students as a necessity but as people who do not have a creative bone in their body. It is a word that sometimes connotes disrespect, because of the business nature of showbusiness and anyone and everyone calls themselves a *producer* when they are "making that deal" or "bottom fishing" in the business. They haunt the film markets looking for that "one" deal, or package and they are the people who call film schools with enticements of multiple picture deals looking for the next Shane Black, John Schlessinger, Brad Silberling, Penelope Spheeris, Mike Werb, Alex Cox or Sydney Lumet, but instead make empty promises to students who are chasing dreams.

Students in my directing classes have told me that the producer is not creatively involved but merely someone who raises the money and turns it over to someone else to provide the creativity to a project. But then I ask them one question: *"Who receives the Oscar® statuette at the Academy Awards® for best picture of the year?"* Answer: THE PRODUCER. Not the director, the writer or the actor. They have their own statues. The Best Picture Award is given to the Producer of the motion picture, who stands with such producers as Steven Spielberg, Ray Stark, Howard Koch, Louis B. Mayer, Jack Warner; all producers whose driving force for their projects is integrity in creativity. Creativity in front, behind, before and after the rolling of the camera. The creative producer thinks inventively and ingeniously whether it is in the telling of the story, the casting of the picture, the selection of the director, the raising of the finances, and in some cases, the marketing of the film. The creative producer at any moment in the life of a project plays many different roles: the mother, the father, the lover, the romancer, the persuader, the psychologist, the soothsayer, the comic, the tragedian, the best friend, the teacher, the warrior, the negotiator, the arbitrator, the dreamer . . . the list seems neverending. The creative producer sees the project completed, dreams the project, gives birth to the project and then holds on as the project takes a life of its own, all the time molding it, shaping it, providing it with content to share with the world, and then leaving it with the hopes that it makes a difference. Does this sound familiar? It's the same thing we hopefully do with our children.

If we took one foot of film from a thousand-foot reel and held it up to the light what would we see? Well, at first glance we would see an image. But then upon further examination and analysis, and as we thought past the physical presence of the film in our hands, we would see actors, wardrobe, makeup, cinematography, sound (encoded somewhere around the image), set, location, props and maybe special effects.

Thinking further, we would realize that it also included everything it takes to do all of the above.

When a creative producer looks at the same strip of film, what he/she should be looking at are the dollar signs. Now imagine one thousand feet of film. In 35mm that represents a little over eleven minutes of film time and in its reeled version is the size of a 78rpm record (a dinosaur today). Imagine that you are holding this in your two hands (and it takes two hands to hold it), and there are nine more reels stacked on top, making the stack quite heavy. Now look at it. You are holding *Titanic*, which cost $250,000,000. Or you may be holding *The Clonus Horror*, which cost $250,000. What is the difference between the two? They look the same; they are the same height, the same weight. But why does one cost .001 percent of the other? What role did creativity play in the planning, execution and eventual completion of these projects that apparently look and feel the same? Does the amount of money spent on a film mean an improvement in the film? Can an understanding of creativity go beyond that which is seen on the screen and include how it got there? What role do the words "ego" and "relationship" play when being creative? These and other questions will be answered throughout this book. You will see various tenets of producing, in maintaining creativity, and be able to make creative decisions based upon the integrity of the work and the ultimate end result of the project.

CHAPTER **1** THINKING LIKE A PRODUCER

"There is nothing more rewarding for a director than being able to collaborate with a creative producer, and there is no better marriage on film or tape than that of a producer and director who collaborate brilliantly."

—Jeff Margolis, Director

END RESULT

The producer is the creative force behind a project. I repeat with emphasis: *The Producer Is The Creative Force Behind A Project.* Contrary to popular belief (and certainly the belief of most film schools) the director is *not* the only creative force behind a project, unless of course the producer entirely relegates that responsibility to the director. Creating a project for film or video is a collaborative effort. It is not like the world of the painter or sculptor who creates alone and then, when finished, the work is presented to the public. It is an art form that requires the collaboration of individual people, each creatively contributing to achieve the end result of the creative vision.

Before anyone else, the producer must know the end result of the project and know what path the project will take after it is completed. This is necessary in order to understand how to guide the various creative contributions to the project. What is its audience? Does it have a limited viewing life? Is it limited in the marketplace by the creative context? Will it be made specifically for one market or another? The producer also has a creative responsibility to try to provide the original investment with return. How will that be done? Will any investment be returned? The end result of the project and its use must be foremost in the producers' mind.

Example #1:

Documentaries are primarily commercially screened on television throughout the world, and many private screening houses are now able to project large screen video. Does this mean that the documentary should be produced entirely on video, or are there creative and aesthetic reasons that require it to be photographed on film and completed in video? Original production in video is less expensive than film but the creative aesthetics between film and video are significant. Perhaps the producer wants the documentary to have moments that feel like the 1920s and decides that the film medium would give the right creative aesthetic element. Therefore the planning for this project would include a creative element.

Example #2:

The story of a narrative project involves a gay relationship between a punk rock musician and a hip-hop musician. Although the characters are well developed and the director believes that the relationships between the two characters are universal, will the project, because of its subject matter, ever see the light of day with distribution? And if it did, what type of distribution would it receive? Will it be an underground or art house project? Or will it make it to the public's eye at all? What is the probability of total investment return?

The concept of focusing on the projects' creative end result and use is an important tenet of producing. This is not an original notion, since the Screen Actors Guild and the Directors Guild of America structure their agreements based on the end use of the product. The concept of end use is one you will be directed to many times as you go through this written diary on independent producing. But first we need to consider independent funding for the project.

THE FIVE QUESTIONS

You have the project, the idea or the vision and now you must give it life. This begins in the Development Phase. This is the period in which the funding comes together. If funding is coming through a studio or other production company, you will work within their dictated guidelines. But if you are raising independent funds, it is often through a legal construct—such as a private placement document or private partnership. These documents must be prepared by a qualified attorney and structured so that the producer, the creative force, is fully protected against any personal liabilities regarding the project. The producer who usually brings the project to the structure is contributing his or her creativity to the arrangement. The clearer this is within the context of the document the more respect potential investors will have towards the integrity of the project. Inexperienced investors often look to see if the producer has his or her own funds at risk before considering investing. They will need to be educated concerning the structure of a film or video project investment and the value of a producer's creativity to the package.

Once the contribution relationship between producer and investor has been clearly explained and defined in the body of the partnership document, there are five questions always asked by investors.

The partnership document must contain the answers to all five of these questions, as they define the risk to the investor and the depth of the creative producer's motivation.

Question #1: How Much Money Do You Want Me to Invest?

This one is easy to answer. The investment is the negative cost of the project with negative cost being defined as the amount of money necessary to come to a completed composite answer print of the project. The negative cost can include the hard cash dollars used on the project as well as any arranged deferred costs. Deferred costs are expenses applied to the project that are paid at some mutually agreed upon time after the completion or during the distribution of the project. The investment proposal may discuss the overall investment and what minimum units of investment might be fashioned as a part of the overall investment. Or it may indicate what sort of investment may be shaped and in what form. But the bottom line is that it will declare *how much money is needed to make the project.*

This brings up one of the big fallacies in the industry as it applies to producers. How can the producer know how much the project is going to cost before it is made? When you are buying a house, the investment is based upon predetermined information. The same should hold true in a movie or video project. But unlike the purchase of a property, the producer—due to lack of knowledge or experience—may first ask various people to provide him or her with information before setting the cost of the project. The unfortunate process for inexperienced independent producers is (all to often), to hire a production manager to create a budget for the project without any dialogue as to the creative producing of the project.

Production managers are not producers, although some may be line producers. They manage the day-to-day operations of film production. They are not involved in post-production, or above-the-line decisions of a project. They have not set the creative or philosophical approach to the producing of the movie, nor are they required to completely understand the demands of a director. So why are production managers asked to prepare budgets? Or more importantly, why would a "soon to be" producer trust the budgetary figures that a production manager provides them with? Production managers will always budget to protect the downside of their job. They will always ask for more dollars than are necessary for their area of responsibility and shortchange those areas that they do not know well or are unfamiliar with. There are not many rules in production, but there is one that is constant about the *process* of production. *"What you do not plan for in pre-production affects production, and what you do not do in production affects post-production."* This chain reaction is what causes any project to go over its budget. So why take a budget prepared by a production manager as gospel as to what the film will cost?

Studios have budget departments that, after reading a screenplay, prepare a budget that is presented to the producer as what the film should cost. Thus studios require producers to be responsible for keeping a project on a budget created by people who have never before made films. Does this make sense? During the development phase of *The Girl, the Gold Watch and Everything*, I prepared a budget based upon the first draft of a screenplay, knowing that I had to keep it within the licensing fee of $1.6 million dollars paid to the studio. The studio's Budget Department prepared a budget for the same screenplay. Their budget was $2.6 million dollars. I was told by the studio to have the script rewritten so that it could be made for the license fee. I remained firm on the screenplay as written and presented them with my budget created from the same screenplay (and my production board), reminding them that I was responsible for the producing decisions on the film. The project came in at $1.37 million dollars.

Question #2: What Do I Get for My Investment?

This is another easy question to answer. The document should clearly spell out what percentage of the film's profits that the investment dollar or any portion of the investment dollar is to receive. Do the investors (often referred to simply as "the money"), share in 50 percent, 70 percent, 30 percent of the profits? Do the first investors who invest in the project (commonly referred to as "first money"), get a higher return on the investment than those who are partially motivated to invest because others have done so? (The thought being that first money is almost always the most difficult to raise.) Whatever the deal may be, it needs to be clearly spelled out in the investment package.

There can be many different types of profit structures each reflecting a different psychological factor to the investment. As an example, a first-time producer may take a smaller share of profit participation, offering investors the larger share as an incentive to invest. Or, the producer might structure their share of profit participation as the source for any profit participation that must be given to secure talent. Or profit participation to secure talent can be taken from the total before investors and producers take their participation. The independent feature *Hunter's Blood*[1] was budgeted at $850,000. It was a genre project, a clash of cultures type of adventure/horror film. Practicing the "End Result Use" tenet, research told us that the project could have a high probability of a return on an investment of this size. It would, of course, depend on the quality and creativity of the producing. We decided to interest passive investors in the investment (a passive investor is one who has never before invested in a motion picture project), who turned out to be a group of doctors from Central Florida. They were a bit shy to invest cash, as they were unfamiliar with entertainment industry investments and it wasn't like investing in a piece of land that you can go to and touch and feel. So we had to find a method of investment that would provide them with the security, and convince them that this particular deal was a low risk investment. We brought in a bank which would provide the funds against letters of credit that were issued by the investors through their respective financial institutions. This gave the group of doctors the psychological security of knowing that a bank had reviewed the investment (*Hunter's Blood*) and had decided it merited the funds against the letters of credit collateral. The bank was not at risk as they had the collateral in place. The investors were more comfortable knowing that another financial entity had reviewed the investment package and decided that the people involved could deliver. The burden of this investment fell to the production, because in order to pay the interest on the loan, we had to factor in another $150,000 onto the negative cost as a bank fee should we have needed to pay the bank back through the end of the terms of the loan. Therefore, through our investors we needed $1,000,000 in letters of credit for the bank. One of the major responsibilities that a producer has when doing a project is to maintain the integrity to the investors and to recognize that the "business" end of the phrase

---

[1] The creative nature of *Hunter's Blood* is discussed in the book *Men, Women and Chainsaws, Modern Horror Film Genres*, by Dr. Carol Clover and published by Princeton University Press.

"show business" is equally as important as the "show." When the picture was completed the negative cost was $750,000 and the bank was paid back within one year of the completion of the answer print of the picture. The letters of credit were never called, the bank received interest on the money, the investors received their percentage of profits and the picture was a success.

In another film proposal, the producers were making their first film and needed to find a mechanism to entice investors to believe in their project. Although they had not done all their homework or research in terms of examining ways to reduce the risk to the investors, they were able to raise the funds by structuring the proposal as a 75/25 percent split between investors and producers with any participation points given from the producers' side. This was further enhanced by allowing the investors to recoup their investment plus 15 percent before there was any profit participation. To the investor this is a very good deal. Now all the investor had to think about was the earnestness and passion of the producer and creative team that was being put together since the return to risk ratio was in the investors' favor.

Although film and video investments may appear to be very businesslike, emotion almost always enters into the partnership. With emotion comes ego, with ego comes motivation and since the producer has to appeal to the investors to get the project funded, the producer should define how the investment is put together.

Question #3: When Do I Get My Money Back (or Any Portion of My Money Back)?

The answer to this question is a bit more complicated. The payout to the producer from any project has its greatest return within the first eighteen months of the life of the project. That is to say, assuming that upon completion of the answer print, a path for distribution and release has been set in motion, the terms of distribution usually reflect the largest revenue coming back to the investors within the first eighteen months of the life of the film. There are several reasons why this is so.

During the first year of the project's completion, distributors provide reports to the producer monthly. The second year, the reports are made quarterly. By the third year, the producer should expect reports biannually. The major thrust for a project in whatever primary markets are determined happen immediately upon the project's release, while ancillary markets such as television, cable, videocassette and DVD may be scheduled sometime after the initial release. All of this usually happens within the first eighteen months of the life of the project.

Advances can also be negotiated regarding any of the avenues of distribution, which will have a direct impact on the percentage of distribution or release fees that will be levied against the product. If these advances are in the form of guarantees made by distributors during the development phase of the project, then the producer is able to unequivocally state when any portion of the investment will be able to be returned to the investor.

However, this type of situation puts a certain amount of fiscal responsibility on the guarantor, or distributor, and therefore the producer usually agrees to other incentives for the distributor when the project is completed. The incentives may be in the form of a high distribution fee taken upfront, total recoupment of the guarantee plus interest, equity participation, creative input or control in the project, or any or all of the above.

The producers of *The Clonus Horror* received a $100,000 advance from their distributor upon delivery of the answer print for distribution. On the surface of it, this seemed to be a fair deal. Not a great deal, but a fair deal, as the picture only cost $250,000 to produce. However, the young producers were not familiar with all of the nuances of distribution and discovered that the distribution fee was higher than it might have been without the advance. Also the distributor charged interest on the advance based upon the prime rate in any year. So although almost 45 percent of the investment was returned within three months of the investment, the balance of the investment took longer to receive. Looking back on the twenty years since its distribution, the profit to the investors would have been sooner and greater had there been no advance.

On the low budget feature *Crime Task Force* ($450,000) the producers did not offer the investors any guarantees or make any warrantees as to when the investment would be paid back. They wanted to return the basic investment as quickly as possible to their investors so they could ask them for funds for a second film. In so doing, they negotiated a $250,000 advance from the foreign market and a $200,000 advance from the domestic market which covered the negative cost of the film, paying back the full investment. But the foreign distributor took a large percentage for a distribution fee and the domestic distributor retained all domestic rights (including any ancil-

---

PRODUCERS VOCABULARY

Negative Pickup—A term used to describe an agreement between a film's distributor and the producer, whereby the distribution company agrees to pay a fee for the rights to distribute said film. The fee typically is not paid to the producer until delivery of the completed and cut negative. (This is the opposite of pre-production financing.) If the pick-up deal is with a major studio, the producer can usually take the agreement to a bank where it can be discounted (e.g., converted into money for a fee). Many productions are financed, or partially financed, this way.

laries that might have been available such as videocassette, DVD etc.) Subsequent funds came in to the producers after the first release of the film, but the percentage return to the investor was much lower than it could have been had the producers not decided on the advances.

So Question #3 begins to introduce to the producer some philosophical decisions that must be dealt with in relationship to the project. The producer must ask some questions: "How badly do I want these investment dollars? How much of the creative element am I willing to give away? Is it a wise decision to get advance guarantees to secure the investment if the investors' opportunity to recoup or profit potential is decreased?"

Question #4: How Do I Know You Are Not Going to Ask for More Money?

More money! More money! More money! This is the producer's undying cry as the film gets into production and the funds are being used up quickly. The investor wants to know if the producer is able to make the project for the original amount that the producer warrants is needed for the project. This is a fair question. The investor wants the assurance that the investment isn't going to be sold off later because of the need of funds for its completion. Certainly, you can talk to the investor until you are blue in the face, trying to convince them that you know what you are doing and that you are absolutely sure that you will not need more money to complete the film—in spite of the fact that your director has a reputation for being slow and not completing a scheduled day's work, and your director of photography loves to "paint" with light until the image is absolutely perfect because that is how they did it in film school. Unless you know how to successfully use the word "no" with these and other situations, *you will need more money!* So don't fool yourself. Protect the investment and find a method that will assure and guarantee to your investors that you will not need more funds to complete the project. This can be done by using a completion bond. The completion bond is an insurance policy purchased through a qualified company made up of certified experts in film and video production. After they have analyzed the documents in the application package—including the script, production board and budget—they will provide a letter stating that in their opinion the project can or cannot be produced in a first class distributable manner. If it can, they will state their willingness to provide the completion bond. If for any reason the project is being produced badly, or the money is being used unwisely in the producing of the project, they, as overseers, will come in and complete the film at their expense. Their letter should state this information as it will provide confidence to investors and provide the answer to Question #4.

If it is that simple, why doesn't every project have a completion bond? Because not every project is bondable! Bonding companies in reality, do not bond (insure) projects; they bond (insure) the people making the project. The last thing in the world a bonding company wants to do is take over a project. So they look to the people making the project as to being reputable, knowledgeable, creative and (they hope) experienced. It is therefore difficult for a first time producer to obtain a bond on a low or medium budget picture. A first time producer may have to align with a bondable commodity such as a director, co-producer or line producer with a positive track record. Bonding companies are primarily concerned with the preparation and production aspects of a project because production can be, and usually is, volatile. The post-production phase is a more fixed and controllable phase at which time the responsibilities of the bonding company may be (but are not always) relieved. Does this assurance for the investor come cheap? No. Is it necessary? Probably. Bonding companies routinely charge 6 percent of the project budget as a bonding fee; if there is no contingency in your budget, they require at the least a 10 percent contingency before determining their 6 percent fee.

As an example: If a project's budget is $2,000,000 and does not contain a contingency within the total amount of the budget, then an additional minimum of $200,000 must be added. The bond fee of 6 percent is then calculated on a budget of $2,200,000, thus adding an additional $132,000 to the budget as a fee paid to the completion bond company. The cost of the project has now been increased by $332,000 to $2,332,000.

However, bonding agreements are negotiable and various terms can be discussed and negotiated as part of the agreement. These terms include such items as the working relationship with the producer, terms and conditions of invading the bond, procedures regarding expenditures of budgetary items, and the bond fee (some of which are discussed in Chapter 4).

Question #5: How Do I Know that the Project Will Get in the Marketplace?

This is the question that requires the most puzzled answer of all. Because *you don't know!* But there are various elements you can pursue that will increase the likelihood of it getting into the marketplace.

1. The producer, director or writer may be someone with a track record and whose previous projects have been released.

2. After researching the marketplace, acquire an option on an actor or actors whose names may encourage distribution.
3. Tie up a distribution deal early on in the package.
4. Or, throw the dice and trust your creative abilities to produce an exciting project with a good story that distributors will want.

Each of these circumstances requires the producer to carefully consider any particulars that may arise. Again by example, should the project include a person with a track record, the back end participation (commonly referred to as "profit points") may be part of the relationship and affect the way the investment is structured. It may very well be that investors are deciding to invest because a writer, director or producer has a proven track record that would logically dictate the purpose of the project. The difficulty in this situation may come from the working relationships of these three people, as they must all have a clear and unified understanding of the vision for the project so that their efforts do not conflict with one another.

If the producer determines that the project needs a viable actor to insure its marketability, a difficulty may arise in acquiring distribution. Although the producer's research might indicate that having a "name" actor tied to the project may ensure distribution, the reverse may also be true. Distributors may decide that the particular actor tied to the project is wrong for the project and they can easily say no to the project because you have given them a way out. And, if the actor is a member of the Screen Actors Guild, and unless you have structured the actor's relationship to the project in a certain way, the actor is paid for the project whether or not it is produced since SAG actors work on a pay-or-play basis.

If the producer agrees to a distribution deal during the development phase of the project, the deal will probably be a healthy one for the distributor and a not-so-great one for the producer. Distributors believe that their involvement makes the project viable, so they negotiate for a larger distribution percentage than they might receive if the project did not need their association to secure the investment. Further, it is not unheard of for the distributor to be involved with the creative side of the project if that relationship is required for investment.

If the producer throws the dice and goes with their belief in the project, its characters and its story, the producer is then in the strongest position creatively, but distribution will rest entirely on the integrity of the work. The producer must convince investors the project will be successful in the marketplace, and will include the right actors, director, writer, cinematographer and composer, all of which will help maintain the quality of the work and motivate distributors to put the project in theaters or on the small screen. Or, the producer must believe in the project so strongly that investors are convinced that the project will be successful on the festival circuit before getting distribution. This can be shortsighted since important festivals are getting very selective about what they accept. In other words, the producer is selling integrity to the investors and attempting to set up a level of trust and mutual respect. This is the toughest road to go since it is built on dreams and passion but it can also be the most gratifying to the producer.

As you can see, the answer to the last question is the most complicated and has a direct correlation to the answers for the previous four. However, if you present these answers clearly in your investment document, your investors will be willing participants.

—— • • • ——

"When dealing with studio 'suits' the real job of a creative producer is simple: lie. Lie like a dog, lie like a rug, lie, lie, lie. Say whatever it takes to get executives out of your way so you can get your project made the way you want. Mostly, this involves the old Hollywood standby—telling them what they want to hear: 'I promise you it will have male appeal' (and it does!), 'If it comes in over-budget, you can take it out of my salary' (but it never does!), 'I know for a fact that the scene will work when its on its feet' (and it does). Don't ever tell them what it will really cost, or how long it will really take to shoot (because they have no imagination or creativity and don't really know production anyway). Once it's made, there's nothing they can do. If it never gets made, there's nothing you can do, except learn from your 'truth mistakes.' In addition, one of the fringe benefits of professional lying is how powerful the truth can be. Once, when I was executive producing a sitcom for Fox Television, we were called into a meeting to explain how we'd fix the show in order to get (a pickup of) the coveted back nine episodes. The show was hanging by a thread, and my studio execs (which studio shall remain nameless), were tap dancing their asses off to get the network to give us the order. I listened silently for an hour, then made my move. I told the network president the truth: that the show sucked. 'It's about flight attendants, for God's sake. We're barely getting the show to stick to the videotape, and the only thing we can tell you without bullshitting you is that we can try a little harder.' There was a long pause as everyone in the room stared at me as if I had just killed their mothers. The network president looked at us and said, 'Thank you. This meeting is over.' No one from the studio spoke to me for the rest of the day. But the next morning, guess what? We got the back nine. Sometimes it actually pays to tell the truth. Who knew?"

—Jamie Wooten, Producer/Writer, *The Golden Girls,*
The Five Mrs. Buchanans, For Your Love

—— • • • ——

CHAPTER 2   UNDERSTANDING PRODUCING

MAKE THE SHOE FIT THE FOOT

We read about projects that go over budget and the lament of projects costing so much money in Hollywood that the projects go to Canada, Australia, South Africa, Eastern Europe or other countries. They call these runaway productions. A lot has been written about runaway productions that seek less expensive locales or government tax credits. Its true that in some instances savings can reduce a budget by as much as 35 percent because of a strong U.S. dollar or government incentives. This is especially helpful on television projects where production costs have risen while the fees networks pay production companies have decreased. Producers blame the rising fees on the craft people, unions and guilds for running projects out of Hollywood. That's not entirely true. What has contributed to running projects out of Hollywood are producers who do not understand the positive side of the words "ego" and "relationship," and who are worshipers of the written word. They believe the words in the screenplay are sacrosanct and should never be changed, so they try to adjust the production (and its budget) to fit the written words.

Let's examine that logic. The words of a screenplay are written by a writer sitting alone in a room, dictated by his or her imagination. The writer has little or no knowledge about the inherent problems to production—and why should they? They are writers, and you are a producer. They write; it's your job to produce. But collaboration is the key to this relationship and you must try to make the shoe fit the foot, with the foot being the budget and the parameters of production and the shoe being the screenplay and the process of production.

What makes an excellent screenplay? Is it the size of the bridges that are blown up or the number of cars that crash in the first ten minutes of the film? Or is it the characters and what they say and feel? We all know the answer to that one. The answer should always be "it's the characters." No doubt about it, when a project has solid characters who feel, speak and interact within a good story, the picture has the potential of being an excellent project.

Crafting a screenplay to include characters who are solid, emoting, feeling characters takes creativity, not money. Blowing up the bridge in the story may advance the story but is it necessary for the characters and to the story? Can the story be advanced and achieve the same thing without an onscreen explosion? The characters' reactions to the dramatic intent of the action or effect should be what makes the project work, not the special effect itself.

So a creative producer who is familiar with reality and is starting to raise the money should first determine, based upon research, how much money can be raised, everything being equal. This is a key phrase! "Everything being equal." This refers to the project before distributors or financiers demand specific requirements, each of which they feel is critical to protect their end of the risk and which will raise the budget of the project. The requirement of a specific actor, for example. Once the budgetary funds have been determined, then the producer working creatively with the writer adjusts the screenplay to work within the available funds (making the shoe fit the foot). A production breakdown on a production board (discussed in Chapters 3 and 11) will identify some of the creative changes that might need to be made. It may mean changing certain locations, which do not work for the production or are too expensive, adjusting the number of characters in the story or perhaps setting certain limitations as dictated by budget. Limitations are always part of the formula. Creativity flourishes within limitations and restrictions. Mozart had a deadline when he was commissioned to write *The Magic Flute;* the Pope continually pressured Michelangelo with deadlines for the completion of the Sistine Chapel. Limitations can force you to stretch your creativity in new (and often cost effective) directions.

As previously mentioned *The Girl, the Gold Watch and Everything* had a screenplay that the studio said would cost over two million to produce. I knew that if I produced the film from scratch and had to find or build all the locations and did the scripted special effects the way that was standard at the time, it would have cost what the studio had projected or possibly even more. This was prohibitive for a movie for television. We were doing a union (IATSE) picture and set construction alone with an IA crew would have taken the entire budget. The final script the studio Budget Department read had already been reworked with the writer with the "shoe fit the foot" theory. I decided to walk the studio soundstages to see what sets were standing and what sets could, with changes to the set dressing or minor alterations to the screenplay, be used for *Gold Watch*. I found a wonderful hotel suite which would match into the Hotel Del Coronado in San Diego, and an interior being used for a romantic comedy which could also be matched with exteriors into the project. This tenet of producing, of maintaining picture quality and creativity and having the "shoe fit the foot" prevailed through the entire production process.

Hunter's Blood was faced with a different problem. The executive producer had wanted the project shot in Florida, thinking that the terrain of northern Florida was more suited to Arkansas and Oklahoma where the story was set. (She was also from Florida.) I was faced with finding locations in Southern California that could work for the picture. I knew that what was important to the movie were the people, not the trees and shrubs (although there couldn't be any palm trees in the film) or how the landscape was dressed. So I needed to find exterior locations that could pass for the woods of Arkansas. I knew the first draft of the screenplay would need changes to coincide with the vision I had of two cultures clashing with one another. I spent weeks looking within a fifty-mile radius of our production office. Finally I found a woods on a "location backlot" in Newhall, California, just behind the Six Flags Magic Mountain Amusement Park. Once I found the woods, I asked the lot manager what else was situated on the lot. He drove me around and I saw areas that—with some rewriting and clever set dressing—could work very successfully for the film project. I also found a practical (that is, working) freight train and about five miles of track. When I showed this to the writer we changed the ending of the picture and added two exciting (but inexpensive) stunts to the project. Once again, the shoe was made to fit the foot!

RELATIONSHIPS AND EGO

You have raised the funds for the project. You have restructured the screenplay so that the shoe fits the foot. Now you are faced with producing the project. But before you begin, there are two words that you must distinctly

---

PRODUCERS VOCABULARY

Lot—The area comprising a production studio; it may include office buildings, sound stages, dressing rooms, etc., and is usually protected by guards at the front gate who regulate entry of non-employees.

grasp. These words may be the most important concepts that you can gain from this book. The words are: *Relationships* and *Ego*.

Relationships

The relationships you build along the path of the profession are the relationships that will stay with you for your entire career. It makes no difference if the relationships are with financial institutions or with grips and electricians. All relationships are equally important. Never burn a bridge. Just reconstruct them! You will learn that the entertainment industry is a very small one and your path will cross the paths of many others again and again. It is your integrity that will keep your relationships in place.

The nature of human relationships relies on the fact that a certain amount of what motivates someone is their relationship to someone else. You may hire a handyman who has worked for one of your relatives for many years to work for you on your house. The handyman wants to make sure he does an excellent job because of his ongoing relationship to your relative as it is important to him to maintain the integrity he has in that relationship. But when he comes to do work on your house, you continually tell him how to do his job. Or maybe it's a warm day and you don't show him the courtesy of offering him a cold drink when you see that he is perspiring. In other words, you treat him with disrespect for his labor and the good rapport he has with your relative. This demonstrates a lack of integrity on your part and will be your downfall in establishing a relationship with the handyman. That disrespect may work against you in the future; he will not be as receptive to your needs the second time you call, and your relative may not be willing to refer people to you.

You will find that as your producing career builds, you will go back to the same people for assistance. They will learn from you and you from them. Producing is an art form and we must remember that, as with any art form, it is never just a job; you will need relationships you have cultivated and nurtured in order to be successful. Always maintain your relationships with people. Above everything else, it is the one skill that will allow you to bring about your passionate lifelong project and have people rally around you when you are ready to produce it. I have never been to a cast and crew screening of any project where each and every person there did not feel like it was their own project. As the film unfolded, they each saw, in the far recesses of their minds, their creative contribution and they knew they were a part of the whole. This is what creative producing does. It helps people realize their potential and appreciates their contribution to the birth of the project.

Ego

The connotation regarding this word is often interpreted as negative, as in "his ego is so out of line that we just can't deal with him!" But there is a positive side to this word and the creative producer understands how to exercise it when producing a project. Something as simple as a producer spending five minutes in genuine discussion with a crewmember can positively enforce the ego of that crewmember. That crewmember unconsciously thinks "this busy producer spent a bit of time to find out how I am doing, and not on a production level but on a personal level." Gil Cates, a favorite producer of the Academy Awards® ceremony, has produced that show longer than any other producer since the inception of the awards. The Oscar® telecast requires a producer with extraordinary skill, taste and diplomacy to carry it off. I have known Gil from the days when he was president of The Directors Guild of America (also known as the DGA), an organization to which I belong. He was one of my "bosses" when he became the founding Dean of the UCLA School of Theater, Film and Television. For eight years, I went to his weekly "Dean's Meetings" during which I would watch him skillfully motivate a variety of egocentric academics into ferrying the school to new heights of professionalism. He handled those meetings like a creative producer and maneuvered his creative academic team to all see the same vision. I may not have agreed with all of the decisions he made, but his ability to finesse the various egos and allow each person to know they were valued while contributing to the ongoing success of the school showed me what creative producing is about.

Although I was only one person on the academic administrative hierarchy, Gil knew that my strength in supporting his vision for the school was as a producer as well as a teacher. Many times he would stroll into my office, seat himself in a chair and spend a bit of time with me. During those conversations we did not speak about the work at hand, but instead discussed our families and our lives. Although I knew his interest was genuine, I also knew that, as a gifted producer, he totally understood the positive side of the word ego and was reinforcing mine. When he would leave my office, I felt that he cared to take the time to visit and find out about "me," and so I wanted to provide more support for his creative vision for the school.

The industry operates on a horizontal basis. If someone works as a grip, then they are thought of as a grip. If someone earns their living as a property person then it is almost impossible for them to be considered for anything other than a property master. What would they know about art direction or production design? While the last sentence is written sarcastically, it is often true. The industry *does* operate on a horizontal basis. In general, producers do not want to take the chance of using someone in a new capacity for the first time. But a producer who clearly understands the positive dynamics of ego, will, when needed, attempt to work against that policy.

In searching out a production designer for the film project *Hunter's Blood*, I found a man who had previously been a property master on big budget major feature films. He came highly recommended by production designers and art directors I had previously worked with but who I could not afford for this particular project. They knew he was a talented property master and probably had the ability to be an excellent production designer if given the chance. After meeting with him, my instinct and their recommendations convinced me to give him a try. I knew that by giving him this opportunity his ego would make him go that extra mile to interpret the vision of the project. Because he was a property master on major films, he knew the volatile demands of production, had the relationships with personnel and prop houses important to the project, and could work within a structured budget. Moving him up to a production designer meant giving him more responsibility, providing him with screen credit in the front titles of the film and allowing him to be creative in a different way than he had been in the past. It also gave him an opportunity to move vertically up the industry ladder and possibly change his position on future projects. Because he wanted this opportunity, he agreed to a lower salary than he would have commanded as a property master, or that I would have had to pay to an established production designer. The result was positive for both of us and all because of understanding the positive meaning of the word ego.

Of course this does not always work, and the risk is based upon the judgement of the producer. Many years earlier I did the same thing on the motion picture *The Clonus Horror*. But in this case, I made an error in judgement and did not check out the candidate with other people before hiring him. On this project, the concept of hiring a property master as an art director appeared to be working quite well, until the art director was to design and build a set situated in a warehouse that we were using as a soundstage. The film had an eighteen-day shooting schedule. During that time a "clone room" needed to be constructed. While we were shooting on location on a Tuesday, the art director was to have been supervising the building of an approved set design that was to shoot the next day. After Tuesday's production day, the director (Robert Fiveson) and I stopped off at the warehouse to see the set and discuss the next day's shooting. When we got there what we found was the art director sitting in the middle of an empty warehouse scratching his head. There was no set. The man had panicked. He had no imagination and was unable to carry out the designs we had discussed. He was a fine property master and set decorator when he was given a set of parameters by an art director or direction from the screenplay, but when he was required to create something that didn't exist, he panicked and failed. It was a judgement error on my part as producer. But as the person ultimately responsible for the creative aspect of the project, I sent the director and "art director" home, and with a couple of carpenters, an ounce of creativity, my wonderful assistant Carolyn Haber and all the gold mylar paper we could find in the city, we built a clone room and the director was able to shoot the next day. So remember *ego* is an important word to understand, but make sure that you truly understand it.

GETTING STARTED

You have your screenplay, you have your budget completed and approved, you have your funding in place and now you are ready to move from the development phase of the project to the production phase. Of the list below who are the first three people you should employ?

	DIRECTOR
	PRODUCTION MANAGER
	CASTING DIRECTOR
	ASSOCIATE PRODUCER
	CINEMATOGRAPHER
	LOCATION MANAGER

If you checked any of those production positions, you are absolutely *wrong*!

The first three positions that you should employ are the *producer's assistant, a production accountant* and a *production assistant.*

The Producer's Assistant

The producer's assistant is your assistant. In other decades they were called secretaries. Today they are referred to as Assistant to the Producer. This is the person who you ask to contact the Screen Actors Guild to get the signatory documents, or to contact a casting director to begin discussions with you. It is this person who is your right hand in getting things together and providing the follow through. It should be someone with whom you can confide and trust. It should be someone you know will get things done in a timely fashion and who will know how you think in terms of creative producing.

The Production Accountant

The production accountant is the person who must immediately set up the accounting systems on the project. This is not the corporate accountant who assisted in the setting up of the project, but someone who knows how to read a production budget, understands in detail all the guild and union agreements, knows all the basic principles of accounting, and knows how to produce a daily cost-to-complete statement. It must be someone who is proficient in the use of computerized accounting programs and someone who is able to give you answers to budgetary questions at the drop of a hat. It must be someone who understands and recognizes the volatility of production, knows how to help you protect your financial downside of the project, and has the respect of the bonding company or financial community. It must also be someone with the temperament to deal with long hours, short tempers, large egos, quick turn around, angry crew personnel and (of course) stress. This person is your right hand in relationship to the fiscal structure of the project and is critically important to your success as a creative producer.

The Production Assistant

While every project requires a number of production assistants, each doing different functions working in different production departments, this specific production assistant is considered the producer's production assistant and will work on getting "tradeoffs" for the film project. A tradeoff is also referred to as a product placement. It takes a great deal of time to put tradeoff agreements in place on a project, which is why the process needs to be started early in the production phase. The production assistant must be a person who has the gift of gab and knows how to sell themselves first and the project second; like any good salesman. The production assistant must be very good on the telephone as well as in person as he or she is representing the quality and integrity of you and the project.

The *tradeoff* [1] agreement is a major assist in helping an independent producer remain within a prescribed budget and providing creative quality onscreen. It allows the producer to save monies in various areas of produc-

---

[1] Tradeoff agreements are not permitted in commercial television, but are permitted in the cable television and feature film markets.

tion, such as locations, properties, wardrobe, set decoration and transportation, etc., by finding mechanisms and methods for displaying product logos
or use of a specific product onscreen. The production budget should be prepared as if no tradeoff agreements are in place, so monies that are saved
from any agreements eventually made can be put elsewhere to be seen on
the screen. Tradeoff agreements for limited budget productions can enhance
the details of picture quality and give a small picture a more expensive look.
But tradeoff agreements take time to acquire. Many producers do not wish
to use product placement as they believe it affects the integrity of the artist
and the film can appear to be one long commercial. However, if a producer
is careful, creative and selective as to how the product is used and identified
onscreen, this perception can be avoided.

The Clonus Horror, produced for $250,000, had tradeoff agreements with
Bell Helmets, Adidas, Schwinn, Dr. Pepper and Old Milwaukee Beer, all of
which were seen onscreen. In one instance the characters, as a story point,
talked about one of the placed products. In another, Robert (the director)
wanted all the clones in the picture to look the same and ride the same bicycles. So in the opening of the movie ten clones ride matching Schwinn bicycles, wearing matching Adidas wardrobe and matching Bell Helmets. If the
production had to purchase the bicycles, wardrobe and helmets, we would
have spent close to $3000 to achieve the look. Through tradeoff agreements
we were able to provide the look and acquire more wardrobe for other
clones for later scenes.

There are companies whose function it is to place product onscreen in
theatrical motion pictures. Product placement companies, sometimes called
"promo houses" are listed in the telephone book and in various industry
production information manuals. Located primarily in Los Angeles and
New York, they get hundreds of calls a day and must be selective as to which
projects they recommend for their clients. Companies not represented in
this fashion can be contacted directly and eventually your production assistant will find the right person to speak to and make the pitch.

That pitch must contain the right information to successfully involve
product placement. Product representatives must know the name of the film
project and the names of the people producing and directing. They must
also be told how the product will be used and which character will be using
the product. They will want to read the script to make sure it enhances the
image of their client. The product representative will ask other specific questions before agreeing to place their product and your production assistant
should be ready with answers. "Who is in the picture?" They need to ascer-

tain the quality of the project in relationship to the creative community. "What company is releasing the picture?" They need to gauge the distribution merit of the project. "When will it be released?" They need to know when they get the exposure. "What type of exposure are you offering?" They need to know how much exposure they are getting. The script will be a key factor in their decision. Language can be an issue. Nudity can be an issue. Violence can be an issue. Budget can be an issue. Now you can see why tradeoff agreements take time.

They are not easy to arrange, but once you have acquired one tradeoff, others may fall into place more easily. One product company, knowing that another product company is endorsing the film by allowing use of its products may agree to become involved *(ego)*. Also, once you have acquired one tradeoff agreement you have established a *relationship* with someone who already said yes to you once. If it is a company that represents various clients, massage this new relationship and ask what other clients might be willing to appear in the film. Your new friend has already okayed all the tough stuff by approving your project so maybe he or she has other clients whose products may work for your film even though you may not have identified them yet.

Hunter's Blood acquired a tradeoff for a Ford Bronco that was used extensively in the film. A product placement company that was headed up by a friend I had known for many years represented Ford Motor Company at the time. After concluding the deal, he then asked me if any characters in the film smoked. The picture is a story of a group of hunters who go camping in the back woods and therefore it could provide an opportunity for someone to smoke onscreen. Before answering him I asked him why he was asking that question. He informed me that he represented a tobacco company and it was getting very difficult in today's environment to place tobacco products in movies. I asked him what he was offering. He told me that he could not provide money for the product to be seen, but that the company would pay for seven dozen three color embroidered cast and crew jackets for the picture. I agreed. And what you see in the movie is one of the characters smoking (which he was going to do anyway), and a 3-second medium shot of a campfire and an empty crumpled pack of cigarettes. In return I received approximately $10,000 worth of cast and crew morale building jackets during a difficult shoot.

The production assistant working on tradeoffs will eventually move to other production tasks on the project once you hire the heads of certain creative departments. Each department head should have their own relationships in place to do further tradeoffs since they each have creative egos which will motivate them. However, in those cases—as in the ones that your production assistant has developed—you must be willing to agree to those tradeoffs. Remember that tradeoffs are important. The producer should always maintain the creative integrity of the project, but should also be open to inspiration, as you never know what will turn up. The skill to negotiate is a key aspect in acquiring tradeoffs.

NEGOTIATING

The producer must possess skills in negotiating. Every aspect of producing involves negotiations in one form or another. It can be as simple as negotiating for a casting director, or as complex as working through distribution deals or talent contracts. The words "relationship" and "ego" also play into the understanding and skills needed to negotiate, and as the producer continues to produce this will become more and more apparent. There are, however, twelve major points to remember when negotiating.

1. **PLAN WITH YOUR LIMITATIONS IN MIND:** Know your limitations. If you have any budget limitations, know what they are. Do your research. Learn about the person with whom you are negotiating if you don't already know them or have a relationship with them. Keep in mind any guidelines you may have and know how they may affect other people and be ready to respond to the unexpected reaction.

2. **ESTABLISH RAPPORT:** If you do not have a relationship with the person you will be negotiating with, then it is important to establish one. Relationships are established by conversation. Often this can come from talking about things outside of your project such as both of your backgrounds, sports, hobbies, families and so forth. Where and how you negotiate will also have an impact on establishing this relationship—many people, for instance prefer face-to-face meetings over telephone conversations. Do you negotiate on your turf or on the other person's turf? Do you meet in a neutral place like a restaurant or coffee shop?

3. **PITCH THE ELEMENTS:** If applicable, paint a visual picture. Describe the elements so the person with whom you are negotiating clearly understands the project. Who is directing? Who wrote the screenplay? Where will it be shot? What is the story about? What will the project do for whom you are negotiating? Where will the project

be distributed? Who will be the cinematographer or the composer? You must clearly describe the elements to excite and embrace the person with whom you are negotiating. Try to get them emotionally caught up in the vision. It will give you strength in the negotiations.

4. **BE HONEST:** Above all, one must maintain integrity, so you must always be honest. But remember, there is honesty and there is *honesty*; while you don't ever want to lie, it may not be critical for everyone involved to know everything about the project. Select your words very carefully so your honesty does not negatively impact the project.

5. **WATCH AND LOOK:** Listen carefully to the other person's words; phrasing or sometimes just observing their body language will tell you a lot. Avoid derision, banter, contempt or mockery. Be careful with humor unless you know the person with whom you are dealing. Some people have no sense of humor and you can blow the whole negotiation if you try to be funny.

6. **APPROVAL:** Give approval and respect to whomever you negotiate. Acknowledge who they are and what their importance is to the negotiations. Appeal to their ego. Since it is usually unexpected it can sometimes give you the upper hand and it may be returned. It shows your integrity and will cement your relationship for future negotiations.

7. **HUMILITY:** Show humility. Being humble can be used successfully when negotiating. It can even provide you with dominance if it is used correctly.

8. **PROACTIVE:** Be upfront and take the initiative when negotiating. Never let the other party take control of the situation. Avoid arguing or debating with someone since that will lead you to a dead end and only cause you future problems.

9. **EXPOSE YOUR WEAKPOINTS:** It's okay to expose your weak points. It can only make you stronger since the person you are negotiating with does not expect you to expose yourself and it may give you credibility. If you establish a sound relationship with the other party, they may try to help solve those weaknesses for you. Our basic nature is often to help the underdog and it can sometimes be in your favor to be seen as the underdog in the need of support.

10. **AVOID BEING A JERK:** Smugness and conceit are relatives to avoid. Use words such as "we" and "us" and avoid using "I" and "me." People want to work with people who respect them and using the collective noun puts you all on the same team and the deal will be easier to make.

11. **TRUST YOUR INSTINCTS:** This is the producer's barometer. Instincts are never wrong. The producer's instinct is his or her creative self and if you listen to your instincts, you will be ahead of the game.
12. **HAVE A GAME PLAN:** Know what you want to achieve when you go into negotiations and know your parameters. Be ready to walk away if it does not meet your game plan. There are many roads to Mecca, and a minor detour should not keep you from getting there.

THE STAGES OF PRODUCTION

The process of production has a path that is broken into four stages. The development stage is the phase in which the producer is developing the major elements of the project in an effort to raise the money to make the project. Usually the development phase is totally at the expense of the producer and any costs that might be incurred during that time are difficult to recoup from the final project. Development can include preparing the production board, the budget and putting the elements together to release the funds to move the project into the next stage.

Development	Pre-production	Production	Post-production

Figure 1—The Stages of Production

The second stage along the path is pre-production. Pre-production is the period that commences as soon as the financing has been secured. The producer hires the staff and formally begins the task of planning out the details of the project. The pre-production phase of the project is a fixed phase and does not involve the panic or volatility that exists in the production stage.

The third phase on the path is production, the most volatile stage in the process. It is the phase in which most problems can occur. Murphy, of Murphy's Law, was an optimist when it comes to the production stage of the film process. Because of this volatility there is no substitution for solid groundwork in pre-production. What the producer fails to do in development will affect pre-production, what the project fails to do in pre-production affects production and what the project fails to do in production affects post-production—all of which will affect the end result.

Post-production is the last stage on the path of the process of production and is the most fixed phase. More than 80 percent of what happens in post-production can be fiscally determined in pre-production. But in order to do so, the producer must have a clear understanding of the entire process or road the project will take to achieve its end result: the finished project or composite answer print. The composite answer print refers to the best possible photographic image (and sound) of the project produced on film as it comes from the original picture negative.

LOOKING BACKWARDS

What the producer fails to do in development will affect pre-production, what the project fails to do in pre-production affects production, and what the project fails to do in production affects post-production—all of which will affect the end result.

This simple statement is a key element in creative producing. The producer ought to clearly know the path the project will take to achieve the end result, the better to see and plan for any of the problems that might occur along the way. To do that the producer should scrutinize that path backwards from the projects completion (answer print) and plan out each phase of the process. If the producer analyzes the path forward, from development through post-production, without seeing the end result first (the answer print), the unknown factor of what lies along the path affects the probability of the project running out of funds before it is completed. In other words, think of planning the project from Z to A, rather than from A to Z. When you do this, you will foresee some of the difficulties in producing and plan for them during the appropriate stages of the process. By looking down the road backwards from its completion to pre-production and by planning carefully for each phase, you will be minimizing any potential troubles and assuring that you will have enough resources for the projects' completion. This way, each phase from pre-production to production to post-production will be much more efficient and productive. In order to try to catch problems before they arise, the producer must start at the very beginning: with the script.

CHAPTER 3 LOOKING AT THE WRITTEN PROJECT

There is no mystery to breaking down a screenplay. Production managers, assistant directors and producers do it all the time. It is simply a method of reading a screenplay and reducing it to the elements affecting the choreography of production. The breakdown directly affects the pre-production and production phases and indirectly involves the post-production phase of the process. Assistant directors and production managers both break down the project and prepare production boards with an eye to their own responsibilities. Each department head on the project will also do their own breakdown and correlate that to the production manager's board. As the producer, your requirements are different than the assistant director's or production manager's because you need to have your board show you creative issues as they will relate to schedule and budget. Also, the departmental breakdowns only consider the production stage since their involvement ends when production ends. Their breakdowns and boards do not ordinarily consider the post-production stage of the process or the way it impacts the production and the post-production budget. The producer must consider the entire process. This chapter will provide you with the appropriate information for the producer's breakdown and ultimately the production board, so you can make intelligent and creative decisions.

BREAKING DOWN THE SCREENPLAY
The first step in breaking down a script is to prepare a continuity breakdown page for each scene in the project. These are pages that indicate the logistical elements of a scene as they relate to time and people. As the scene changes (since it may be rewritten), the elements on the continuity breakdown page may also change. These pages become the overall "bible" for the written elements in each scene, since they can pertain to setup and shooting

duration during production. They are kept together in a notebook and referred to by either the producer (or sometimes the director), the production manager or the production coordinator. Specific elements from the continuity breakdown pages are translated to production strips, which are then placed on a production board. The production board is used as a mobile tool to assist in the time and labor management of production on a day-to-day basis.

A script must have numbered scenes in order to be broken down. The numbering of scenes is an organizational technique that references story moments for everyone involved in production. It also is a structural guide for post-production editing, and makes for a smooth transition to the post-production stage. Only scenes or slug lines are numbered. To repeat: *Only scenes or slug lines are numbered!* A slug line shows whether the scene is an interior (INT) or exterior (EXT) scene, its setting, and whether the scene takes place during the day or night. For example:

```
21. INT. EYAN'S APARTMENT - NIGHT
```

Sometimes a screenwriter will number the script and in so doing number the shots they may have written into the script. With the exception of the occasional POV shot which sometimes must be written in, screenwriters should avoid writing specific shots into a script. The director interprets a story the way he or she creatively wishes after conferring with both the producer and the writer. Shots may be discussed at that time, but a writer must allow the director the creative freedom to interpret the screenplay and tell the story.

Sometimes writers do not write scenes out completely. They may simply indicate the action. The producer must go through the screenplay and make the appropriate changes to clearly define the breakdown of the story. For example:

```
21. INT. - EYAN'S APARTMENT - NIGHT
    Eyan comes into the apartment and puts the
    shopping bag down on the sofa. He notices the
    time on the hall clock and moves into the hall
    singing HAPPY BIRTHDAY. As he moves quickly
    down the hallway, a masked burglar, hearing
    Eyan, lies in wait in the bedroom. Eyan
    strips off his clothes and drops them in the
```

```
hall, finally walking into the bathroom and
into the shower, drawing the shower curtain
behind him.
```

By examining this scene carefully, we are able to see there are four different locations: 1) the main room off the front door, 2) the hallway, 3) the
bedroom where the burglar waits, 4) the bathroom in which there is a shower. In the middle of this scene, the picture cuts to the bedroom to see the
burglar waiting, or the burglar may be just inside the bedroom door and
lean his head out into the hallway as Eyan passes. How this moment is to be
shot depends on the final choice of location, the ability to have both actors
available on the same day, the director's concept and the time it may take to
do the sequence. Because there are multiple variables, upon first breakdown
of the scene, the producer should rewrite it to read:

```
21.  INT - APARTMENT LIVINGROOM - NIGHT
     Eyan comes into the apartment and puts the
     shopping bag down on the sofa. He notices the
     time on the hall clock.

22.  INT - APARTMENT HALLWAY - NIGHT
     Eyan moves into the hall singing HAPPY BIRTH-
     DAY. As he moves quickly down the hallway.
     Eyan strips off his clothes and drops them in
     the hall.

23.  INT - APARTMENT BEDROOM - NIGHT
     A masked burglar lies in wait, hears Eyan
     singing. As he hears Eyan go past the door,
     he carefully opens the bedroom door and leans
     his head in the hallway.

24.  INT - APARTMENT BATHROOM - NIGHT
     Eyan walks into the bathroom and into the
     shower, drawing the shower curtain.
```

Once the location has been secured and if the configuration of the apartment is one that does not have a hallway leading to a bathroom, the above
breakdown is the only way one can see the details of each moment and

adjust for them. If the location is going to be a set that is constructed accordingly, then the scene may remain as previously written. This will depend on the producing philosophy of the project and the ability of the producer to have the shoe fit the foot. However, please notice that the scene numbers are different. This is because there may be separate camera positions in each of the locations as the dramatic intent of the story shifts from each location. If it is to be a continuous action sequence then a single strip on the board will reflect scenes 21, 22 and 24 to be shot at one time, with scene 23 being a separate scene in the bedroom.

Sometimes the writer may write a scene and indicate it as a montage.

```
35.  RODEO DRIVE MONTAGE
     Eyan  takes  Trish  to  various  stores  along
     Rodeo Drive to get a new wardrobe.
```

Here again, since "various stores" indicates more than one but as yet we do not know how many, the scene may have one breakdown page indicating the montage. But a notation should be included that once the stores have been secured, a breakdown page for each store will have to be created. Production will demand new camera position setups in each location and will therefore require separate breakdown pages. However, the scene number for each page is still 35 and it may include a letter after the number, such as 35A, 35B, 35C, etc. Although the sequence is shot in several locations, they are all part of Scene 35 because the dramatic intent of the story calls for Eyan to shop with Trish making the emotional attitude constant. The dramatic intent of the story for that montage has not shifted.

At times, the writer may write a telephone conversation and indicate that it is *intercut.*

```
53.  INT - DOWNTOWN PHONE BOOTH - DAY
     Eyan is on the phone talking to Trish, who is
     at home waiting for him to arrive.

                    EYAN
          I'm going to be late, darling.


INTERCUT
```

> TRISH
> But I have made a wonderful
> dinner for us tonight!
>
> EYAN
> It can't be helped dear; I'm work-
> ing late.

The camera reveals that Eyan's assistant
Meredith is in the phone booth with him.

> TRISH
> How late are you going to be?
>
> EYAN
> I don't know as yet. It depends on
> how soon I am able to get into the
> case with the client.
>
> TRISH
> Okay. I'll keep things warm.

She hangs up the phone and puts the dinner in
the oven.

Upon examining this scene we see that the writer wrote it as a two-loca-
tion, three-character scene. Because there are two locations for the scene—
the downtown phone booth and Trish's house—each location will have the
same number: 53. But one will be 53A and the other 53B. They will be shot
at different times in the production schedule and in all probability the actor
playing Eyan will not be present when the actor playing Trish is doing her
dialogue and vice versa. The writer gives an indication to the editor and producer to intercut the scene as they wish which is why the word INTERCUT
is written in the margin.

In another example, the writer may have written a scene that calls for the
characters to watch something on television. If the sequence on television
has to be shot as part of the story, then the sequence on television will have
a scene number that will indicate that it works as part of the scene. If the
director wants to see the actors watching the sequence then the production

will have to schedule the television sequence before the scene in which the characters are watching the television.

Another example may be a screenplay that indicates a POV. Although writers should be discouraged from writing specific shots or angles in their screenplays, they often include a POV as a characters point of view. For example:

```
75.  INT - TRISH'S KITCHEN - NIGHT
     Trish puts the letter down and pours a cup of
     coffee. She hears a car pull up and walks over
     to the window and looks into the alley. From
     her POV she sees Eyan getting into his car
     with Meredith and driving away. She begins to
     cry as she lowers the blinds and closes the
     kitchen curtains.
```

The POV shot is really another scene and the sequence should be rewritten as:

```
75.  INT - TRISH'S KITCHEN - NIGHT
     Trish puts the letter down and pours a cup of
     coffee. She hears a car pull up and walks over
     to the window and looks into the alley.

Her POV

76.  EXT - ALLEY - NIGHT
     Eyan gets into his car with Meredith. They
     drive away.

77.  INT - TRISH'S KITCHEN - NIGHT
     She begins to cry as she lowers the blinds
     and closes the kitchen curtains.
```

From time to time a writer may write a sequence that takes place in a vehicle.

```
82.  INT - 1963 VW BUG - DAY
     Eyan and Trish are traveling home from the
```

> airport. There is a definite sense of neither
> one of them wanting to be with one another.
>
>   EYAN
>   I'll drop you off and then go to
>   the office.
>
>   TRISH
>   Why? So you can meet Meredith?

Although the scene is set in a car, the scene location is not the car but instead is the street or highway. The production elements will dictate how the director interprets the sequence. The director can show the car traveling along the highway while the audience hears the dialogue over the exterior shot, or the director can shoot the actors in the car, which will have to be towed by another vehicle.

These examples indicate your need to read the script carefully and attempt to visualize the choreography of production, all while minimizing the dialogue as it has little relevance to the choreography of production.

Once the project is appropriately numbered you are ready to break down the screenplay to its choreographic elements and complete a continuity breakdown page for each scene. The breakdown elements will have a direct correlation to the amount of time and the number of dollars it may take to visualize the scene.

TITLE: The name of the project.

PROD NO.: (Production Number): Sometimes, for accounting purposes, production companies may want to assign a production number to a project. This is especially applicable in television when there are multiple episodes in various stages of the production process.

DIRECTOR: The name of the director (and/or producer).

SET: Description of the setting as indicated within the slug line of a scene. In the first example above *EYAN'S APARTMENT* is the setting in the slug line of scene 21.

SCENE #: Denotes the scene number, which is opposite the slug line of the script.

B.D. (Breakdown) PAGE #: The consecutive numbering of the breakdown pages. Scene numbers and the breakdown page numbers may not always be the same. Scene numbering may vary depending on the script but the breakdown pages will be consecutive.

CONTINUITY BREAKDOWN PAGE

TITLE: *LOVE IN A HANDBASKET*   B.D. Page # *55*

PRODUCTION # *348910*   Sequence : *INT*

DIRECTOR: *J. Moore,*   PRODUCER: *C. Bradley*   Day or Night: *Day*

SET: *Downtown Street Phone Booth*   Location/Studio: *L*

SCENE # *53A*   Script Pages: *5/8*
     64

Synopsis:
     Eyan tells Trish he will be late for dinner.

Cast	Atmosphere	Props
Eyan *Meredith* *Trish (VO)*	*10 Passerby*	*Phone Booth*
Bits	**Special Effects**	**Vehicles and Livestock**
	Sound *Record Sound*	**Music**

Notes
     Use voice of Trish from scene 53B. Carry phone booth on prop truck

SEQUENCE: The INTERIOR (INT) or EXTERIOR (EXT) indication of the scene found in the slug line. Because interior and exterior production choreography have different lighting and set up requirements this can translate to increased production time.

DAY OR NIGHT: The DAY or NIGHT indication of the scene is found in the slug line. This does not indicate the time of day the scene is to be shot, but refers to whether the dramatic action in the story takes place during the day or night. Production choreography shifts dramatically between scenes that are INTERIOR DAY, EXTERIOR DAY, INTERIOR NIGHT or EXTERIOR NIGHT.

LOCATION OR STUDIO: An indication as to if the scene is shot on a location (either distant or local), or at a studio or studio backlot. There are significant differences in organizational techniques between location and studio production.

SCRIPT PAGES: Script pages are broken down into 8ths. Eight/8ths equal one page. This is the yardstick that is used when discussing the length of specific scenes. It permits the director to discuss specific logistics of a scene in relationship to the time it takes to complete a scene. And the scene is talked about in terms of number of pages it takes to present the scene. When indicating the page count do not reduce the 8ths to a common denominator (such as 4/8ths becoming 1/2); keep the count in 8ths. However, if a scene is more than one page do not count the page as 8/8ths, count it as one page. Only count portions of pages in 8ths. So a page and a half scene has a page count of 1 4/8ths, not 12/8ths. One bit of warning however. Because a scene may be 1/8th of a page it does not mean that it will take a brief period of production time to shoot. That 1/8th page might read: *"The Indians attack the village"* and may require two or three days of production depending on the creative and dramatic vision of the producer and director. *NOTE: Write the page number of the script where a scene begins underneath the Script Pages space. This becomes a quick reference if you need to refer to the script.*

SYNOPSIS: Write a short one or two phrase description of what happens in the scene:

i.e. *"Eyan comes into the apartment,"* or *"Eyan takes a shower singing Happy Birthday,"* or *"Eyan and Trish buy clothes on Rodeo Drive."*

CAST: This refers to any member of the cast of characters who says a line or words in the scene. It is listed separately from those members of the cast without speaking parts because actors who deliver lines are usually paid more money than those who don't. These characters will be the characters who move the action and the story forward. It is important to read the screenplay carefully because a cast member may speak in one scene but not speak in another. Provided they speak somewhere in the script, they are considered a speaking member of the cast. In some instances a major character endemic to the story may not speak at all. In those cases, the character is listed under *Cast*.

BITS: This is shorthand for "silent bit" and refers to any onscreen talent that does not speak in a scene but does interact with principle actors. Often they are indicated in the description of a scene by a generic name such as waiter, doorman, waitress, bellboy etc. *"The waiter brings Eyan and Trish's meal to the table."* All silent bits in a scene are listed on a breakdown page since they usually receive a higher wage than talent who appear as atmosphere, but a lower wage than actors with speaking parts. The term "bit" is also used to denote a cast member who has one or two lines and works as a day player. They are often referred to as "bit players" since their role is very small in the project. Because they speak they are included in the breakdown page under "cast."

ATMOSPHERE: Cast members who "people the scene" creating the background are defined as atmosphere. They are sometimes called the "wallpaper" of a scene since the right atmosphere will create an aesthetic texture that translates to the scene. This may be written in the screenplay in the following manner: *"Eyan and Trish walk through the crowd of people on their way to the airport gate."* As the producer you will determine the numbers and genders of people who make up the crowd when you break the scene down as you will be thinking about the budget as you do your breakdown. If a specific atmosphere character is required, than the character is listed separately under this category. For example, if the description above read *"Eyan and Trish walk through a crowd of people on their way to the airport gate. They pass a tour group of Asian senior citizens."* The Asian senior citizens would be listed as atmosphere but separately from the other atmosphere in the scene and you should determine the number of seniors in the group.

SPECIAL EFFECTS: Indicates any mechanical or makeup effects that might be required for the scene. Mechanical and makeup effects require specialists who will need time to set up for whatever effect is required. If the work is done by an effects company, you will have to know which specific scenes they will be required for. Further, you will need to determine the coordination needed so the effect can be carefully executed on a precise cue as needed creatively by the director. Since the breakdown process is a process that permits the producer to manage time in relationship to creativity, it is important to have special effects for each scene listed.

A mechanical effect is any visual effect that is created mechanically during the production process. Today's technology permits the producer to digitally create effects. Digital effects are handled in post-production, although images needed for the effect may need to be created during production either by first unit photography or second unit photography. In such cases the project will employ a visual effects supervisor whose job it is to coordinate the elements. Mechanical effects can be anything from mist rising over a river, to blowing up a bridge, to *Gone With the Wind's* burning of Atlanta.

A makeup effect is required by the story and performed on an actor to create a specific effect. Jim Carrey went through many hours of makeup effects to become the Grinch before starting work each day for Universal's *How the Grinch Stole Christmas*. If a character dies onscreen and the script calls for a visible gaping wound, the scene will require a makeup effects supervisor. These effects will take time and you will need to know for which specific scenes they will be needed, so they are included on the breakdown page.

When determining what production effects are needed, the producer must read the script carefully and logically think the elements through. Examples of a special effect may be as vague as: *"Eyan and Trish make love in a steamy shower."* The actors would not really be acting in a shower that was so hot that it created steam. But since the writer and director call for the steam as an effect to translate the creative internal characterizations of the moment, the steam would have to be created by an effects person.

SOUND: This box is used to indicate whether a scene is to be shot with sound or silently. Most scenes have dialogue and therefore production sound needs to be recorded. But directors and producers like to record sound for all scenes whenever possible whether there is dialogue or not. The ability to record sound during a scene requires placement of a microphone, which can affect the time it takes to do a shot. However, in many scenes it is not necessary to record sound as the sound can be added in post-production. For those scenes this space on the breakdown page is marked with the letters M.O.S. According to film lore, the acronym M.O.S. has its origin in the early days of sound when well-known German directors were asked to come to Hollywood. As I heard it, the great German director Ernest Lubitsch was directing a scene that had no dialogue and just before the camera rolled Lubitsch was asked by the soundman if he wanted the sound recorded since there was no dialogue. Mr. Lubitsch responded very dramatically "No, ve vill do this scene mit out sound." And to this day, the expression "mit out sound" is translated to M.O.S. If a scene is written in the script as *"The van pulls up to the curb and stops,"* it is not necessary to record the sound since the sound effects would be added to the scene later and you can make the decision to do the scene M.O.S.

MUSIC: This space indicates if music is needed to shoot a specific scene. If it is, it will require the ability to have pre-recorded music played back or the recording of live music in the scene. This will require more production elements than are customarily used in production and will add time to the production of the specific scene.

PROPS: Although the property master will do a breakdown, the producer must indicate any items that are handled by actors or help to create the mood that are written into the description of the scene.

"The camera moves past a lantern, an ax stuck in a tree stump, and a rusty wheel barrow before it settles on Eyan and Trish who are sitting having lunch." The lantern, ax, and wheelbarrow would be written on the breakdown page under props, as would be the lunch. Writers include props and descriptive elements to point up the creative intent of the story. By indicating what props are called for in the script the producer is able to see if there will be any major prop issues that may be problematic or need to be solved by tradeoff relationships.

VEHICLES AND LIVESTOCK: This space lists any vehicles or livestock that might be required for the scene. This does not refer to vehicles or livestock that may be needed to transport production elements but refers only to those that appear onscreen. Including them in the breakdown again provides the producer with the opportunity to see if there are any major vehicle or livestock problems that may be problematic or solved by tradeoff relationships. It may also be necessary to schedule a vehicle or animal on a production board as one would an actor. This is the case when the vehicle or animal is specific to a character and you need to know on which day it appears in the schedule. They will require personnel to monitor or transport it for the sequences.

NOTES: At the bottom of the breakdown page is a space for the producer to indicate any ideas or additional production elements for the scene. *"Trish and Eyan are walking on the beach at sunset."* A special note for this scene might refer to shooting it at magic hour or using a steadicam.

Computer programs like Movie Magic and Turbo Budget A/D are used commonly throughout the industry. These programs permit the input of

---

PRODUCERS VOCABULARY

Magic Hour—The time of day on exterior locations just before the sun rises or sets. This usually lasts about 20 minutes.

the data that appears on every breakdown page. They also allow for other information eventually used by the production manager or first assistant director, such as the whereabouts of each set or location. As these programs manipulate data, they easily permit the production manager to quickly generate the schedules and lists used during production. They are also able to create a breakdown format from a computer-generated screenplay and the breakdown information will be as accurate as the accuracy of the data in the screenplay. Therefore the producer should check the breakdown for accuracy.[1] These programs will also generate strips which are inserted into colored sleeves for a production board. While these are wonderful time-saving tools, when you prepare the strips *by hand* you begin to see the choreographic elements of production and there is something quite visceral with this process that brings you closer to the vision of the project. Once the screenplay is accurately broken down the next step is preparing the production board.

PREPARING THE PRODUCTION BOARD

A production board has two, four, six or eight panels. A six or eight panel board is the standard board for a feature length project. Each production board consists of at least one header and various color strips. The header is placed at the front of the production board and captions out the specifics of what may be indicated on each strip. Strips are narrow color cardboard bands on which specific information is transferred from the breakdown sheets that correspond to the captions on the header. At least four different colored strips are needed for the board representing interior day, exterior day, interior night and exterior night. By seeing these colors at a glance you immediately know that each have their own production requirements. If the project calls for scenes that would have unusual production characteristics (such as scenes that take place in moving vehicles), it is not unusual for these to be indicated with another color strip as well.

The Header

The first task on the header is filling in the title of the project, and the name of the director (if known) and the producer and the date of the most current script used in breaking down the board. *All work is done in pencil, so it*

---

[1] The computer programs do not make decisions. They merely look for like notations. The producer makes creative decisions while working on a breakdown: i.e. number and gender of atmosphere, characters in scenes who may not speak in the scene but appear elsewhere in the script, etc.

THE HEADER

Breakdown Page
Day or Night
Location or Studio
Sequence
No. of Pages

Title	Love in a Handbasket
Director	J. Moore
Producer	C. Bradley
Asst. Dir.	R. Robles
Script Dated	2/04/01

Character	Artist	
Eyan Hayes		1
Trish Malone		2
Suny Malone		3
Angela Hayes		4
Tommy Joe		5
Delphine		6
Meredith		7
		8
		9
		10
		11
		12
		13
		14
		15
		16
		17
		18
		19
		20
		21
		22
		23
		24
		25
		26
		27
		28
		29
		30
		31
		32
		33
		34
		35
		36
		37
		38
		39
		40
		41

Figure 2

can be erased. In the blank area between the number of pages and the title, you should provide a brief legend as to a color explanation of the strips.

Cast

Primary characters of the story should be listed first. They are written on individual lines under character. (See Figure #4)

You will note that a number is automatically assigned to each characters' name. This is the number that will be used to identify the character whenever the character is in a scene. Usually we list the main characters first, and

HEADER WITH SEVEN STRIPS

Breakdown Page							
Day or Night							
Location or Studio							
Sequence							
No. of Pages							
Title Love in a Handbasket							
Director J. Moore							
Producer C. Bradley							
Asst. Dir. R. Robles							
Script Dated 2/04/01							
WHITE= Exterior Day							
BLUE = Exterior Night							
YELLOW = Interior Day							
GREEN = Interior Night							
RED = Car Interior							
Character **Artist**							
Eyan Hayes	1						
Trish Malone	2						
Suny Malone	3						
Angela Hayes	4						
Tommy Joe	5						
Delphine	6						
Meredith	7						
	8						
	9						
	10						
	11						
	12						
	13						
	14						
	15						
	16						
	17						
	18						
	19						
	20						
	21						
	22						
	23						
	24						
	25						
	26						
	27						
	28						
	29						
	30						
	31						
	32						
	33						
	34						
	35						
	36						
	37						
	38						
	39						
	40						

Figure 3

work our way down the list to characters that have smaller speaking roles. All *speaking* roles are listed by character on the header.

Some screenplays have many more speaking roles than there are lines on the header. In those cases the header is altered accordingly. As the speaking roles get smaller, there is less of a likelihood of those smaller roles working together. Therefore we are able to re-number a portion of the header to adjust for this phenomena. (See Figure #5)

Character		Artist	
Eyan Hayes			1
Trish Malone			2
Suny Malone			3
Angela Hayes			4
Tommy Joe			5
Delphine			6

Figure 4

Character		Artist	
Eyan Hayes			1
Trish Malone			2
Suny Malone			3
Angela Hayes			4
Tommy Joe			5
Delphine			6
Meredith	7	Policeman #1	16
Annette	8	Policeman #2	17
Bob	9	Tyler	18
Don	10	Teacher	19
Elizabeth	11	Nun #2	20
Bernie	12	Adam	21

Figure 5

Bit and Atmosphere

Once the cast of characters (speaking roles) has been penciled on the header, the next step is to create a legend for the bit roles. Each day the same silent bit character works, the actor portraying that character gets paid. If a bit character is assigned dialogue because of on set inspiration by the director on any day, and the project is a signatory to the Screen Actors Guild, the actor receives a "bump" in salary to that of a speaking role wage. And for every subsequent day worked by that bit character, whether or not he or she has dialogue, the actor continues to receive the higher wage.

A simple technique of creating a separate legend over four or five lines on the board works well for indicating bit characters. Each bit character is assigned a letter and the boxes corresponding to the numbers would reflect the letters of the bit characters needed for the scene. Also, select one num-

Character		Artist				
Eyan Hayes						1
Trish Malone						2
Suny Malone						3
Angela Hayes						4
Tommy Joe						5
Delphine						6
Meredith						7
Annette						8
Bob						9
Don						10
Elizabeth	11	Mary				15
Bernie	12	Policeman #1				16
Fireman #1	13	Policeman #2				17
June	14	Tyler				18
Waiter **A**	Bartender **E**	Teacher **I**				19
Waitress **B**	Rabbi **F**	Nun #2 **J**				20
Traffic Cop **C**	Nun #1 **G**					21
Atmosphere						22
30 beach marines						23

Figure 6

bered line for atmosphere required in a scene. (See Figure #6). The box on the strip corresponding to this number will indicate the number of atmosphere needed in the scene. Special atmosphere should be listed underneath.

The Strips

Once the header has been prepared in this manner, the producer is ready to transfer the information from each breakdown page to individual strips. For purposes of this explanation we will look at the top part of the strips first.

1. In the box on the strip opposite the Breakdown page line, write in the number of the breakdown page.
2. In the box on the strip opposite the Day or Night line, write either D or N as it applies from the breakdown page.
3. In the box on the strip opposite the Location or Studio line, write either L or S if you intend on shooting at a studio or on location. The amount of studio work will be reflected in your budget as will travelling to locations.
4. In the box on the strip opposite the Sequence line, write either INT. or EXT. as it is indicated on the breakdown page.
5. In the box on the strip opposite the No. of Pages line, write in the page count of the scene as indicated on the breakdown page.
6. In the long space on the strip write in the setting of the scene exactly as indicated on the breakdown page.

You will notice that there is no specific space on the strip to indicate the scene number. This is because sometimes scene numbers will change, but the breakdown page numbers do not. However, it is much more efficient to indicate the scene number on each strip even if the scene number eventually changes. Therefore:

7. In the box on the strip opposite the line that has the words "character" and "artist," write in the scene number as indicated from the breakdown page. (See Figure #7)

Breakdown Page	1	2	3	4	5	6	7	8	9	10
Day or Night	D	N	N	N	D	D	N	N	D	D
Location or Studio	L	L	S	L	L	S	L	L	L	L
Sequence	EXT	INT	INT	INT	EXT	INT	EXT	EXT	INT	EXT
No. of Pages	7/8	5/8	2	2	1 1/8	3 1/8	2 4/8	1/8	5/8	1 1/8
Title: Love in a Handbasket Director: Jason Moore Producer: C. Bradley Asst. Dir.: R. Robles Script Dated: 2/04/01	Eyans Apartment	Eyans Bedroom	Trish's Livingroom	Eyan's Bedroom	Beach	Euclid County Jail	Alley behind Euclid Jail	Beach Pier	Neighborhood Italian Restaurant	Eyan's Apartment
Character Artist	1	2	3A	3B	4	5	6	7	8	9

Figure 7

For the remainder of the strip, only information that is applicable to the ongoing creative producing decision-making process is taken from the breakdown page. Most important are those elements that appear in front of the camera, such as actors, atmosphere, animals and bit performers. Information regarding vehicles and props are not boarded unless they are important to, or indicative of, character in the story. As an example, in *Hunter's Blood* I chose to board the Ford Bronco because this was a tradeoff product and it was needed on specific days. This required coordination with Ford as the Bronco was on loan for the picture. Also, it made sense creatively to board the Bronco since in the story it represented a safe place that the hunters were trying to get to while they were being hunted. It therefore served as a character in its own right.

It is not necessary for the producer to indicate on the board as to if a scene is to be shot M.O.S. This can be determined later during production meetings and will be of concern for the assistant director. During their own preparation the Property, Set Dressing and Wardrobe Departments will build on top of what is written in the script and flesh out their contribution to the visuals of the vision.

Figure #8 demonstrates the way the appropriate information is translated to each strip. Each bit of information has a direct correlation to each other bit of information and it permits the producer to see quickly the many

		#	Eyan /Trish arrive at Apt.	Trish /Eyan make love	Suny /Angela Argue	Trish on phone	Trish/Eyan almost drown	Angela Bails Suny out	Trish/Mered. Argue	The heist is planned (pos. magic hour)	Trish & Eyan join the plan	Eyan's Apt is on fire
Eyan Hayes		1	1	1			1				1	1
Trish Malone		2	2	2	2	2	2	2	2		2	2
Suny Malone		3			3		3	3		3	3	3
Angela Hayes		4	4		4		4	4		4	4	4
Tommy Joe		5	5									
Delphine		6							6			
Meredith		7							7			
June		8								8		
Bob		9							9			
Don		10								10		
Eyan's Stunt Double		11					11		11			
Trish's Stunt Double		12					12		12			
Delia Varni		13										
Charlotte Silver		14										
Cop #1 15	Mary	19	15				15		15			
Cop #2 16	Monica	20					20		16/20			
Fire #1 17	Leslie	21	17				21		17			17
Tyler 18	Gower	22					18		18		22	
Waiter A	Nun D	23	C/D						E		A/B	
Waitress B	Teacher E	24							C			
Rabbi C	Librarian F	25										
		26										
		27										
		28										
Atmosphere		29					4					2
30 Beach Marines		30					30					
		31										
		32										
		33										
		34										
		35										
		36										
		37										

Figure 8

choreographic permutations of production. Each of these permutations have a fiscal relationship to the creative process.

The following is taken from each breakdown page:

1. In the box on the strip opposite the apropos character indicated in the scene, write the number that has been assigned to that character.

2. Note that depending on how the header is prepared it is possible for one box to have two numbers in it. This is certainly the case with larger projects with many speaking roles. (Refer to lines 15-22 in Figure #8)

3. In the assigned number boxes opposite the "Bit Legend" use letters to indicate the appropriate bit player on the breakdown page. (Refer to lines 23, 24, 25 in Figure #8)

4. When atmosphere is required by a scene and is indicated on the breakdown page, place an X in the box on the strip opposite the numbered line that has been assigned on the header for "atmosphere." This is usually somewhere near the end of the strip, but before the summary.

   When atmosphere is needed for a scene, many producers often leave it up to the director and assistant director to determine the gender of the atmosphere. The director may determine that the scene requires not only adults as atmosphere but children as well. However, the director and assistant director might not take into consideration that welfare workers are required on the set when children are used. The director is also limited in the amount of time that the children are able to work due to work laws for minors. This will create production time limitations. Further, depending on the time of day that the atmosphere is to be used, the producer may have to provide meals. This can be costly. So the producer should be involved with atmosphere decisions because they relate directly to not only the visual creativity but also the creative use of the budget. Therefore, on the producers' production board, where atmosphere is indicated, a number should be placed in each quadrant of the X. The four quadrants represent "men," "women," "boys" and "girls,"thus providing a sense of what the atmosphere in a specific scene may look like early in the preparation phase. This method allows the producer to make creative adjustments before the preparation gets too far underway and this detail is missed.

5. About six rows up from the bottom of the strip, write in the brief summary of the scene indicated on the breakdown page.

6. If there are any special notes indicated in the breakdown page, then those same notes can be indicated in the bottom summary space. (Refer to Strip #8 in Figure #9)

7. If there is an indication on the breakdown page of a mechanical or makeup effect for a specific scene, then indicate the need for this by placing a bold (colored) dot on the strip where the set or location is indicated. (Refer to Strip #10 in Figure #9)

8. Finally, if there are any other specifics that, as the producer, you wish to indicate on the production board which may have a direct correlation to fiscal and creative decisions, then find a method of indicating that. The board is for you, so prepare it so you can understand it and can use it to communicate to others your ideas for the logistics and choreography necessary for a creative production period.

Figure #9 is a portion of a producer's production board not yet broken down into shooting days, and it breaks the project down to the visual basics. The production board speaks to the producer. It indicates which scenes may be problematic and which scenes may work better if consolidated with other scenes. It tells the producer where money can be best used on the screen in telling the story. By reading the bottom summary in a continuous manner, the producer is able to see the action of the film unfold. A glance at the numbers denoting when specific cast members work can tell the producer how the Screen Actors Guild (also known as SAG) budget may lay out. Because the strips are of varying colors, a glance at the number of Exterior Day or Exterior Nights can highlight possible production problems which may occur on exterior locations.

Note that the header in Figure #9 also indicates the color of the strips and what they designate. This legend must be posted so others can understand the board without supervision.

Miscellaneous Boarding Issues

Since breakdown pages are directly correlated to the structure of the screenplay, many times there will be more strips than there are spaces on a six or eight paneled production board. The screenplay may change continuously especially if the project adheres to the shoe fit the foot theory. Because each strip represents specific production logistics the project takes shape as shooting locations are secured and as the screenplay goes through various revisions. The strips may therefore change, and it is very likely there will be scenes that can be consolidated on a single strip.

THE COMPLETED HEADER AND ELEVEN CONTINUOUS STRIPS

Color legend:
Blue: Ext. Night, Green: Int. Night
White: Ext. Day, Yellow: Int. Day
Red: Traveling sequences

Title: Love in a Handbasket
Director: J. Moore
Producer: C. Bradley
Asst. Dir.: R. Robles
Script Dated: 2/4/01

	1	2	3	4	5	6	7	8	9	10	
Breakdown Page	1	2	3	4	5	6	7	8	9	10	
Day or Night	D	N	N	N	D	D	N	N	D	D	
Location or Studio	L	L	S	L	L	S	L	L	L	L	Airplane Landing
Sequence	EXT	INT	INT	INT	EXT	INT	EXT	EXT	INT	EXT	
No. of Pages	7/8	5/8	2	2	1 1/8	3 1/8	2 4/8	1/8	5/8	1 1/8	
Location	Eyans Apartment	Eyan's Bedroom	Trish's Livingroom	Eyan's Bedroom	Beach	Euclid County Jail	Alley behind Euclid Jail	Beach Pier	Neighborhood Italian Restaurant	Eyan's Apartment	

Character	Artist	#	1	2	3A	3B	4	5	6	7	8	9
Eyan Hayes		1	1	1		1	1		1		1	1
Trish Malone		2	2	2		2	2	2	2		2	2
Suny Malone		3			3		3	3		3	3	3
Angela Hayes		4	4		4		4	4		4	4	4
Tommy Joe		5	5									
Delphine		6							6			
Meredith		7							7			
June		8									8	
Bob		9							9			
Don		10									10	
Eyan's Stunt Double		11					11		11			
Trish's Stunt Double		12					12		12			
Delia Varni		13										
Charlotte Silver		14										
Cop #1 15	Mary	19	15				15		15			
Cop #2 16	Monica	20					20		16/20			
Fire #1 17	Leslie	21	17				21		17			17
Tyler 18	Gower	22					18		18	22		
Waiter A Nun D		23	C/D						E			A/B
Waitress B Teacher E		24							C			
Rabbi C Librarian F		25										
		26										
		27										
		28										
Atmosphere		29					3 ✕ 2 (4)					4
10 beach marines		30					30					

Scene descriptions (by column):
1: Eyan/Trish Arrive at Apt.
2: Trish/Eyan make love
3A: Suny/Angela Argue
3B: Trish on phone
4: Trish/Eyan almost drown
5: Angela Bails Suny out
6: Trish/Mered. Argue
7: The heist is planned (pos. magic hour)
8: Trish & Eyan join the plan
9: Eyan's Apt. on Fire

STOCK FOOTAGE: 1/8, EXT, SF, D, 11

Figure 9

The Production Board Eventually Becomes an Extension of the Creative Producer.

One example of scene consolidation (and one that is most common), are continuous dramatic action scenes in one setting that are intercut with other scenes. In this case it is acceptable to consolidate the scenes on one strip since the action and emotional content are continuous. In all probability the director will shoot all of each location's scenes as if they were one scene because there are no dramatic changes in time which might call for a redress of setting, costume changes or emotional shifts of the characters. The top section of the strip might look like Figure #10, as it would reflect information from three separate breakdown pages.

45, 47, 49
D
L
INT
2 1/8
One room schoolhouse
40, 42, 44

Figure 10

Note that once the dramatic time in a location changes, a new strip must be prepared.

Many times a screenplay will call for the use of stock footage. Stock footage is already existing film (shot by other people) that is purchased for use in the project and licensed through a film footage library. Usually it involves imagery such as an airplane taking off or landing, or historical footage such as that used in the motion picture *Forrest Gump*. A production board must contain every scene whether the director shoots it or not. Therefore, a strip must represent stock footage as well. However, since it will not be part of the production's obligation, a strip is prepared detailing in the summary what the scene is, and the words STOCK FOOTAGE written over the length of the strip. It is then placed in the production board upside down. (See Figure #9) The same is true if the project incorporates a second unit production team. Separate colored strips of those scenes to be shot via second unit should be prepared and included in the producer's production board.

The preparation of the board raises the chicken and egg question that students always ask me. The practice of studio production and budget departments is to create the production board from the screenplay, and then create a budget from information that the board provides. This philosophy is based on the assumption that the project is writer driven rather than producer driven. In this case a screenplay written by a writer without any regard or knowledge of the logistics of production is given to a group of people none of whom have the responsibility for the creative result of the picture. They read the screenplay, prepare a board and create a budget, all without first getting input from either the producer or the director. At best this will lead to pre-production, production and post-production problems. At worst, this process will undermine the ability to creatively tell a story successfully. Elements that increase the cost of a project are primarily visual elements. In projects employing visuals to tell the story, the budget will reflect what is needed to create those visuals. If it is an historical project, or crosses various geographic regions, it will require a budget to support those requirements. If a project requires specific casting then the budget may reflect an increase to accommodate those casting elements. Therefore the producer must start out with a sensible budget plan and look at the screenplay from that perspective. Writers do not consider budget limitations or production elements when they work from their imaginations which is why the producer should employ the shoe fit the foot theory from the genesis of the project. (Besides, what makes a good narrative relies on the depth of the characters and what they say and feel, not just visual effects).

It is critical for the producer to know the choreographic elements of production through the production board process. Preparing the board gives the producer the opportunity to see any potential production problems or problems in the writing and make appropriate changes either in production or in the writing before these problems have an affect on the production process. The production board should be the producer's tool and when interpreted by the producer will provide needed information for quick and easy creative decisions. Therefore the producer should be the first author of

— • • • —

I was given a licensing fee of $1.4 million dollars from the network for the television movie The Girl, the Gold Watch and Everything. *As already mentioned, studios require the producer to be fiscally responsible by signing off on a budget. The studio production and budget departments prepared a board and budget from the screenplay. When the budget department came in with their budget of $2.6 million it was partially due to the special effects called for in the story. We wanted to "stop time" on exterior locations. The studio production department said the budget was too high due in part to what the script called for and I was instructed to have the screenplay rewritten to allow the effects to happen on interior soundstages in a simpler and less expensive fashion. But I had prepared my own board and budget and knew we could create the exterior effects through an experimental videotape transfer to film process that was the forerunner of high definition television. I knew that by using this experimental process the special effects would cost 1/10th of what they might cost if they were attempted entirely on film. It could also be done in half the time. I told the studio that the effects would cost no more than $30,000, and showed them the item in the budget that I had prepared for the project. My executive producers backed me all the way on this issue and we went ahead and made the film. The special effects did cost $30,000 and the picture was finally produced for $1,360,000—below the licensing fee—and the studio suits were astounded when they saw the results onscreen.*

— • • • —

a production board (and budget). Every production is different and when the board is arranged and rearranged for the needs of production, the project takes on its own personality. The producer *must* be in synch with that personality.

The production board is the producer's bible. It is the map that allows the producer to make instant creative decisions in relation to the budget and the visual needs of the project. It allows the producer to examine the choreography of production and see the creation of the visuals from a fiscal point of view. There is no mystery in the preparation of a production board. The mystery lies in the laying out of the board. (This will be addressed in Chapter 11.)

———— • • • ————

"The film business is simply that—a business. Like any Fortune 100 business, it is driven by creativity and product with the common denominator being cost and profit. Throughout my career to date, I have been fortunate enough to have enjoyed a creative and collaborative experience with some of today's hardest driving, most creative and knowledgeable producers and directors (James Cameron, Danny DeVito, Michael Douglas, Peter Guber, Gale Anne Hurd, Mark Johnson, Barry Levinson and Joel Silver to name a few) ... Producers often find themselves pitted against, on one side, the studio or bankers who put up the funds to make the film, and on the other— their director. Producers must walk a fine line between guarding the creative vision, guarding the budget and maintaining the relationships and confidence of the studio, distributor, bankers, financiers and completion bond companies. At the end of the day we must remember that the film business creates entertainment, enjoyment, visual dimension and expressionism—but is a business that needs profit to maintain its existence. Art, on the other hand, is the guy down the street who owns the pawn shop."

—Steven R. Benson, Visual Effects Supervisor, Producer,
Studio Executive, *Austin Powers, International Man of
Mystery; Aliens, The Crow I, The Crow II, The Jewel of the
Nile, Sniper, Commando, Prefontaine, Spy Hard*

———— • • • ————

CHAPTER 4 THE PRODUCTION BUDGET

An independent producer's responsibility is to know the budget backwards and forwards, inside and out, and creatively finesse the resources so that every cent will be seen on the screen. The beacon phrase must be "every quarter spent on the project should look like a dollar and a half onscreen."

The production budget is the independent producer's guidebook. The producer should prepare it as if no deals or tradeoffs were granted for the production. The final production budget will have a direct correlation to the philosophy of production and will be reflected by the production board.

There is a philosophy in production planning that prescribes breaking down a script first, then preparing a budget based upon the script breakdown. However, an illogical factor drives that philosophy. The writer of a screenplay rarely focuses on the problems inherent in production while writing a narrative. As an example, a screenplay whose story is based upon character and not special effects, may include a scene that reads:

```
43. EXT - HOUSE - NIGHT
    A barrage of bullets scatters across the
    front of the house. After one last warning
    shot, Suny comes out of the house to face his
    accusers.
```

Although the "barrage of bullets" might provide an exciting visual, this 1/8th page scene can cost hundreds of thousands of dollars to create. Because the strength of the scene lies with a dramatic way to force the lead character from the house, it may be possible to find another solution equally dramatic and visual but considerably less expensive to create:

```
43. EXT - HOUSE - NIGHT
    A barrage of bullets scatters across the
    front lawn of the house, shattering the mail-
    box and the flower boxes along the path.
    After one last warning shot, Suny comes out
    of the house to face his accusers.
```

If we were to attempt to do the description of the scene as originally written, we would have to either damage the front of the house which would need to be restored afterwards, or build a false front that can be damaged. If the effect did not work successfully for some technical reason the first time it was attempted, a new wall would have to be brought in. By using the lawn and mailboxes and flower boxes you can buy at a discount store, the effect is much simpler to create and still provides the desired effect.

So, if the "shoe is to fit the foot" before the screenplay is budgeted, a creative producer will guide the creativity of the screenwriter in a direction that will work for a plausible independently raised budget. More money for a project does not reduce the problems of producing a project. A $100,000,000 project will have $100,000,000 worth of problems.

THE BUDGET TOP SHEET

The top sheet of a budget provides a summary of the details within the body of the budget. (Figure 11)

The legend at the top of the page provides general information used in structuring the budget and includes the name of the producer and director who will be most directly responsible in assuring the production stays within the budget. It gives information relating to principle photography—the date the picture is to be started and completed —and a statement as to the foundation for the budget. This information is critical in understanding the creative dynamics of the specific budget. Should any one item in this legend change, it may cause a shift in one or more line items in the budget. It is important to note (and will be mentioned many times), that the production stage is the most volatile phase of the process. The volatility is due to potentially unknown factors such as weather, locations, actors, production problems, etc.

PRODUCTION BUDGET TOP SHEET

Title			Producer	
Travel Days			Director	
Rehearsal Days			Start Production	
Distant Location			Finish Production	
Local Location Shooting			Total Production Days	
Stage Shooting		Answer Print Due Date		Total Days
Budget Based On		Script Dated		Script Pages

Acct. #	Classification	Page #	Budget Notations	Totals
100	Story & Other Rights			
200	Continuity and Treatment			
300	Direction and Supervision			
400	Cast, Day Players, Stunts			
500	Travel and Living			
600	Extras			
700	Fringe Benefits			
	TOTAL ABOVE THE LINE			
2000	Production Staff			
2100	Visual Preparation			
2200	Set Dressing,			
2300	Set Construction			
2400	Properties Department			
2500	Special Effects			
2600	Camera Department			
2700	Electrical Department			
2800	Set Operations/Grip Department			
2900	Wardrobe Department			
3000	Makeup and Hair Departments			
3100	Sound Department			
3200	Transportation Department			
3300	Location			
3400	Stage & Process – Production Effects			
3500	2nd Unit, Miniatures, Prod. Effects			
3600	Production Film and Laboratory			
3700	Tests			
3800	Fringe Benefits			
	Total Production Period			
4000	Editing – Picture and Sound			
4100	Music			
4200	Post-production Sound Laboratory			
4300	Post-production Film and Lab			
4400	Fringe Benefits			
	Total Post-production Period			
5000	Publicity			
5100	Insurance			
5200	Miscellaneous			
5300	Fees and Other Charges			
	Total Administrative Charges			
	TOTAL BELOW THE LINE			

	ABOVE-THE-LINE	
+	**BELOW-THE-LINE**	
=	**DIRECT COSTS**	
+	**CONTINGENCY FEE**	
+	**COMPLETION BOND FEE**	Prepared by
=	**TOTAL**	
+	**OTHER FEES**	
+	**Deferments (if any)**	Signature for Approval
=	**TOTAL NEGATIVE COST**	

Figure 11

The budget is divided into two sections: above-the-line and below-the-line. The below-the-line section is subdivided to include the production period, the editing period and miscellaneous overhead expenses that relate to the entire project.

ABOVE AND BELOW-THE-LINE

Prevailing wisdom has it that in the old studio days elements that were considered more creative, the script, producers, directors and actors, were separated on a budget from other production cost elements with a big thick line. As a result, all of the costs associated with those categories were called above-the-line. Everything else was called below-the-line. These terms are still used today, even though many of the below-the-line categories are readily acknowledged as being creative. Certainly a cinematographer, a composer, an editor, a costume designer, a production designer, an art director and a sound designer are all creative. Yet their cost centers are found below-the-line. An independent producer should recognize that everyone working on a project is creative in their own way, since doing a project is a collaborative effort. Wise producers will let everyone know that they are appreciated for creatively contributing to making the project work, whether the line item is above- or below-the-line.

Above-the-line might refer to those positions on a film project that could be part of a recognized guild bargaining organization prevalent in the entertainment industry. There are three guilds that define specific creative personnel on a project: the Writers Guild, the Directors Guild and the Screen Actors Guild. Unlike the motion picture labor craft unions, the American Federation of Musicians (also called the AFM) and the Teamsters, all found to be below-the-line, the guilds are not sanctioned but recognized by the American Federation of Labor even though production managers, and assistant directors are members of the Directors Guild of America and found below-the-line in a budget. The reason for this rests in the history of the Directors Guild. Production managers, assistant directors, and stage managers and production assistants in videotape are major administrative production support personnel and provide the guild with contract negotiating strength with the motion picture producers.

Everything else in the budget is below-the-line.

Adding together the total of above-the-line and the total of below-the-line provides us with the direct costs of the project. However, the direct cost on a *preliminary* budget, only covers what are intended to be the direct costs for the project. It does not allow for any unforeseen exigencies. It is imperative that the project's budget includes some protection against those unforeseen elements. Therefore we add a line and call it a contingency. This is usually a

PRODUCERS VOCABULARY

Budget—The listing of every possible expense in the making of a project before it begins production. Accurate budgets can only be created after completely breaking down a script and preparing a production board; industry practice calls for the budget to be prepared by the production manager or, for studio pictures, by the studio's Estimating Department.

predetermined percentage of the overall budget. A 10 percent contingency fee should be the least percentage included, but budget contingencies have been as high as 35 percent or 40 percent. With at least a 10 percent contingency, the producer has fulfilled one of the requirements for obtaining a completion bond. The direct costs, plus the contingency, plus the completion bond fee (if required) renders the total cost of the project.

In some instances the top sheet may reflect "other fees" such as a finders fee (for the entity who found the resources), banking interest, or other fees that have no direct correlation to what is seen on the screen, but may be necessary for funding the project. Unless there are agreed upon deferments, the total is the negative cost of the project. However, necessary deferments are also included on the top sheet and may be part of the negative cost. A deferment is often used when a producer decides that the "hard cash" available for the project may not be enough to secure talent or services. The concept of a deferred payment is not a new concept. It developed from the independent movement of the 1970s. The upside of such a concept is that one does not need the immediate cash to secure the talent or pay for services for the completion of the project. The downside is that the talent or service entity might, as a condition of deferment, hold a security interest in the project, or require a premium for being in a deferred position. (see Chapter 11) Also, once a budget top sheet reflects expenses for other fees and deferments, the producer has developed a profile or structure for the project that,

———— • • • ————

A producer must not only be creative and knowledgeable in business matters, but must also be one hell of a salesman. The art and the craft of being a creative producer is finding a way to support and enhance the creative elements while, at the same time, operating within the constraints of the money available and the contractual obligations of what, where and when to deliver the finished project. The experienced creative producer, like Schreibman, utilizes every resource available to achieve his or her goal of getting the most "bang for the buck" and knows that in this endeavor the staunchest ally is his or her friend, the Completion Bonder.

—Lionel A. Ephraim, Senior Vice President
Cinema Completions International, Inc.,
*Crouching Tiger, Hidden Dragon; Traffic, What Women
Want, The Thin Red Line, The English Patient*

———— • • • ————

although not translated creatively, will affect the structure of the investment. The total plus fees and any deferments will render the final negative cost of the project.

THE COMPLETION BOND

The line item in the bottom portion of the budget top sheet identified as COMPLETION BOND is for the fee that is required to secure a security bond for the completion of the project. As stated in Chapter One, unlike a completion bond in the construction business, a completion bond on a film or video project guarantees to the investment or funding institution that the project (barring an Act of God) can be produced in a first class distributable manner for the money stated in the budget.

There are many companies that offer completion bonds. However, there are only a handful of insurance companies that provide the insurance to the companies. Therefore the producer should be looking for a bonding company that offers them:

a. professional production expertise
b. a successful track record in keeping projects on budget
c. integrity and security for the investment

Before a bonding company agrees to bond a film project it first reads the screenplay, examines the budget, the production board of the project and the various supporting documents of the people involved with the project. They review the script from the standpoint of production logistics and choreography and explore the post-production avenues that the project will take to its completion.

They will ask specific questions concerning the philosophy of the production, the specifics of certain production aspects and will question the professional integrity and expertise of both the producer and director. The producer must be prepared to provide the answers to any questions relating to how the project will be produced before the bond is put in place as the bonding company must be convinced that it will not have to take over the picture and complete it on behalf of the investment. When a bond is placed on a project the bonding company may immediately freeze the budgets of the Legal and Music Departments. The reason for freezing the first is to make sure the projects budget can pay any legal costs involved with their invasion of the bond as well as take care of all the legal issues surrounding the completion of the project. The reason for freezing the second involves more of an explanation.

Most bonding companies know nothing at all about the music business and therefore do not have the relationships that are necessary should the bonding company be required to complete the project. Also, music is so important to the creative tone of the film, and since bonding companies do not get involved in the creative, the proposed budget allocation is needed to complete the music as creatively planned.

In addition to freezing these two cost centers (and perhaps others as well), the bonding company requires another major guarantee from the producer and director, which, if violated, constitutes grounds for the bonding company to invade the project. It is a guarantee as to the amount of film stock that will be purchased for the project. On the surface this may not seem to be a big deal. But the amount of film stock shot has a direct correlation to the amount of money being spent on the project in terms of the time it takes to shoot and post the project. The director and producer must plan out the shooting ratio of the project very carefully, because in all likelihood, once it is approved as part of the final budget, it is locked in stone!

The completion bond fee is no more than 6 percent of the direct costs, plus the contingency fee, which must be no less than 10 percent. In most cases a bonding company will rebate a percentage of the bonding fee if the project comes in on time and on budget because bonding companies *do not* want to take over a project. This percentage rebate to the producer is an incentive to keep the project on time and on budget. Usually the rebate is about 50 percent of the fee. In some instances the rebate has been as high as 75 percent of the fee, thus making the bonding fee only 1.5 percent of the budget of the project. This will depend on the integrity and track record of the producer. The fee for bonded projects I have produced has never been more than 2.5 percent of the direct costs plus contingency. There is, however, a bottom line. Since bonding companies are backed by insurance companies—to which they must pay a premium—and since the bonding company itself is in business to make money, there is a bottom line fee that a bond company will assess a production for a bond.

A wise producer will consider the bonding company a colleague on the project and will often work with them to create a "good cop/bad cop" relationship with production personnel. As an example, if there is a belligerent director who is insisting on a production element that the producer knows will throw the budget off, and at the same time not benefit the artistic vision, the producer might say to the director, "That's a terrific idea, but Mr.

Jones of the bonding company will be on my case if we fall behind in our schedule. I don't know what he will do if we do what you are asking." The director may now rethink the request and see its impracticality. A savvy producer will remember that the bonding company is an ally and not an enemy.

FINANCIALLY PROTECTING THE CREATIVITY

The producer must protect all aspects of a project and do so without squelching the creativity of others who contribute to the vision. The producer must always be alert to creativity getting away from the vision—and gently pull it back in relationship to the fiscal limitations. Although a budget is created for a project it should be considered as a guide for making deci-

— • • • —

The director on Hunter's Blood *was continually getting behind schedule. He came from the commercial world and, while talented, his inexperience with the scope of features and the specific limitations of time and money were difficult for him to handle. The bonding company was concerned about us being behind schedule and asked me if we could pick up the time and still finish production on time and on budget. I told them that I believed we could pick up the time lost and I knew how it could be done. I told them that I was trying to make suggestions to the director to pick up the time but he would not heed them. So they devised a plan to make the point to the director of the importance of being on time. We were scheduled to shoot road sequences on a Saturday and Don Parker of the bonding company asked me when we would break for lunch. I estimated the time and he instructed me to make sure I was going to lunch with the director at a designated restaurant near where we were shooting. When we arrived at the restaurant Don was there having lunch and asked us to join him. We did and, over the course of our lunch, Don casually asked the director why he was so far behind. After listening to his cast and crew problems, Don leaned across the table, looked him right in the eyes and in his most serious steely voice told him that I was a very experienced director and producer and he had to listen to me about picking up time in his schedule. It was a meeting with the godfather and the director got the point. As we left the table Don winked at me and I knew then and there that the bonding company was my new best friend.*

— • • • —

sions and something that will be flexible within the parameters that it sets. The budget must never ultimately go outside of the basic parameter of the negative cost of the project. If it does, you will find yourself searching for additional funds to complete the project.

When developing a philosophy for a project, a producer should visualize a four-burner stove. On one front burner is the working budget, on the second front burner is the screenplay, on one back burner is the creative vision of the project, and on the second back burner is the end result of the project. As the philosophy develops (cooks) all four burners are working and eventually you, the chef, find yourself moving the items around on the burners as the project gets made. As the project takes on a life of its own, you will have to safeguard the creative vision and make sure it is not lost in the shuffle on the stove. In the next several chapters we will see methods of assuring this protection and how, through creative use of budget funds, you can protect the creativity by quietly increasing your budget without requesting additional funds. The wise producer will use that knowledge to maintain a creative environment and protect the project against damage—despite the volatility that often emerges during the production of a project.

CHAPTER 5 ABOVE-THE-LINE

"The most creative producer I have worked with is Lorenzo O'Brien. His talents include handling enormous numbers of people with great tact and efficiency, protecting the director from unnecessary slings and arrows, and providing unusually perceptive script and story notes. On one occasion he provided me with the entire script, El Patrullero (Highway Patrolman), and then found us the money to make it. I owe Lorenzo the best work of my career."

—Alex Cox, Writer, Actor, Director, *Repo Man, Sid and Nancy, Fear and Loathing in Las Vegas*

STORY AND DELIVERY
Rights

We begin our discussion of above-the-line cost items and their relationship to the creative process by examining the cost centers indicated in Figure #12. A project's origin begins with the rights to the project. If a project originates with a book or a newspaper article, then the producer must acquire the rights to that book or article before a screenplay can be written. If a screenplay is an original screenplay, then the producer is purchasing the rights to the story that is inherent in the screenplay as well as the screenplay itself. No matter what the project, there will be underlying rights that must be optioned or purchased.

The rights must be in writing and it is important that you do due diligence in finding the existence of any underlying rights. A handshake deal is not enough. Not only is getting things in writing good business practice, in this case it is necessary in order to obtain an Errors and Omissions Insurance policy (see Chapter 10). Being able to get an E&O policy is a mandatory delivery item for distribution. This relates to the "end result" concept of producing and becomes evident when you analyze the process from Z to A as mentioned in Chapter 2.

During the development stage of *Hunter's Blood*, the executive producer needed to make a film for no more than $1,000,000, since she felt she could raise that amount easily. So we looked around for a project that had interesting character points and could be made for under $1,000,000.

The original screenplay for the project was submitted through a writer's representative. Upon reading it, I found myself interested in the clash of cultures that existed in the story and the notion that the characters who

Acct.	Account Name	Unit x	Rate =	Amount	Sub Total	Total
100	**STORY/OR DESCRIPTION**					
	Rights					
	Total 100					
200	**STORY DELIVERY**					
01	Writers					
02	Clerical Assistant					
03	Research					
04	Story Editors & Consultant					
05	Script Timing					
20	Other Charges					
	Total 200					
300	**SUPERVISION**					
01	Executive Producer(s)					
02	Producer(s)					
03	Associate Producer(s)					
04	Assistant to the Producer					
05	Director(s)					
06	Second Unit Director					
07	Dance Director (Choreographer)					
08	Dialogue Director(s)					
09	Assistant to the Director					
10	Clerical Assistant					
11	Casting Director					
20	Other Charges					
	Total 300					

Figure 12

Note: Units in the budget are by weeks, months, footage or flat.
Unit x Rate = Amount (Example: 4 wk. x 2000 = 8000)

appeared to be the "good guys" were really the guys who initiated the trouble and upset the sociological culture of another group of people. Although the screenplay was weak and had exploitive elements (like cannibalism and salacious nudity), I was led to the same conflict of culture issue that had been part of the John Boorman film *Deliverance*. I knew *Hunter's Blood* could be made for under $1,000,000. When I asked about the origin of the story, I was told that it was based upon a "pulp novel" of the same name written by Jere Cunningham. We have all seen those types of books in the supermarket or on the rack in a convenience store. Their cover artwork designed to intrigue every man who might peruse the stand, just as romance novel covers are meant to attract women. The writers' representative told me that his client had optioned the novel at one time in order to write the screenplay on speculation and that the writer no longer owned the rights to the story. I researched the rights to the novel, found they were available and that its author had recently signed with Creative Artists Agency for representation as a writer of feature films. I contacted his agent, who turned out to be someone I had known for years (*relationships*). Although he knew of Cuningham's screenplays he had never heard of this novel. I was honest with the agent and told him what we wanted to do and the agent allowed us an

——— • • • ———

Several years ago I was the creative producer of the development of the New York stage production of On the Waterfront. *The notion to do this as a play came from my experiences in working with actors on scenes from the film, and my realization that the film had all the elements of good theater. I was under contract to Columbia at the time and was able, through studio research, to find out that neither the studio nor Sam Spiegel owned the rights for a stage presentation. The original agreement indicated that these rights reverted back to Budd Schulberg, the author of the screenplay. After contacting Budd, he informed me that he had also written a novel called* Waterfront *and that the movie's screenplay was based on a series of articles in a New Jersey newspaper detailing mob like crimes on the docks of New York. On advice of our attorney we needed to obtain the rights to both the novel and the articles before proceeding with the play. They and the screenplay became part of the entire rights deal before the play was written.*

——— • • • ———

exclusive short-term free option to the rights in order to raise the funds to do the project.

Once we had a green light, the purchase price for the rights to the novel was to be $15,000. Two percent of the budget, or $20,000, was allocated towards acquiring the rights *and* the screenplay. The writer of the screenplay was not a member of the Writers Guild of America so we were not bound by WGA minimums. The original screenplay, written on speculation, was no good without the underlying rights, which we now owned. So we offered the screenwriter $5,000 for the screenplay that he wrote several years before. For that amount we also wanted one supervised rewrite to make the shoe fit the creative parameters of the foot. He agreed to this arrangement.

Writers

The writer writes the narrative or screenplay. Often more than one writer works on a project and the structure of each writer's deal can vary depending on the needs of the project. In the entertainment industry the employment of professional writers of movies and television shows is often (but not always) governed by the Writers Guild of America (WGA) and the 1998 Theatrical and Television Basic Agreement. The present agreement includes a standard Internet contract for writers. In general, the agreement is for writers who render their services in the United States or Canada or whose deals were negotiated in the United States. This also applies to those writers who live in the United States but who are transported abroad for their services. The agreement covers most forms of writing, from the original story and screenplay to simple polishes that a producer may want for a screenplay. It is important to note that the writer must be a dues paying member of the WGA and the production company must be a signatory to the WGA in order for this agreement to be binding. WGA members are not permitted to

---

PRODUCERS VOCABULARY

Deal Memo—A short, written statement outlining the terms of an agreement. It outlines information regarding services, compensation, etc., and, if not used as a final contract signed by both parties, can serve as the basis for further negotiation or for preparation of a lengthier or union-required contract. Until a formal contract is drawn and signed, the deal memo is fully binding to all parties.

First Look—A deal wherein a company has the first right of refusal on a project.

Greenlight—When a production is given the go-ahead from a studio.

WGA—Writers Guild of America , in the United States, the union for film, television and radio scriptwriters. Writers Guild of America, East, headquartered in New York City, represents scriptwriters east of the Mississippi River; Writers Guild of America, West, headquartered in Los Angeles, represents scriptwriters west of the Mississippi River. The two are affiliated; each offers a script registration service to members and nonmember writers.

work for a non-signatory production entity, and a signatory production entity is not permitted to hire a writer who is not a member of the WGA. Also, the Writers Guild requires scripts to be submitted to signatory producers or companies only through qualified agents, managers or attorneys. So understanding how this guild works in relationship to the industry is important.

The guild requires the production entity to be responsible for writers' pension, health and welfare, and residual payments under the agreement. A residual payment is made when the project is distributed in various markets (free television, pay television, basic cable, CD-ROM, DVD, videocassettes, multimedia games etc.)

It is not uncommon for non-guild writers to use the basic wage scale terms of the WGA as a yardstick for their deals with a producer. Flat compensation for theatrical features is based upon the stated verified budget of the project. A project budgeted less than $2,500,000 is considered low budget and a project higher than that amount is considered high budget. As an example of the rates under the current agreement, a scale rate for an original screenplay, including a treatment, for a low budget feature is $43,952, and for a high budget feature is $82,444. This may change after the new contract is negotiated with the Writers Guild in June of 2001. Scale is the minimum a producer can pay. When a scale deal is negotiated (of any sort, with any guild) it is negotiated as a scale plus 10 percent deal, as agents are not permitted, by their sanctions with the guilds, to take a commission from their clients when they work for guild minimum. The 10 percent goes to the agent of the writer, director or actor. You should check with the Writers Guild to get the specific terms and details of their agreement. There are also compilation books that provide a digest of all guild and union agreements.

Many times a producer will option a writer's work before purchasing the project. An option is an agreement that gives the exclusive rights to a literary property, such as a novel or play, for a period of time (the term of the option), in order to turn the property into a motion picture or video. The acquisition of literary rights can be structured as an outright purchase or as an option/purchase agreement. Producers often prefer to take an option on a property to reduce the up-front risk. A fee is paid against (or in addition to) the agreed upon purchase price and authors of any literary works must warrant that they own free and clear, all the rights they are selling.

An option gives the producer the *exclusive* right to purchase the rights within the period of the option. The exclusivity makes it impossible for someone else to purchase the rights during the option period and for the writer to interfere with the purchasing of those rights. Once the option expires, however, the writer retains the option money and the rights as well. If the option is exercised the producer owns the rights outright. When negotiating the option for a property, you must also negotiate the terms of the purchase so that once the option is exercised the literary purchase agreement is automatically in force. If you enter into an option agreement without negotiating the underlying literary purchase agreement, you have bought a useless option because all you have is the right to enter into an agreement in the future should you want the rights. The writer is under no obligation to sell on the terms you want to propose. One other important thing to remember when negotiating the purchase agreement is to include a provision that states that you are under no obligation to actually produce the project. You want the right to make the project but not be obligated to do so.

You should also seek the rights to renew the option before it expires. In this case you will probably pay an additional fee for the period of the extension but you should do it before your original option period expires. Otherwise the writer can refuse to grant or extend your option. Renewals essentially let you extend your option without exercising it. The standard option fee according to WGA rules is 10 percent of scale and is often for a period of eighteen months. Renewals should be based upon that yardstick.

It is not uncommon for writers to require clerical assistants or researchers for projects. I know one writer who writes through dictation. He spends a great deal of time researching the characters before writing and then when

---

PRODUCERS VOCABULARY

Colored Pages—Whenever a project has been fully prepared for production and is in the hands of the appropriate personnel, the script pages are usually white. Once revisions of any kind are made, the new pages are printed on colored paper (beginning with blue, then pink, yellow, green, etc). The date of the correction on the page is marked on the top of the page and an asterisk is noted in the margin by the precise changes on the page.

Longform—Narrative television project that is longer than an hour in length.

Spec Script—A screenplay written on speculation. The writer spends his own time and money researching and writing the script, with hopes that a producer will buy it. If a writer sends a spec script directly to a producer who did not request it, it is also called an unsolicited script and may be returned unread. A spec script can also be used as a writing sample, especially by an unproduced or aspiring screenwriter; it also can be submitted in scriptwriting competitions.

Step Deal—A method whereby decisions (and payments) are made at various steps towards completion. This usually pertains to the story and is broken out by synopsis, treatment, first draft, second draft, and final screenplay.

Turnaround—The negotiated right of a writer or producer to submit a project to another studio or network, if the company that developed the property elects not to proceed with production. Typically, the right is subject to the condition that the developing company's investment is repaid; it also may require the developing company to retain an interest in the film's earnings.

he begins he acts out the characters while his assistant, in shorthand, writes what he says, both the dialogue and the action. A producer may require a writer to work with a consultant or a story editor to help get the screenplay to the point where it is ready for production. These key personnel all assist the writer in delivering the best possible project in a written form.

Script Timing

Determining the running time of a script is the function that is often relegated to the continuity person (discussed later) and is called script timing. A scene in a screenplay written as:

```
67. EXT - PRAIRIE - DAY
    The Indians attack the village, pillaging the
    rival tribe of its valuables.
```

is written as 1/8th of a page may take many days of production to shoot and might be seen onscreen for a minute, five minutes or longer. Since it involves a creative relationship to the story, the producer and director should determine its length onscreen. One of Hitchcock's continuity people once said that one page of script written in proper screenplay format will play 47 seconds onscreen, everything being equal. So a 100 page screenplay should roughly run eighty minutes and a 120 page script, approximately 110 minutes. Some continuity people use the scale of one page equals one minute. Although necessary for television, script timing may not be a necessity for feature films. Commercial television formats rely on precise timing for the insertion of commercials. Therefore it might be beneficial to have a teleplay timed for onscreen running accuracy. The creative side of television requires aesthetics different from theatrical presentations, so the style of production and direction is different. Television makes more use of close-ups, and employs a more confined story structure through the dialogue of the characters rather than the spectacle of production. Whatever the decision might be for having a script timed for running accuracy, preparing for that requires the funds for this line item.

The Producers—Executive Producer, Producer, Associate Producer

The person responsible for the project being financed is the executive producer. This can be someone who provides the funding for the project or puts elements together (such as the cast or a director) that may trigger the financing. The executive producer's main duty is usually completed once the project is in pre-production, although they may still be involved in arranging for the distribution of the project. Because of this, the executive producer is generally non-exclusive to a project and may be involved with more than one project at any one time. It would not be unusual to see the salary for an executive producer be lower than a producer's salary. This may not always be the case since people like Francis Ford Coppola and Steven Spielberg, when acting as executive producers, may be receiving a salary equal to or more than the producer's. Their involvement may have been the reason the project was funded.

The producer is exclusive to a project. The producer's salary is the *only* item in your budget that you always have *absolute* control over. You can determine your own financial needs and structure this area accordingly. If you are a first-time producer, your motivation may be getting the project made and not the amount of money you might earn as the producer. Your ego is motivating you to establish yourself in the profession and you may only be looking for enough money to pay your bills.

On the other hand, if you have a proven track record, your fee may be one that reflects your status and strength on the package of the project. Unless the project is one that an established producer is extremely passionate about, the fee will probably not be any lower than the last project he or she produced. This is especially true if the producer is not a primary owner of the project, but a hired hand.

In some instances it might be necessary for a first time producer to bring aboard an established producer to provide credibility to the project. If that is the case, then more than likely there will be two fees set aside for producing, one lower than the other, to accommodate for two producers. In other instances a project may have a producer whose reputation and expertise is that of a production manager but who wants to be more involved with the creative side of the project along with the management side of the production. In that case, the producing fee may be lower since the person is making a vertical career move to establish themselves as a producer, a practice discussed in Chapter 2. Above-the-line producing salaries are often high because narrative projects today may have three, four and five producers each involved with the project in some way. It is not unusual for the director to also be a producer. Directors are realizing that in order for them to have more creative authority, they have to be a producer on the project.

What is an associate producer? By definition it is someone who is a producing associate given some limited creative responsibility towards the producing of the project. It can be someone who is solely involved with the producer, or someone who may have another responsibility on the project, like editing or production management. The associate producer title may be given to someone in the latter instance if they have been effective in the pre-production creative decisions that involve the producing of a project. The distinguished Film Editor Richard Marks (*Broadcast News, Apocalypse Now, Terms of Endearment*) was also the associate producer on *I'll Do Anything*, a film written and directed by James L. Brooks. An associate producer might be involved only with supervising the post-production on a project or just the day to day activities of the production period. Associate producers do not have as much creative responsibility for the whole project as the producer does, but they assist the producer in achieving certain creative producing assignments. It is also a title that you can keep in your arsenal of negotiating techniques for above-the-line creative talent. Maybe you want to have the writer on the set for necessary rewrites during the production process, and you offer the writer an associate producer credit in an effort to pay less for these and other creative services of the writer. Here this technique approaches two principles discussed in Chapter 2: appealing to the writers' ego, and elevating the writer to a different category within the industry. A smart producer will not underestimate the value of the associate producer title on a project.

Producing and Directors

The Director of a project is creatively responsible for the interpretation of the vision and has the final word as to what happens in front of the camera during the production. A wise producer will select a director who shares the same vision of a project and will collaborate to bring the project to fruition. Independent producers in the United States are faced with directors who may or may not be members of the Directors Guild of America (DGA), the bargaining organization representing directors, second unit directors, assistant directors, associate directors and production managers. A director who is not a member of the DGA is free to enter into any agreement with the producer for services on the project, providing the producer's company is not a signatory to the DGA agreement. If the company has signed an agreement with the DGA then it must only use members of the Guild, or the director it wishes to hire must join the Guild. The strength for the directors in the Guild rests with the production managers, assistant directors and associate directors who also make up its membership. These people provide the primary support for directors to do their jobs successfully and they, through practices established by the DGA, are trained in specific techniques in assisting the director and being responsible for production logistics and schedules.

Minimum fees for DGA directors are set by contract with the Guild. Once a DGA director is employed, he or she is paid regardless of whether the picture is made. This is called pay-or-play and is required when the producing company is a DGA signatory. When producing a low budget film or a project for the Internet, independent producers often believe that they are not able to use Guild personnel because of their fees. This notion is no longer true. The Directors Guild has afforded producers with the opportunity to hire its members for independent projects based upon the budget of the project. Briefly stated, if the budget of the project is at least $3.5 million but less than $6 million, 70 percent of the applicable minimum salary may be paid to the director with the remaining 30 percent deferred. In addition, the director must receive an additional 25 percent on deferral for agreeing to defer the payment. Deferrals are paid once the project has reached breakeven, which is defined as 200 percent of the production costs. If the budget of the project is at least $2.5 million but less than $3.5 million, 60 percent of the applicable minimum salary may be paid, while 40 percent and an additional 25 percent may be deferred until breakeven on the project.

Further, if the budget of the project is at least $1.2 million but less than $2.5 million, all conditions of employment, including compensation and deferred compensation, are open for negotiations between the producer and the director.

PRODUCERS VOCABULARY

Coverage—(1) A brief analysis of characters and story line of a project as prepared by a story analyst or script reader. The coverage will include a recommendation for any further action on the project. Story analysts are subjective in their views. Many story analysts are writers themselves whose egos often may not permit them to see the potential or the vision of the creative work that is the passion of the producer. (2). Shooting a scene from various angles and setups to provide options for the editor.

Cover Shot—An additional take of a shot that is printed in the event that the preferred take is unusable or damaged. Directors will often do a second take of a shot for safety purposes or in the hopes of getting a better performance from the actors.

DGA—The Directors Guild of America is the collective bargaining unit for directors, assistant directors, stage managers, and production assistants (tape television) in the industry. Founded in 1959. Based in Hollywood, California.

Director's Cut—1. Version of a film approved by the director after the initial assembly of footage by the editor; guild contract may allow the director a specified length of time to produce his cut before the producer may suggest changes, if at all. 2. Commercially released version of a film conforming to the director's personal editing choices; typically, this is a version of the theatrically released film that contains unused or deleted footage. For example, there are six different versions of James Cameron's *Terminator 2: Judgment Day* (1991) available on laser disc, many of them featuring special editions, added footage, etc. Also called a director's special edition.

Finally, if the budget is less than $1.2 million, the producer and director may set any terms they wish including salary and/or deferrals. In other words, the basic motivation for a director at this level will clearly be his or her own creative ego. (They may even work for food.)

There are also minimums for television work depending on the use for television: i.e. network, syndicated, cable etc. They have also struck a separate agreement for a standard Internet contract.

DGA directors are entitled to certain creative rights by the terms of their contract, such as a director's cut. Other issues open for negotiation by all directors (DGA and non-DGA) may include final edit of the project, creative control, casting approval and their choice of assistant directors. These are all issues that must be worked out before the director is hired and are all based upon the producer's trust and collaborative relationship with the director.

The press sometimes reports directors leaving projects due to "creative differences" with the producer. Although this may or may not be true, certainly when this happens, people are not able to collaborate with one another. The working relationship between the producer and director is the most important working relationship towards the success of a project. While the final responsibility for everything on the project falls in the lap of the producer, directors should keep in mind three basic responsibilities: The first is the responsibility to the audience in telling the story, the second is the responsibility to the producer, without whom there would be no project, and the third is to the director's creative self. This third responsibility must be nurtured by the creative producer.

There are specific recommended guidelines for producers when working with a director. First, make sure the director has the ability to work with actors or any talent in front of the camera. The only person on a set during the making of the project with that responsibility is the director, and a director who is intimidated by actors, or who cannot communicate with sensitive onscreen talent, will be the downfall of the project. I have seen talent take control of a set when the director did not feel comfortable with their communication. This is not unusual since actors often talk back to directors if they believe the director has not been clear about what is wanted or needed, or if the director has not provided a creative atmosphere in which actors can work.

Second, do not interfere with the director on a set. The director must be absolutely in charge on the shooting set. If a producer interferes with what the director is doing in front of a cast or crew it will demoralize the director and damage the working relationship with the production company. If the producer wants to talk to the director about something during shooting, it is best to do it in private away from the cast and crew or to wait until there is a break, or before or after the day's work. This way the producer is maintaining the collaborative and respectful process of production.

The medium is collaborative whether you work in film, video or digital. The collaboration begins with the producer and the director and the trust and confidence that each must have with one another. If this is in place then the trust and confidence will be there through the entire production.

Third, and most important, make sure the director does his or her homework on the project. Directing is not only creatively handling actors and interpreting the screenplay, it also includes the ability to complete a day's work on time and on schedule. A director who is properly prepared allows for the creative, while planning for the inevitable problems. A director who

——— • • • ———

I teach a course at UCLA in the collaborative nature of production between the producer, director and the cinematographer. One year a student producer, who was also the writer of the project, took the course having already had extensive professional experience. He met with one of the directors' two days before the actual shoot date and planned out the creative aspect of the story they were to shoot on that day. On the day of production the director decided at the last minute to totally change certain characteristics of the main characters, without discussing it beforehand with the producer. On the set the producer tried to carefully adhere to the practice of not interrupting the set activity, and not waiting for a specific break in the activity, quietly addressed the question with the student director. The response he received had no logical answer directed at the story. The student director threw his hands in the air and yelled, "because I want to be creative!" Needless to say, this interaction infuriated the student producer who had a difficult time holding his temper in front of the rest of the student crew and actors. When we talked about the incident later in class, the students all agreed that the director was arbitrary and non-communicative and the producer should have taken the director aside during a lull in the production and discussed the matter in private. The situation never should have happened if the director and producer had discussed the change before coming to the set.

——— • • • ———

is able to think creatively while making instantaneous decisions based upon the pressures of production is a successful director.

All the previsualization in the world won't prevent problems from occurring if a director doesn't have the ability to creatively improvise. Cinematographer Tom Denove tells this story about a director with whom he worked. It was the director's first picture; his background was in animation and he spent hours doing his homework, elaborately sketching out each shot on paper so he was able to show Tom exactly what he wanted as an image. One day he came to work and, as he faced the set, the door in the set was on the left and the door in his sketch was on the right. He stood and looked at the real set, and then at his sketch, and then back at the real set. He couldn't figure out how to stage the scene to make it work because the set was not as he had sketched it. Many people, including the actors, gave him suggestions, but he was so locked to his previsualization that he couldn't unfreeze his thinking to create on the spot. This went on for several hours until he realized that by turning his sketch over and holding it up to the light, the door that was on the right in his sketch was now on the left. He was then able to figure out what to do. But by then time had passed and the day's work could not be completed on schedule.

Some productions will require a second unit director. Second unit is a second production crew that shoots selected sequences of the production board either before, during or immediately after the main production unit shoots the majority of the project. Many times this involves stunts, special effects, establishing shots or images that do not involve speaking or identifiable cast members. It can also involve shooting performers or main actors on a green- or bluescreen stage for photographic or digital effects as in the case of *X-Men, The Cell* or *The Matrix*. The logistics of the production defined by the production board, or by the needs of the director, often dictate the necessity for a second production unit, that is headed up by a second unit director or in some cases, the visual effects supervisor. Collaboration is necessary between the project's director and the second unit director before second unit production takes place so that the second unit director clearly understands the creative style of the project set by the cinematographer and director. In the case of stunts, the second unit director is often a stunt coordinator who knows the best angle from which to shoot a stunt. A production budget will contain a "mini-crew" just for second unit photography. This is a smaller crew but mirrors the first production unit. (Many directors will do first and second unit direction themselves.)

Casting Directors

The casting director is the producer's face to the acting community during and after pre-production. Selecting the right casting director can give actors' agents and managers an idea of the quality and integrity of your project. There are many people in the industry who call themselves "casting directors," and many more being added every month. They may have experience at casting companies as receptionists or assistants, or may have come from the ranks of management, but that doesn't guarantee they have any real creative casting experience. So check them out for the casting quality. There are several questions that a producer needs to ask about a casting person before hiring their services. What is their casting track record? What projects have they cast recently? Have they worked only on low budget action projects and is your project a romantic comedy? Do they have an excellent creative sense of the characters in the project? A quality casting director can be invaluable to the producer when it comes to finding the right actor for the part.

One of the most important questions a casting director can ask of the producer is; *"If you had all the money in the world, whom do you see in these roles?"* This question quickly removes any fiscal limitations from a creative casting discussion. What is the casting directors' relationship to the actor/agent/management community? Find out what their reputation is with producers, agents, actors and managers. Do they primarily work with the "A," "B" or "C" level theatrical agencies? Agencies sanctioned by the Screen Actors Guild can be classified in terms of the actors they represent. The William Morris Agency, Creative Artist Agency and United Talent Agency are three of many "A" agencies that generally represent actors of excellent quality who may be considered a *name*, are packagable or are up and coming in the acting community. The size of these agencies varies as many of the smaller "boutique" agencies also fall within this category. These agencies are aggressive and are always seeking new and exciting material for their clients. "B" agencies are smaller agencies that represent quality actors who may be experienced in theater or commercials, but who have little film experience. These agencies are always looking to move their clients up the talent ladder and into new arenas of performance. "C" agencies represent actors with little or no experience. They may be excellent actors but they may or may not be members of the Screen Actors Guild. "C" agencies often work the hardest since their clients are unknown commodities. These agencies deal in volume in the hopes that one of their clients clicks. Casting directors usually work with specific agents and agencies that trust their judgement on projects. These relationships are strong and are based on years of successfully working together. If an "A" agency knows that a casting director they respect is casting a specific project, they may be willing to submit their clients even for smaller or lower budget projects than they might usually consider. The concept of *relationships* discussed in Chapter 2 is very important to a producer when considering a casting director.

Casting directors usually work on a flat rate for the job, as most of them work as independent entities. The rate will be based upon the amount of casting the producer is asking them to do. You may hire the casting director to cast only certain roles, thereby using the relationships the casting director may have with certain agencies to find specific acting talent. You may decide that you want someone in-house to cast the smaller roles or hire a casting associate to work with the casting director. Or you may want a casting agency to cast the entire project and will negotiate a fee for those services. The fee is generally based upon the budget, the status of the casting agent and the amount of work expected for the project. It will also have a direct correlation to past or ongoing relationships with the producer and the quality of the project. An interesting, exciting and creatively strong project may be enough to motivate a strong and effective casting director. Getting the project to that point will cost you absolutely nothing but your own innate creativity.

When a project is ready to hire actors, casting directors contact the agencies and managers with specific descriptions of the characters that have been approved by the producer. In Los Angeles, Vancouver and New York City, the project is submitted to Breakdown Services, a company that performs a reading and descriptive breakdown of the synopsis and characters for the producer at no charge. They also gather other important information supplied by the producer that may affect actor submissions (union/non-union, etc.). Once Breakdown Services has created the approved information, they send it out to those agencies and managers that subscribe to their service. There are also trade newspapers for actors like *Back Stage West* and online Internet sites at which a producer may post descriptions of their cast of characters. The producer must be prepared to receive hundreds, and in some cases thousands, of submissions for the project. Weeding through those submissions is a laborious chore best suited for casting agencies. The final decision on casting rests entirely with the producer and director. But a wise producer will find a casting director whose creative instinct for talent can be trusted. Listen to them and consider their ideas carefully. Casting is a very small world, and establishing a supportive relationship with a quality casting director can be very worthwhile.

CAST—ACTORS—ONSCREEN TALENT

The single most volatile segment of a production will be within the CAST budget. There are many variables involving the onscreen talent (including their own egos') that have an impact on what and how they do what they do.

The Screen Actors Guild is the bargaining organization that represents actors in the industry. Producers, of course, can use actors who are not members of this guild. They are referred to as non-SAG actors. In order for an actor to be a member of the Screen Actors Guild, a production company who has agreed to only use SAG actors must hire them. These production companies are called signatory companies. Once a company is a SAG signatory it agrees to use *only* dues-paying members of the Screen Actors Guild and non-SAG actors are unable to work on the project. A SAG actor who works on a non-signatory project bares the burden of that responsibility, as they can be penalized or even ejected from their guild for doing nonunion work. The producer cannot be held responsible since the company is not a signatory to the Screen Actors Guild. It is therefore critical that the producer makes it clear at the time of the casting announcement as to whether the project is SAG or not. Be warned!

Agents that are franchised by the Screen Actors Guild may not submit their clients to a non-SAG signatory project. Occasionally, an agent who believes in the talent of a non-SAG actor will attempt to find work for the actor in a SAG signatory film. But it is usually very difficult and the main avenues of exposure for that actor lie with student films or nonunion projects. These rarely provide financial incentives for agents but they are necessary for the actor to build a career. Acting for the camera has different technical requirements than acting on the stage and actors must learn both of these techniques. Also actors usually work in student or nonunion films with the promise that they will be given copies of their work which they can include in their product reel. If you make those agreements, make sure you honor them. The actor you work with today may well be the actor you need to get your project made tomorrow.

The independent producer is usually faced with the need to secure "name" acting talent as part of the package to entice the financing of the project. You can rest assured that these actors will be members of the Screen Actors Guild and will only work on signatory productions. It is important to note that SAG has jurisdiction in the United States or any commonwealth, territory or possession of the United States in which the Guild has established a branch. However, if the production company has a representative or is based in the United States and wishes to use an actor who is a member of the Screen

Acct. #	Account Name	Unit	Rate	Amount	Sub Total	Total
400	**CAST**					
01	Principle Characters					
02	Supporting Characters					
03	Day Players					
04	10% Agent Commissions on Scale Actors					
05	Stunt Coordinator					
	Stunt People					
06	Stunt Adjustments					
07	Overtime – ADR - Other					
08	Miscellaneous Cast Expenses					
	Total 400					

Figure 13

Actors Guild, it must become a signatory even if the project is being made outside of the United States. The Guild includes actors, performers, professional singers, stunt performers, stunt coordinators, airplane and helicopter pilots, dancers and puppeteers who appear onscreen. (SAG also covers extras, but only under certain conditions which are discussed later in this chapter.)

Often new independent producers will feel somewhat intimidated by the size and power of the Screen Actors Guild. They fear that the Guild will make it impossible for them to produce their projects. This statement is far from the truth. The Guild wants their members to work and has become very "producer friendly" in establishing various agreements under which a producer may do a project in film, video or digital. They also recently approved an agreement for their members to work on projects made for the Internet. This agreement provides basic coverage that includes pension and health contributions. It does not as yet specify minimum rates although the producer can negotiate with SAG; the starting salary for negotiations is the basic minimum daily rate of $617. This contract is available from SAG on a case-by-case basis but in the new film and television contract negotiations they will probably seek to include some language that will give more explicit administration over made-for-Internet product.

The Screen Actors Guild recognizes the need for various types of agreements based upon the budget and motivation of the project. They were one of the first Guilds to work with producers and to attempt to structure agreements that allow their members to exercise their creative egos while maintaining dignity and integrity in their work.

All SAG agreements are based entirely on the end use of the project. The Basic Codified Agreement is the basic SAG agreement and includes pay schedules and terms for full budget theatrical feature film, commercials and television.

The Basic Agreement

To qualify for the basic agreement, at least one month prior to the start date of pre-production the producer should contact one of the SAG offices located in twenty-three cities throughout the United States. SAG requires the project to have a verified copyright number issued by the copyright office of the Library of Congress in Washington, D.C. They will also require a copy of the script and the proposed shooting schedule, after which they will send a packet of documents for the producers' signature. Within the packet of information will be the minimum (scale) rates for performers who work both on a daily and weekly contract, and information regarding the use of

---

PRODUCERS VOCABULARY

Callback—I. Invitation for an actor to audition again (after the field of competition has been narrowed). For SAG members, there is a limit to the number of callbacks an actor may have before being paid. 2. Actor's automatic invitation to continue working as a day player, unless specifically notified by the end of the shooting day that he has been laid off.

Drop and Pickup—A specific SAG rule which applies to their basic agreement that states that there must be ten free days between the last day that an actor works and the time he/she next works on a production otherwise payment must be provided for all intervening non working days. This applies to weekly and daily performers and is waived on certain SAG agreements. This rule can be applied once per actor per production.

Principal Players—Members of the cast comprising the main featured actors.

SAG—The Screen Actors Guild is the collective bargaining unit for actors and performers in projects released in film and film television. In the United States, the union for actors working in motion pictures, television and commercial productions shot on film and released on film, videotape or videodisc. Founded in 1933 and based in Hollywood, California, with offices around the United States.

SAG extras in the New York and Los Angeles Zones (discussed later in this chapter). Note: The New York Zone is within 300 air miles from Columbus Circle, including New York City, Boston, Philadelphia and Washington, D.C. The Los Angeles Zone includes Los Angeles, San Francisco, Sacramento, San Diego, Las Vegas and the islands of Hawaii.

As part of the package of documents the producer will be asked to sign a certificate assigning the negative of the project as security for assurance that their actors will get paid the necessary residual and Pension, Health and Welfare payments upon the project's exhibition in ancillary and subsequent markets. Once the distribution deal for the project is in place, then the producer must obtain an executed Distributors Assumption Agreement which will release SAG's security interest in the project's negative. If the project is made as a theatrical project the producer is entitled to distribute it worldwide theatrically without additional compensation to the actors. When the project is distributed beyond the theatrical market, and moves into ancillary markets (such as foreign, television, video and DVD), the producer is required to pay residuals to the principal performers (SAG members). Residuals are paid each calendar quarter and are generally based on a percentage of the Distributor's Gross Receipts (DGR). The percentage is then divided up amongst the performers based on their salary and the amount of time they worked on the project. These percentages vary depending on the contract. Currently the contract calls for residuals to be paid as follows: free television—3.6 percent of DGR; videocassettes and DVDs—4.5 percent of 1st million of DGR and 5.4 percent thereafter; basic and pay cable—3.6 percent of DGR. The Pension and Health Plans' contributions are included in these percentages. (These percentages may change as a result of the current contract negotiations.)

The Low Budget Agreement

The Low Budget Agreement is one that may be used when the producer is doing a project shot entirely in the United States for an initial theatrical release but with total budget less than $2,000,000. This agreement allows for certain benefits for the producer and the actor. First is the waiving of the consecutive employment policy for day or weekly performers. This allows the performer to be dismissed and recalled for the actual days worked rather than paying the performer for days for which they may be on hold or waiting to be used. This can save the producer and the production the expense of paying an actor who may not be used daily, as the volatility of production can cause a ripple in the production schedule which could force an actor to be rescheduled for another date. The downside of this benefit is that the producer may not ask the actor to be exclusive on days that the actor is not scheduled (the consecutive rule is not waived when the actor is on an overnight location). In addition this benefit allows the actor to work weekends without benefit of weekend premiums. The second benefit is a lower scale rate of salary for weekly and daily performers. As an example: $466 for a daily performer, vs. $617 and $1,620 for a weekly performer, vs. $2,142. The third benefit is that SAG is amenable to reducing the number of extras employed under the extra performers agreement. The fourth and final benefit rests with a reduction in the overtime rate. In this agreement, overtime is paid at 1½ times until the 12th hour and then double time thereafter. *It is important to note that if a project is budgeted under $2,000,000 and a producer makes the project under this agreement, the producer must distribute the project theatrically before going to any other markets.* If it first plays in another market (such as television or videocassette) the project will be upgraded to the terms of the Basic Agreement and the producer will be obliged to pay the difference *including* the consecutive employment. Thus the need for adhering to the End Result Use theory.

The Affirmative Action Low Budget Agreement

This agreement can be applied when the producer is shooting a project in the United States for less than $2,750,000 and is initially for theatrical release. Fifty percent of the roles and the days of work must be for performers of color, women, seniors, and/or performers with disabilities. Twenty percent of the roles and days of work must be for performers who are African-American, Latino, Asian-Pacific or Native American. When applying to SAG for this agreement the producer must present a list of characters identified by category before SAG will provide its approval. The benefits are the same as the previous agreement, except that it permits a ceiling of a higher budget than that for the low budget agreement.

The Modified Low Budget Agreement

This agreement is applicable when the producer is shooting a project for theatrical release that is shot in the United States for less than $500,000. The production benefits include no consecutive employment (except on overnight locations) and significantly lower scale rates of $248 for a daily performer and $864 for a weekly performer. This agreement also permits the producer to negotiate in good faith with the Guild before hiring extras, and allows for a reduced overtime rate for its performers. The Distributors

Assumption Agreement requirement is the same with this agreement as it is with the others regarding residual responsibilities, however under this agreement the percentages of Distributor's Gross Receipts (DGR) are different. The percentage of DGR for free television is 7.2 percent, videocassettes and DVDs are 9 percent of the first million and 10.8 percent thereafter, and 7.2 percent for basic and pay cable. These percentages may change as a result of the current contract negotiations.

The Limited Exhibition Agreement

This agreement is applicable when the producer is shooting a project for the experience of doing the project. It cannot cost more that $200,000 and must be entirely shot in the United States. The intention of this agreement is to allow the producer to do a workshop or training project. The benefits under this agreement include no consecutive employment (except on overnight locations) and a six-day workweek with no premium pay. It also covers professional performers and professionals only when they are hired as extras. The rate for these performers is $100 a day when they have one or two days that are guaranteed, and $75 a day when three days are guaranteed. The producer is free to distribute this project *only in* film festivals, limited run art houses, or on basic cable and public television that allow for an "experimental/independent producer" type of format. Any other type of distribution will require the professionals' (SAG performers) salaries to be upgraded to the rates in the SAG agreement that is applicable to the form of distribution. The residual payments that are due beyond the initial distribution market are the same as the Modified Low Budget Agreement.

The Experimental Film Agreement

This agreement is applicable when the producer is shooting a project for the experience of making the project. It is intended for projects that are workshops or training situations. The total budget of the project must be less than $75,000, and the project must be shot entirely in the United States. The benefits to the producer include no consecutive employment and completely deferred salaries for the performers. No premiums are levied and the

---

PRODUCERS VOCABULARY

Pictures Gross—The gross revenue a project earns before expenses are assessed to the project. Box-office grosses are part of the Pictures Gross.

Producers Gross—Producers profit revenue before expenses.

Producers Net—Producers profit revenue after expenses.

agreement only covers professionals. This means that the producer may use SAG players alongside non-SAG players. *The producer is entitled to distribute this project at film festivals only and for limited distribution for Academy Award® consideration.* If the producer wishes to distribute it beyond film festivals, each SAG performer must be contacted, provide a written consent and negotiate compensation with the producer for any further distribution. This negotiation must reflect the rates in the SAG agreement, which are applicable to the initial distribution beyond festivals.

The Student Film Agreement
This agreement is applicable when the producer is a bona fide student shooting a project affiliated with their course of study. The student must submit a copy of the final shooting script, a detailed budget and a letter of intent itemizing the project specifics. The student must also have a letter from the instructor at the school confirming that the student is enrolled at that educational institution and is undertaking the project as a course requirement. The project must not be more than thirty-five minutes in length and have a cost of no more than $35,000 with no more than twenty consecutive shooting days. SAG actors may waive compensation, but agreements must be entered into as if they were getting paid for their services under the SAG agreement. This means that all time sheets must be kept as if the actors were receiving payment. Student projects must carry workers compensation insurance. The project may be exhibited in the classroom for a grade, or as a visual resume to demonstrate before established members of the entertainment industry the merits of the student's filmmaking capabilities. It may also be exhibited at student film festivals and for possible award consideration before the Academy of Motion Picture Arts and Sciences. If the project earns $1.00 in any form, or is exhibited in any public forum, then the student is required to pay all SAG actors for services performed on the project. The specifics of the Student Film Agreement may change from school to school. SAG has altered the agreement for schools based upon the structure of each schools' curriculum.

The Screen Actors Guild agreements are renegotiated every three years at which time new areas of concern are discussed. Terms of the new contract and these agreements are currently up for review and the terms of the new contracts are expected to be in place by June 2001.

The Screen Actors Guild agreement covers many areas affecting the working conditions of performers. It not only includes provisions for minimum wages, but it also deals with such issues as nudity, per diems, travel, meal periods, rest periods, retakes, added scenes, looping, wardrobe fittings, night premium, overtime, forced calls and so on. The contract is complex but the details of the contract are generally known and understood, not only by the production accountant, but also by the second assistant director. It is important for the producer and the director to be cognizant of some (if not all) of the basic aspects of the contract since it will affect the creative use of talent.

Dressing Rooms
Each actor is entitled to an individual dressing room when working. In most cases they are small cubicles where they may rest. In other cases it may be a separate room or a motor home dedicated to the comfort for the actor.

Travel Time
Travel time to and from a distant location is considered work time for an actor. If the actor travels to a location (as opposed to reporting to the studio) and that travel begins on any day that the actor is not scheduled to work in front of the camera, the actor is compensated for a days pay with no overtime over eight hours. If the actor travels on a holiday such as Independence Day or Christmas, the actor is paid time and a half for the travel time. If the actor works and travels the same day and should overtime occur caused by travelling, then the actor receives time and a half for the overtime for that day. If the actor lives or works in any area in which there is a SAG branch and the actor is brought to the set or distant location in a different area of the United States for any purpose, the actor will receive not only the transportation to that area but an additional $75.00 a day from the time the actor begins travelling to the time the actor is put on salary.

Replacement of an Actor's Voice
The producer is not permitted to replace an actor's voice without written permission of the actor or in certain other circumstances. Generally it is not necessary to replace the voice of an actor but on occasion, in order to make delivery of the project possible, it may be required. Under those circumstances working with SAG is especially recommended. During post-production on *The Clonus Horror*, one of the female actors refused to loop (replace) her voice, which had been recorded badly during production. I spent many hours with her on the phone trying to get her to agree to loop. She finally told me that she would come in only if we gave her the negative footage of the partially nude love scene she did with the main actor. She honestly

believed that we were going to sell the footage to a pornography company and destroy her career. Of course this was ridiculous but she was insistent upon this as a condition of her looping. The investors and the production company owned the negative and we could not fulfill her demand. I was faced with a predicament. I called our representative at the Screen Actors Guild who warranted that her fears were unfounded since she was protected by our agreement with SAG against misuse of the nude scene footage. Knowing this, I asked the representative to speak with her. She did, and then notified me that all was fine and the actress would loop the scene. Thinking everything was resolved, I called the actress to schedule her time and she continued to find excuses why she couldn't loop. It seemed that the excuses, whether true or not, were all connected with her work as a model for a magazine photo shoot. When she told me the name of the magazine, I called my representative at SAG and explained that the actress she spoke to would still not appear to loop because of her commitments as a model for a magazine photo layout. This did not faze the representative until I informed her that the actress had said that the magazine was *Penthouse.* Our SAG rep immediately ended our conversation with eight words; *"You have SAG's permission to use another voice!"*

Nudity

Performers must be notified in advance of the first audition if nudity or sex acts are expected in the role. When an actor signs in for the audition, be sure to indicate that nudity is required for the role on the sign-in sheet. That way you will have a signed acknowledgement that the actor is aware of the nudity. A performer has the right to have a person of their choice present at the audition. The producer should require the performer to sign a written consent as part of the contract when it concerns nude or sex scenes. It is a good idea for the producer to require the actor to authorize the doubling of the actor in these types of scenes if that is agreed upon by the actor. This will protect the producer should an actor who has consented to this type of scene subsequently withdraw that consent. The producer will then be able to double the actor and the scenes that have already shot may be used under the conditions granted in the original approval. Of course, if a double is used, doubles are not entitled to any residuals or screen credit. Finally, when

PRODUCERS VOCABULARY

Voiceover—Dialogue or narration coming from off-screen, the source of which is not seen.

nude scenes are done, the set must be a "closed" set to all people not having any connection or business with the project.

Overtime

The director should know under what contract the actor is employed. The basic agreement provides for overtime to be paid for a daily player contracted for less than $1200 per day at 1½ times over eight hours up to ten hours and double time after ten hours. If the actor is contracted for more than $1200 a day, all overtime is paid at 1½ times over eight hours at the maximum daily rate of $225 an hour. If the performer is on a day player contract, overtime begins after eight work hours. If the actor is on a weekly player contract the overtime begins after ten workday hours on a forty-four (studio) or forty-eight (location) cumulative hour week. That is to say that weekly contracted actors who work past ten hours a day receive overtime for that day and if on a cumulative weekly basis they work over forty four hours (forty eight on location) they receive weekly overtime payments. Weekly contracted actors who are employed under the terms of special employment indicated in the SAG rules as Schedule C and F receive overtime payments only on a daily basis, as any weekly overtime is included as part of their weekly fee. This is in excess of ten hours on any day and is a double time rate based on $190.91 per hour. If the project is made for television, the overtime rates are somewhat different depending on the rate and terms of employment.

This does not mean that the director must adhere to completing the actors' work within the eight or ten hour day, but it does signify that the director must be aware of these conditions and should plan the use of the actor with these conditions in mind. Second assistant directors on the set are responsible for keeping track of the actual time each actor works. Although they should not bother the director with the conditions of employment for the actor, they should bring any overtime concerns to the first assistant director who in turn should gently nudge the director about being cost effective with the actor. The actual time the actor works is the time that is reflected on a sign out sheet, which is kept in the care of the second assistant director. The actor is normally permitted fifteen minutes to get out of makeup. Therefore, even though the director excuses an actor from the set, the additional fifteen minutes can put the actor into an overtime status. Some actors know that their time is based upon what is on the sign out sheet, so upon being excused by the director, they will purposely wander around, perhaps have a cup of coffee at the craft service table and chat with another actor just to delay signing their time out form so that they will get the extra overtime. This is especially true with actors who are working for minimum scale.

Rehearsal Time

Rehearsal time is work time according to the SAG agreement. Rehearsal is a luxury on low or efficiency budget projects. Although the actor or director may want to rehearse, the budget may not allow for a rehearsal period. The producer should not worry or panic or think that rehearsal is absolutely necessary. The creative process for the performer, or the process that permits the performer to feel and experience the role usually happens when the performer is put in the actual location and wearing the appropriate wardrobe. This does not totally happen until they are on the set and working. There is a style of directing that will permit the director to get quality rehearsal time with the performers and not slow the production process during the actual day of shooting. An experienced and skilled director knows and utilizes this technique. Rehearsal that involves getting actors on their feet with the script in hand to stage a scene definitely counts as work towards shooting the project. This notion comes from the rehearsal process employed in theater. When this is done you will have to pay actors because this sort of rehearsal constitutes official work time. But a group of people getting together for dinner, during which they discuss the story, character and relationships is certainly not a rehearsal. It will not feel like a rehearsal to actors and therefore they will not have a notion of "needing" to get paid for that evening. Yet this will provide actors with the security that their egos need to fully grasp the work and relate to their fellow players. An informed gathering like this gives the director the opportunity to introduce the actors to one another and to view the interchange of creative ideas and thoughts; it also provides the producer the opportunity to nurture a creative environment for the "in front of camera" talent, without officially putting performers on the payroll.

Meal Penalties

SAG requires that their performers sit and eat a meal within six hours of their reporting to work. The meal period is deducted from the performers work time and must be no less than thirty minutes and no more than one hour in duration. Each additional mealtime is to be within six hours of the preceding meal. But if the six-hour period ends while the camera is in the actual course of photography, the shot may be completed without a penalty being levied to the producer. For the first half hour or fraction of violation of the meal period, the performer will receive $25.00; for the second half hour or fraction of violation the performer will receive $35.00; and for the third half hour and each additional half hour thereafter or fraction of violation the performer will receive $50.00. So if the performer sits down to eat a meal 7½ hours after they have started work, they are to receive $110.00 (non-taxable) from the producer. Meal penalties occur more times than they should, primarily due to poor planning on the part of the director.

Wardrobe Fittings

If a producer asks a day player to go to a wardrobe fitting any day prior to the day the actor works, the day player is entitled to be paid for the amount of time they are required for the fitting, unless the day player is receiving more than $950 a day for their performing services. However, a producer may require a weekly player to go to a wardrobe fitting without additional compensation as the producer is entitled to four free hours of fitting time on two separate days for each week the performer works on the project. Any more than four hours or additional days requires the producer to pay the performer for their time.

Forced Call

The producer must schedule performers so they are able to have twelve hours between the time they are dismissed from any days' work to the time they are called in to work the next day. The twelve hours may sometimes be reduced to ten hours (only once in three days), only if the next day's schedule is a location other than an overnight location and exterior scenes are required on the day before and the day after the rest period. On theatrical projects with overnight locations, the producer may give a performer eleven hours of rest on any two non-consecutive days. A performer must also be given thirty six consecutive hours of rest within the workweek. This usually reflects the amount of time that is taken during a six day shooting week, which is customary on overnight locations. If the workweek is a studio workweek, then the rest period the producer must provide for a performer is fifty-six consecutive hours. The penalty for any of these violations, known as a forced call, is one day's salary. *This penalty may not be waived under any conditions without the specific consent of the Screen Actors Guild.* Forced calls are common when the director has not planned out the shooting day, or does not know how to work creatively with performers in relationship to production schedules. Directors who are not skilled with directing techniques to avoid forced calls are usually first-time directors whose experience has been on low budget films where fourteen to sixteen hour production days are the norm. Will Gotay, one of the stars of the film *Stand and Deliver,* was employed under a SAG agreement for a series of commercials to be shot in Mexico. Eight of the nine days he was working were forced call days. He came home with enough money to purchase a new automobile outright while the producer had to go back to the advertising agency and try to explain why the lead actor's salary went triple over the projected budget.

Day Out of Days

The production board comes in handy when estimating the probability of forced calls. This will depend on the complexity of the production elements on any specific day and on the director's preparation. The production board will also provide information about other actor scheduling problems. From the production board the producer is able to establish a *day out of days.*

The day out of days in Figure #14, taken from the production board tells the producer many things; *"sw"* indicates start work, *"w"* indicates workday, *"fw"* indicates finished work, while *"h"* indicates that the performer is on hold for that day. A hold day is a standby day in case the director needs to call the performer in to work because of new scenes, rescheduling of scenes, or scenes that were not completed from another day. A wise producer will also use the hold day to schedule actors for looping or rerecording badly recorded dialogue for scenes that have already been shot. This may avoid additional payments to the actor for looping during post-production. The day out days in Figure #14 tells us that the character Eyan Hayes will need to be hired on a weekly contract with one-week guarantee. Although the character works seven days, four of them are in the first week and three of them in the second. Without including the words *"one week guarantee"* in the contract, we would not be able to pay the performer for 4/5ths of a week for the second week of work. The performer would have to be paid for the entire week, since he would be employed as a weekly performer without a

Week Days		1	2	3	4	5	6	8	9	10	11
Character Artist											
Eyan Hayes	1	sw	w	h	w	w		w	h	w	fw
Trish Malone	2		sw	h	w	w	w		w	w	fw
Suny Malone	3			sw	h	w	w		w	fw	
Angela Hayes	4	sw	h	w	h	w	w	fw			
Tommy Joe	5	sfw									
Delphine	6							sfw			
John	7							sfw			
Annette	8								sfw		
Bob	9							sfw			
Don	10								sfw		
Eyan's Stunt Double	11					sw	w	fw			
Trish's Stunt Double	12					sw	fw				
	13										

Figure 14

mention of a guarantee. The same holds true for the performer playing Trish Malone even though her week begins a different day than the actor playing Eyan's. It should be noted that both characters have the appropriate two days off and the producer and director have to make sure that they have fifty six hours of time off from the time they are released on the last day of their work week to the time they start their second work week. If they do not, the first day back becomes a forced call.

The character Angela will have to be hired on a weekly as well. But with her there is a fiscal question. She is scheduled to work the sixth day of a five-day week with only one-day off before working again. Unless the project is being done under one of the other SAG agreements (other than the Basic Agreement), the sixth day will be a double time day and the seventh day of work will be a forced call day. If this is the case, the producer will have to re-schedule this character by reboarding if possible, or plan for the extra funds needed to pay the actress playing this character. The characters Tommy Joe, Delphine, John, Annette, Bob and Don are all day players who are scheduled to start and finish work on the same day. The key issue in their cases is the eight hours of work before they reach an overtime status. Remember, over-time for a day player contracted for less than $1200 per day is at 1½ times over eight hours up to ten hours and double time after ten hours. If the actor is paid more than $1200 for the day, overtime is paid at 1½ times at $225 an hour.

Finally, the day out of days indicates that Eyan's stunt double is working on a day that Eyan is not scheduled. Although this seems strange, it really is not. It means that the stunt that Eyan does in the project will be done by the stunt double on the last day of the workweek and the performer playing Eyan is not needed. In this case, the director has made a definite creative decision not to see the actual performer playing Eyan when the stunt is being done. In *Hunter's Blood*, the shooting schedule was based on a six-day week for the crew, but a five-day week for the actors. We were able to board the project so that Sam Bottoms was the only actor to work on the sixth day in two successive weeks, and we planned to pay him for that sixth day pur-suant to the SAG agreement as an overtime day. We just had to make sure that he had the appropriate turnaround time before beginning his next week of work.

As the schedule changes for whatever reasons, the day out of days will change and will inform the producer and director of other creative and fiscal issues that might become problems. In reality, this puzzle changes constant-ly and a smart producer will stay on top of this major issue since it has such a huge creative impact upon the project. This will be discussed in greater detail in Chapter 11. A word to the wise: "What goes on behind the camera during the process of production can be learned from a book, but what goes on in front of the camera, or the story, can take a lifetime to learn."

The Loanout Agreement

Actors, writers and directors who receive very large amount of monies for their creative work are usually hired through a loanout company. The loanout company is a separate corporation that lends the services of the actor to the producer for a prescribed period of time. The actor is an employee of the loanout company. The loanout company must be a signatory to the appointed guild. Because the salary is very high (six figures or more) it is not unusual for the agreement through the loanout company to be all inclusive of overtime, looping and other services. In a loanout agreement, the lender (company) agrees to cause the employee (the actor, writer, director) to render the services required by the producer and to comply with all reasonable requests and directions associated with those services which must include matters of artistic taste and judgement. The agreement with the loanout company will be an exclusive agreement for a prescribed period of time, which may include pre-production (and post-production if it does not conflict with the artists' schedule). The loanout agreement may contain clauses concerning deferred payment, equity point participation and residual structure within the initial compensation. If the artist is an actor they must fall within the guidelines of the Screen Actors Guild basic agreement. The same is true of the DGA if the loanout is with a DGA director. The financial value of a loanout company to the producer will be discussed later in this chapter under fringes, but with a loanout company the producer has no responsibility or liability for tax withholding, or the health and welfare pension plan for the actor (or director or writer). However, the producer should expect to pay additional compensation to the loanout company for the health and welfare pension plans. The loanout agreement will include other provisions for the talent such as travel expenses, transportation, living expenses on distant locations, size and type of dressing room accommodations, credit onscreen and in advertisements, and any other matters which might be negotiated between the talent's representative and the producer. Although SAG agreements are pay-or-play agreements, in the case of loanout compensation should the producer suspend production of the project due to force majeur (an Act of God or an unexpected uncontrollable event that stops the project) and fail to recommence the project, the producer may be liable to the loanout company only for that portion of the guaranteed payment that had already been paid prior to the suspension of production. (Your attorney should prepare loanout agreements since they are very complex.)

THE SAG BOND
Creative Budget Protection #1
There are several methods of protecting against the possibility of overages through various fiscal techniques of money management. We will refer to them as creative budget protection techniques. Placement of the SAG bond is one of them.

The Screen Actors Guild requires the producer to post a financial bond with the guild to assure that their performers will not only get paid but that the Pension, Health and Welfare monies for the performers will also be paid. The amount of the bond is based upon the producers stated cast budget and the day out days submitted to the Screen Actors Guild. SAG calculates the amount of the bond and the posting must be done before the start of principal casting. The signed signatory documents and the posted SAG bond complete SAG's immediate requirements for the producer. Once the performers have been completely paid and the Pension, Health and Welfare monies for the performers have also been issued according to the agreement, the bond is then released back to the producer. If the producer wishes, the bond can be used to pay the Pension, Health and Welfare. When posting the bond with SAG, the producer should require that the bond be put in a separate interest bearing account. Once the bond is released, the interest will also be released and will be given to the producer along with the bond. In that way, the bond will have earned interest which can then be used for the project. This is the first method of providing fiscal security to protect possible budget overages.

Penalties
Producers generally leave the details of the administration of the actors to production personnel. On set, it is the second assistant director; away from the set, it can be a production assistant, a casting director, an associate producer, the production accountant or a variety of other assigned personnel.

PRODUCERS VOCABULARY

Force Majeur—An unexpected or uncontrollable event that upsets one's plans or releases one from obligations; an act of God. A force majeur clause is often found in contracts above (or below) the line.

However, they generally manage the situations after they have occurred. Unfortunately the people involved do not usually have enough authority or know enough to prevent expensive situations from happening. Each penalty has a dollar fine assessed to the producer that is never translated to the screen. We have already talked about two of them—the meal penalty and the forced call. There are several others with which the producer should be familiar.

Once the SAG performer has been hired and before the performer begins work, the producer must, either through the casting director or the production staff, attempt to get a positive report from Station 12 of the Screen Actors Guild. This is referred to as a "must pay" status of the performer and provides assurance to SAG that the performer being used is a dues paying member in good standing with the guild. A delinquent member with SAG must correct the status before employment begins. (Producers are often surprised when they find out who is delinquent with their dues. It is usually the people you least expect.) If the performer is not in good standing with the guild and works on the project, then the producer is fined $500. The best advice here is to have whoever it is who is contacting Station 12 to log in the date, time and person they spoke with at SAG who provided them with the information. In that way, later on, should there be a dispute, the producer has kept a paper trail.

The producer must give *preference of employment to SAG members* for any speaking roles in the project. Failure to give preference to qualified professional members or failure to employ a nonprofessional who meets appropriate recognized exceptions will result in the producer paying a fine of as much as $700.

The standard exceptions to employing only Screen Actor Guild members are the casting of people of a "name" specialty group (such as Cirque Du Soleil or a professional sports team), the casting of important, famous or well-known persons who portray themselves, and military or government personnel who must be used because of government restrictions that prevent using non-authorized persons. Other exceptions can be children under eighteen or the driver of an unusual scripted vehicle or some other scripted piece of equipment that is not available to the production without employing its operator.

The producer can also use nonmembers of the Screen Actors Guild when the script calls for speaking roles for characters with a special skill or who have an unusual appearance that is required for the project when no qualified SAG members are available who have the same special ability or appearance. A nonunion extra who might be hired as a cast person when the director or producer adds a non-scripted line due to a flash of on-set creative inspiration is also an exception to the preference rule. Finally, the first hire of a professional actor who can show sufficient training and/or experience for an acting career *and* who intends on pursuing the career (full time) by always being available for work may also be considered an exception. This often happens when the actor is working as a paid professional in another medium. In these cases, the people are hired under what is commonly referred to as a Taft-Hartley. A Taft-Hartley report of their hiring must be filed with SAG for approval.

The Taft-Hartley report must be submitted to SAG in an acceptable format. The report should include the pertinent information as to how the performer is to be employed, the work dates, shooting location and the reason for hire, stating the appropriate preference information. It must also include the signature of the producer as well as a contact number. When a person is hired under the Taft-Hartley Act, they are paid as a member in good standing in the Screen Actors Guild, receiving at the least the minimum scale pay-

———— • • • ————

Taft-Hartley Act—*In the United States, another name for the Labor Management Relations Act of 1947, which states that a nonunion worker can be hired for a union job (e.g., a nonunion actor for a role in a movie) if the employer (producer) can justify in a waiver application to the union that no union member is equally qualified to perform the job ("She's going to have to be Taft-Hartley'ed if we want to hire her for the role."). Once employed under the Taft-Hartley waiver, the worker has a finite period of time to join the union; once a member of the union, he or she will be able to continue working with or seeking employment from union signatory companies as long as he or she remains a member in good standing (e.g., pays dues on time and follows union regulations). A person can be Taft-Hartley'd three times before being required to join the union.*

Taft-Hartley form—*In the U.S., a union form used for processing U.S. citizens and foreigners who are not union members and who have been offered employment with a U.S. producer. Besides the required information, a résumé and photo of the individual must be attached.*

—Ralph S. Singleton and James A. Conrad,
Filmmaker's Dictionary, 2nd Edition (Lone Eagle Publishing)

———— • • • ————

ment for their services. From that moment on, each day they work on the project they must receive the same amount of pay and work under the same conditions as a SAG member. So, if a director becomes inspired and in the course of a production day decides to give an extra a line or two in a scene, the next day that person comes to work as an extra, they must continue to be paid wages equal to that of a speaking role. On *Hunter's Blood*, I had an actor who read for one of the redneck poachers, but I was unable to cast him since he was not a member of the Screen Actors Guild. From his reading, and through conversation, I knew he was a brilliant talent. I was disappointed that I couldn't use him in one of the speaking roles since he didn't qualify under any of the exceptions, so I offered him the opportunity of being in the background as an extra so he could get the experience of working on a movie. He jumped at the chance. On the last day of the shooting schedule and after a brief creative story conference with the director, I was struck with inspiration and decided to add a line of dialogue for him to say. That day we filed a Taft-Hartley report with his SAG day player contract. The contract and report bore my authorized hiring signature. The next week he went down to the Screen Actors Guild and joined. That actor is Billy Bob Thornton.

Many times on independent projects, members of the production company or casting personnel who might be members of the Screen Actors Guild may also wish to act on the project. They cannot. Although this was a common practice several years ago, when actors utilized multiple production skills the SAG agreement clearly states this is a violation that will cost the producer up to $800. The only exception that is recognized by SAG is in the case of animal handlers, directors, writers or producers who are also actors and who were formerly hired by written contract before the start of principal photography, or are hired in a bona fide emergency on the spur of the moment on location.

Other penalties resulting in various monetary fines include safety violations, failure to honor a contractual billing agreement, late payment of salary, replacing a performers voice with another voice without approval, failure to deliver a written contract to a weekly performer and the reuse of film or video from another production without negotiating the right to use it.

The details of the Screen Actors Guild rules and regulations will be given to the producer once the project begins the process of becoming a signatory. A representative is assigned and always available to assist the producer in getting over the necessary hurdles to work with SAG and its members. SAG encourages the recognition of the dignity of the actor and the integrity of the producer.

———— • • • ————

When you are working with a creative producer it really adds a whole other dimension to the film process, because a creative producer can visualize and understand things while dollars and cents producers often have no clue as to what you are talking about as a director trying to create your vision. A creative producer is the ultimate for any director, cinematographer, or even an actor or writer who has a vision and is trying to capture it on film. Creative producers understand the nature of the artistic temperament and how to successfully build and engineer a group of people—like the director, the production designer, and the writers—on a path that will make it possible to shape a movie for a particular dollar figure and how to make a platoon of people come together so the work becomes famous. That's what a creative producer does!

—Debbie Allen, Actor, Choreographer, Director

———— • • • ————

CASTING PHILOSOPHIES

Casting a project is one of the single most important aspects of the project. The onscreen talent will have an immediate impact upon the End Result Use of the project. Robert Altman once said that if you cast a project right, the director and producers' jobs are 75 percent completed. Casting is not a simple process because every one of the people you come in contact with during the process will have an agenda. But you should try to get the best possible cast, keeping in mind the end result of the project and its fiscal limitations. You and the director try to find the right ensemble of talent to express and develop your vision; the agents try to get jobs for their clients and the highest possible salary; actors' managers are interested in not only getting a high salary but also in the amenities and publicity the project will generate for their client, and actors are just concerned about getting the job and exercising their creative muse. Of course in the scheme of things, the whole driving force may be the producer's ability to get the project into some marketplace.

A casting philosophy that eliminates the agent and manager's financial motivation from the formula and focuses the project entirely on the creative actors ego is to declare the casting of the project as a *favored nation* project. The favored nation concept is based upon a "most favored nation" clause provision that ensures equal opportunities to parties involved. This tenet in casting is sometimes used when the above-the-line cast budget of the project is not large enough to attract acting talent who normally receive very high pay checks for their services. With this concept, the producer publishes in Breakdown Services that the project will be cast under the favored nation clause and files it with the Screen Actors Guild. Basically, this provides for a stated number of cast members to all receive the same salary and be treated equally in terms of work conditions while everyone else in the cast will receive a salary lower than those stated (which is usually scale plus 10 percent). The question of billing is agreed upon by the parties or they are often listed in alphabetical order. This casting tenet immediately tells managers and agents that there is no room for money negotiations and that if their clients are interested in the project their interest must be on the project's creative merits alone. Often, producers will take this approach with a project when they strongly believe in the aesthetic and creative merits of the characters and believe the ego of the actors (once they read the project) will be enough to motivate their participation. The 1992 motion picture *Glengarry Glen Ross*—directed by James Foley, based on the David Mamet stage play and produced by August Entertainment—was cast using the favored nations concept. Its cast included Al Pacino, Jack Lemmon, Alex Baldwin, Alan Arkin, Kevin Spacey and Ed Harris, all award-winning and highly paid actors. Understandably, the motivation for these actors to do this project remained with the characters, the story and the opportunity for them to not only work with one another in one vehicle, but to also work with one another in a vehicle that would permit them the opportunity to "chew the scenery." Money is not what makes the characters interesting and exciting in terms of what they say and how they feel. That involves the creative patience of the producer nurturing the writer to make the characters come to life on the page so that an actor, upon reading, knows that they *have* to do the project. *Hunter's Blood* was an example of favored nations casting; six characters received double scale, everyone else received scale plus 10 percent—and much scenery was chewed up and spat out triumphantly.

PRODUCERS VOCABULARY

Principal Photography—Segment of production during which all scripted material covering all speaking parts is filmed. Second unit material (of locations and containing no speaking parts) may be shot at approximately the same time. It is possible for second unit photography to be shot either before or after principal photography

Q-Rating—Another name for "TVQ," a rating for television popularity, issued in the United States by Marketing Evaluations of Port Washington, New York.

From time to time a project may allow for "name" actors to play roles for which they would not normally be considered. For example, an actor may continually be cast playing romantic leads, and a creative producer may have a notion to cast him as a villain. The ego of the actor and the possibility of playing an against-type role may be the overriding factor in securing the actor. In those cases, the agent may agree to take less for the actor's services than the actor might usually receive. Once again, it will come down to the quality of the character in the story. *Hunter's Blood* had some of the best character actors in town in the supporting roles as the backwoods poachers. They included Billy Drago, Bruce Glover and Lee DeBroux. They were all actors who usually received large salaries for their work; they agreed to do the project because I promised each of them a wonderful death scene in which they could "eat the scenery."

The production board may indicate a possibility of another philosophy in casting when fiscal restraints exist. A cameo role will show itself by the number of days that a character works in the project. Cameo roles are usually small roles in terms of screen time, but important roles in terms of the story. Diane Baker had a cameo in *Silence of the Lambs*, in which she played the Senator whose daughter was being held hostage by the serial killer. She had that wonderful unforgettable scene with Sir Anthony Hopkins as Hannibal Lecter in which he is wheeled in on a furniture dolly, wearing a facemask. It was one, or possibly two, days work for Diane. In such cases it is possible to budget a substantial salary for the one or two days that are boarded and hire the name actor on a day player contract. Once again, however, the actor's ego will enter into the scenario and it will come down to the quality of the role in relationship to the agreed payment. The down side of this concept is in the day player contract. The actor goes into overtime after eight hours and although the maximum that can be levied for a day player earning more than $1200 a day is $225.00 an hour, you want to make sure that you minimize any overtime for the actor. The trick here is in analyzing the production board and seeing if it is possible to schedule all of the work done by the actor within a one or two day period. It may require rewriting the script to accommodate this limitation. This does not mean sacrificing the story; creativity flourishes when confronted with limitations and restrictions and often new and improved inspiration can create the solution. *The Clonus Horror* adhered to this casting tenet. When this (now cult) film was originally produced, the only market available to protect the return on the investment was free television. I wanted to make sure that revenue from the television market would pay for the investment and knew we had to cast visible and recognizable actors for that market. *Mission: Impossible* and *Bewitched* were two popular television shows at the time so we were able to create a two-day cameo for Peter Graves of *Mission: Impossible* and a three-day cameo for Dick Sargent of *Bewitched*. To help the End Result Use of the project, my producing partner (Robert Fiveson, who also directed the film) and I decided to cast an actor who was known to major theatrical distributors. We cast Keenan Wynn (176 movies, including *Dr. Strangelove, The Great Race, Finian's Rainbow* and *Stagecoach*) in a one-day cameo. This same concept can be used for a weekly player if you are able to schedule their work all within a one-week period. The negative budget on the entire project was $250,000. As a side note, our casting director on *The Clonus Horror* was Susan Arnold, who today is a major producer of such movies as *America's Sweetheart, Forces of Nature* and *The Haunting*. Without her insight into the creative side of the characters we would have been lost.

Many independent producers often employ one or more of these casting concepts. As an example, *The Bone Collector*, produced by Martin Bregman and Michael Scott Bregman, had Denzel Washington and Angelina Jolie in the cast. The project was produced before she won the Oscar®. Denzel Washington plays a quadriplegic and his scenes all basically take place in one interior location. Logic dictated that his work was done during a prescribed period of time unaffected by the rest of the picture shot in New York and Montreal. It is possible that Angelina Jolie—not yet having received her Oscar® — wanted to do the project because it was based on a bestseller, and directed by the talented Phillip Noyce. Perhaps knowing that Denzel Washington was the male lead motivated her towards the vehicle as well. Her fee for this project was probably nowhere near what her fee would be today. Denzel Washington would have been the strong element to the project and his fee might have been based upon the amount of time he was needed or his desire to work with Noyce.

Another example is the remake of the project *12 Angry Men*, written by Reginald Rose and produced by Terrence A. Donnelly for Showtime Television. The story primarily takes place in one location and the jurors are well-developed characters. Directed by William Friedkin, much of the project is performed continuously—as you would see it staged in the theater. The cast included Jack Lemmon, the late George C. Scott, Armin Mueller Stahl, James Gandolfini, Hume Cronyn, Ossie Davis, Tony Danza and Edward James Olmos. The opportunity for the experience of acting in a great screenplay, directed by an actor's director and within a highly creative environment was clearly the motivation for these actors, as the economics of television production do not normally allow for a large budget for above-the-line casting.

The theatrical project *The Big Kahuna,* based upon the play *Hospitality Suite,* has three characters in the entire film. Elie Samaha and Andrew Stevens produced the project. (Kevin Spacey is also listed as a producer, a credit that may have been offered to Spacey to secure him to the project.) This then brought in the talents of Danny DeVito and Peter Facinelli. The project is not a big project, but the characters are full and rich in their relationships to one another and the project provides DeVito, Spacey and Facinelli with the kind of roles they might not normally be able to play.

Actors are usually most concerned with the material and the director. They want to have the confidence that they are in good hands and that they are doing a role that is unique to them. It is their soul that brings life to the written character and they must feel confident that the character is worthy of that life. You must not underestimate casting concept tenets for an independent project. It should be foremost in your mind when you begin and complete the casting process. It all begins with the script, then moves to the director. For the creative producer there is no alternative for the creative thought and nourishing attention that goes into the responsibility of casting.

Stunt Coordinator—Stunts

The stunt coordinator is the person who takes on the responsibility of assisting the director in the staging and execution of stunts on a project. A stunt is any action that is performed by a performer that could potentially cause injury. It can be as simple as a performer jumping off a three-foot wall or something as complex as the action performers appear to do in projects like *X-Men, Saving Private Ryan, Traffic* or *Crouching Tiger, Hidden Dragon.* A stunt coordinator is the expert who understands and suggests the most effective camera placement, as well as instructs the stunt people on the dramatic execution of the action in terms of telling the story. Stunt coordinators, indeed all stunt people, are members of the Screen Actors Guild. There are some stunt people who are non-guild as well. Sometimes a stunt coordinator is also a second unit director and is given the entire responsibility of executing the stunts without the presence of the primary director. Stunt coordinators may be employed weekly or daily for a project and it is a good idea to have them available even on days when stunts are not scheduled. A stunt coordinator may be needed to help the director instruct an actor on how to throw a realistic punch, or provide safety equipment for an actor being required to do action for the camera. Stunts can be performed with stunt people playing specific characters or working as doubles for a specific actor playing a character. Sometimes the actor cast in a role may also perform stunts. It all depends on the visuals and the creative approach the director takes towards the action in the story. You must make sure that the actor is capable of doing the stunts and, if not, you will have to provide training to prepare the actor. A stunt person may be asked to drive a vehicle for specific photographic effects when the camera is attached to the vehicle (as in the case of a point of view shot of a vehicle going through rough land terrain). In all cases a stunt coordinator will be necessary. So it makes sense to hire a stunt coordinator for the entire project.

Stunt coordinators may be hired two different ways. First is on a *flat deal basis* for which no overtime, penalties or premiums would apply, provided that the coordinator is hired at a rate at or higher than those listed by SAG as minimum wage scales. This payment would be inclusive for on camera work of the coordinator. The second is for those employed on a less than the flat deal basis and under those conditions the stunt coordinator should be paid no less than the minimum for a stunt performer. In this situation the producer also has to pay for overtime, penalties and premiums as they apply.

Unlike an actor, the turnaround for stunt coordinators is eight hours since they often need to come to work earlier than an actor or another stunt person in order to work with the director in planning for a shot or a sequence of shots. A creative producer will employ a stunt coordinator at or above the minimum scale who is about the same size as the principal actor in the project so that the stunt coordinator can double for that actor. Thus the producer will be saving on the day wage another actor would get as the principal actors' double. Female stunt performers must double female performers while male stunt performers must double male performers. Children are usually doubled in stunts by both genders depending on size and body type. There are stunt people who may perform many different kinds of stunts but who may specialize in certain types of stunts. There are others who limit the type of stunt they will do. An experienced stunt coordinator or production manager will know who these people are. Stunt people may have agents of their own or they may be represented through either The Stuntmen's Association or Stunts Unlimited. A creative producer should rely on the knowledge of the stunt coordinator to locate the right stunt person for the right stunt because it is the stunt coordinator's ego and reputation that are on the line in making sure the stunts look creatively and dramatically right for the project. The producer should not just leave it all up to the stunt coordinator, however, because all stunts involve some danger and risk. The end does not always justify the means when stunts are concerned and the producer and director should make sure that safety is always a priority. Accidents happen, and when they do you want to make sure that it was not due to the negligence of someone involved in the planning and execution of the stunt.

Stunt people are generally paid the minimum scale as a performer for the day or the week, or if they are an important stunt person, they may expect above scale as a performer. They get paid an additional fee for performing the actual staged stunt. This is called a stunt adjustment and is agreed upon by the stunt performer and the production manager (on behalf of the producer), before the stunt is performed. This is done so production is not delayed while the compensation for a stunt is determined. Stunt players may negotiate a fee for the stunt based upon the difficulty and danger connected with the stunt. The more hazardous the stunt, the higher the adjustment. These adjustments are considered salary and overtime and other premiums are figured on the base rate and the stunt adjustment together.

The adjustment is paid each time the stunt is performed—providing retakes are not due to the fault of the stunt person. When a stunt is planned, the director and cinematographer, along with the creative producer, must consider whether the stunt needs to be done multiple times with one camera being moved to different camera positions, or performed one time with multiple cameras positioned in different camera positions. (For example, there is a spectacular train wreck in the 1993 film, *The Fugitive*. Because this was clearly a "one time only event," the production used nine separate cameras in different positions to film it.) The cost and time factor, and the creative quality of the lighting for either of those two scenarios will have an

——— • • • ———

The first challenge of a stunt coordinator is to devise a stunt according to the script and the director's interpretation of the story, while remaining within the margin of safety and budget. If it becomes an impossibility than the next challenge is meeting with the producer, and director and creatively reworking the stunt to be as spectacular as possible within these guidelines.

—Rawn Hutchinson, Stunt Coordinator,
8 Heads in a Duffel Bag, Waiting to Exhale,
The Linguini Incident, The End of Innocence

——— • • • ———

influence upon the decision. There may be material costs involved in doing a stunt so they should be talked through very carefully, and storyboarded either through 3D animation or with hand drawn storyboards to insure that everyone involved is seeing the same vision.

Overtime—ADR and Other

Overtime and penalties have been mentioned several times. They are unavoidable. They will happen. One more time: The cast or SAG budget is often very volatile as it becomes a direct reflection of the production life of the project, which often appears to be chaotic, personal and fraught with unpredictable human elements involving ego and creativity. Therefore the cast budget must have a line item that prepares for these fluctuations. This line is called OVERTIME—ADR and OTHER. ADR is automatic dialogue replacement, also known as looping, and is discussed further in Chapter 9. You can see an example of ADR in the motion picture *Postcards from the Edge.* In one sequence, Meryl Streep's character, after a violent argument with her mother (played by Shirley MacLaine), runs out to a looping session at which she is shown a scene and asked to replace the badly recorded dialogue with new dramatic intonation, while keeping the same tempo and rhythm as the original. This is done by first listening and watching the scene to get a sense of the rhythm. Then, the actor repeats the dialogue attempting to match the synchronization of the image. The sounds of crowds (who are usually shot silently) are also recorded at ADR sessions. This is usually done during the post-production process by actors who are expert at improvising dialogue based upon what they see on the screen. These are almost never the same extras who are visible onscreen and instead are very specific professionals. They are generally members of the Screen Actors Guild and are covered by the terms of the Basic Agreement. Companies such as The Loop Group, Voiceworks or I Love Looping are available to a producer for a flat fee. Post-production sound houses, editors and post-production supervisors are familiar with these and other companies. Many of these companies utilize wonderful, creative and highly expert actors who can improvise dialogue on the spot based upon simple dramatic direction they may be given by the producer. You must remember to have the performers at these sessions sign written waivers for the use of the dialogue in the project since it is now added dialogue (albeit in the background), and not part of the original script.

No less than 35 percent of the entire cast budget should be allocated to the Overtime-ADR and Others line item (See Figure 13). It is not unheard of for it to be equal to 100 percent of the cast budget. However, when the bonding company sees 100 percent, they may think that the producer and director might not be able to make production decisions very easily.

Travel and Living Expenses

Travel expenses are required when above-the-line personnel are going to a distant location. It covers payments for transportation and housing accommodations. Although people may wind up sharing a hotel room, it is appropriate for the producer to provide individual rooms for everyone. Living in a hotel room is tough enough, but living in a hotel room with someone you work with all day can be tortuous. Per diems are funds provided for incidental and meal expenses associated with being on a distant location. It covers those meals that are not provided by the producer. Per diems are usually $12 for breakfast, $18 for lunch and $30 for dinner, although—depending on the person and the cost of living in the location—per diems may be higher. The production board will assist in determining the calculations for housing, per diem and travel. The producer should also provide flight insurance if air travel is required.

Acct. #	Account Name	Units	Rate	Amount	Sub Total	Total
500	ABOVE-THE-LINE TRAVEL AND LIVING EXPENSES					
01	Travel					
02	Housing					
03	Per Diems					
	Total 500					

Figure 15

Extras

Extras include the people who populate a project in front of the camera but do not have specific characters and do not speak onscreen. It includes stand-ins, atmosphere and bit characters (extras with a special ability). Atmosphere extras have sometimes been referred to as "human wallpaper," since they are people who populate a scene providing it with the human texture and character required by the story. Brilliant directors like Martin Scorsese and Francis Ford Coppola use their atmosphere as if it was its own individual character in the story. How can we ever forget the opening of *The Godfather* when, at the wedding reception, we see hundreds of invited guests and know they are all friends and relatives of the Corleone family?

Extra players in the motion picture and television industry are represented by two labor groups: SAG, and the American Federation of Television and Radio Artists (AFTRA). The SAG Extras Agreement currently runs through June 30, 2001. There are different union rules for extras hired on the West Coast than for those hired on the East Coast. There are also different union rules for extras when they work in projects whose end use is television rather than theatrical. In all cases, the producer is able to mix union extras with nonunion extras, but only within certain set formulas. The wage of a nonunion extra can be set by the producer, but in general the minimum wage that a nonunion extra can be paid per hour is the higher of federal or state minimum wage.

In theatrical projects originating on the West Coast, the producer must hire up to forty union extras per day before hiring nonunion extras. In New York, the minimum is eighty five. In television originating on the West Coast the producer must hire fifteen extras per day before nonunion extras may be hired. In television originating from New York, the minimum is twenty-five.

In all cases stand-ins are not included in these counts. A stand-in is an extra who is employed as a member of what is commonly referred to as a second team. After the director has staged a scene and before the director of photography has determined its lighting, the first assistant director will call for the second team to step in front of the camera. Stand-ins then take the same positions the actors were in when the scene was staged by the director. The use of stand-ins allows the director to work creatively with the main actors off the set, while the director of photography creates the look of the shot. Usually the same stand-ins are used every day of production, and are approximately the same size and coloring as the principle actors they are representing. The current SAG agreement for extras provides for different minimum wage scales for general atmosphere, special ability extras, stand-ins and choreographed swimmers and skaters. Dancers are covered as principal performers under the SAG agreement for actors. The Pension, Health and Welfare contribution is 13 percent of the salary. An extra is hired on a daily rate for eight hours and is paid 1½ and 2 times the hourly rate at specific increments after eight hours. The precise number of hours differs from the West Coast and the East Coast, but extras who work in excess of sixteen hours must be paid a penalty of one day's pay for each excess hour or fraction of an hour past sixteen hours.

Extras who appear in a scene and are required to look or do something specific may be asked to bring specific items to use in the scene. It may be a

Acct. #	Account Name	Unit	Rate	Amount	Sub Total	Total
600	**EXTRAS**					
01	Stand-ins					
02	Atmosphere					
03	Special Ability and Bits					
04	Choreographed Swimmers & Skaters					
05	Extra Personal Equipment					
06	Casting Fee – Extras					
07	Welfare Workers/ Teachers					
	Total 600					

Figure 16

vehicle (such as an automobile, moped, bicycle, unicycle or motorcycle), or a specific prop (such as golf clubs, skateboards, tennis racquet, skis or a headset radio). They may even be asked to bring their own pet. In each of these cases, the extra is paid an additional fee allowance by the producer.

When there are unusual conditions of employment for extras the producer will also be required to pay additional compensation. Examples of such conditions include working in water, snow or smoke, or the wearing of body makeup. You should keep in mind that when you require extras (or anyone) to work in these circumstances, you need to provide an element of comfort for them when they are not on camera or doing their jobs. This will also involve additional expenses.

An extra player who speaks unintelligible background words (commonly called "walla") only receives the basic wage for the particular call. Cheers or words coming from a crowd on camera are considered walla. However, extras who are required to speak dialogue in unison are reclassified as actors which will increase the basic minimum each of them will receive for the day. The exception to this is when there are groups of five people or more and they are required to utter in unison exclamatory words or phrases, or are required to speak in unison using traditional dialogue that an ordinary person could be presumed to know (such as The Pledge of Allegiance). Another exception is based upon the creative inspiration of the director. It involves groups of fifteen or more extras who are photographed as a group and who are asked to speak unscripted lines in unison decided on at the spur of the moment. But if the director thought of the lines the day before and asked the group of people to memorize them, then the extras must be reclassified as actors and paid a higher wage.

If the scene is unusually complicated with a great many extras as atmosphere, it might benefit the producer to have a casting company that specializes in the casting of extras provide supervision of the extras behind the scenes. Finally, directors often want to have realism with the extras who populate a scene. Realism may call for the use of minors. When using minors onscreen, the producer must remember that the project must adhere to state and federal child labor laws that require welfare workers or teachers on the set.

The inclusion of extras in the project can be costly. You should make sure that if the director requires a specific number of extras for a specific scene that those extras are utilized. You also want to make sure that the utilization of extras is cost effective to that production day. If not, you may find that you will have to provide meals for more people than you estimated for, or the payroll for the extras may be higher than estimated for that day. SAG extras fall within the same work conditions guidelines as actors, and that must be taken into consideration. It is not uncommon for the producer to require the director to consider how extras will be used. There is no doubt that they are necessary for the creative texture of the project. You only have to look at a Martin Scorsese film to see how extras can be used to great effect. The scene at the Copacabana in *Goodfellas* demonstrates just how integral extras are to the story. When watching the scene, you know that each of those extras has a life of their own, since they are so animated and involved in the scene. It is clear that extras used in that manner are equally as important as the actors in telling the story. So plan for it. It is an important creative detail that can be cost effective.

FRINGE BENEFITS ABOVE-THE-LINE
Creative Budget Protection #2 and #3

Fringe benefits are fiscal responsibilities that the producer has for the cast and crew of the production outside of salaries and any fiscal requirements that are mandated by state, local or federal laws. It includes the Pension, Health and Welfare payments for those people who are members of the Screen Actors Guild (SAG), the Directors Guild of America (DGA), and the Writers Guild of America (WGA) and the American Federation of Television and Radio Artists (AFTRA). Pension, Health and Welfare (and Vacation and Holiday) fringes for below-the-line personnel must be paid for

---

PRODUCERS VOCABULARY

AFTRA—An abbreviation for the American Federation of Television and Radio Artists. The U.S. union for performers working in live and electronically recorded television and radio commercials, live and recorded television programs (series, talk shows, specials, etc.), and related areas. Founded in 1937 and based in New York City, with offices around the United States.

Waiver—To waive one's right; typically, giving up something that is contractually called for.

Walla—Noise from the background, typically, indistinguishable voices.

Acct. #	Account Name	Amount	Computed Rate	Sub Total	Total
700	**FRINGE BENEFITS Above-the-line**				
01	WGA Pension Health Welfare		12.5%		
02	DGA Pension Health Welfare		12.5%		
03	SAG Pension Health Welfare		13.15%		
04	SAG Pension Health Welfare - Extras		13 %		
05	AFTRA Pension, Health and Welfare		13.15%		
06	Payroll Taxes		17%		
	Computed on $				
	Total 700				

Figure 17

those employees who are members of the International Alliance of Theatrical Stage Employees/Teamsters (IATSE) and the American Federation of Musicians (AFM). With the exception of production managers and assistant directors (who are represented by DGA below-the-line) SAG, DGA, WGA and AFTRA are all above-the-line. The percentage of the salary for the Pension, Health and Welfare program of the Writers Guild and the Directors Guild is 13.5 percent, but there is a salary ceiling of $200,000. The pension percentage for SAG is 13.15 percent with a ceiling of $200,000. For the sake of budget simplicity the producer should use a 13.5 percent of gross wages percentage for all above-the-line guild members up to a salary ceiling of $200,000. Therefore regardless of what the salary is for the writer, the director or any actor, the maximum that may be appropriated for Pension, Health and Welfare is $27,000 (or 13.5 percent of $200,000). The Directors Guild contract is up for negotiations in May 2002. Pension, Health and Welfare percentages and other issues may change at that time.

In the United States, employees of the producer or the production company must have taxes taken out of their wages. If you contract with a loanout company the contract is for services performed by the loanout company and that company is responsible for those fringes and no deductions are taken from the fee paid to the loanout company. The various funds you deduct from your employees' gross wages are OASDI, Medicare, FIT, SIT and SDI.

OASDI or FICA
Old Age, Survivors and Disability Insurance is more commonly known as Social Security. It is the largest program funded by the Federal Insurance Contributions Act (FICA) and provides pensions to retired persons age sixty-two or older, payments to disabled persons and benefits to dependents of insured workers who have died or become disabled. All employees must contribute a percentage of their wages into this fund.

Medicare

This is the federally funded health insurance program for persons age sixty-five or older and/or disabled. All employees must contribute a percentage of their wages into this fund.

Federal Income Tax (FIT)

The Tax Payment Act of 1943 and the 1986 Tax Reform Act require employers to deduct estimated taxes from employee taxable earnings and remit these deductions to the Internal Revenue Service (IRS). These estimated taxes are called withholdings. Employees are entitled to withholding allowances/personal exemptions based upon marital status, dependents and other specific criteria. The employee informs the employer how many allowances/exemptions they are claiming by filing a W-4 form with the employer when they are hired.

State Income Tax (SIT)

This tax is similar and follows the same parameters as FIT with the remittances being sent to the state of the employees' employment. The following states do not currently have employee state income taxes: Alaska, Florida, New Hampshire, South Dakota, Tennessee, Texas, Washington and Wyoming.

State Disability Insurance (SDI)

This tax is required by several states, and provides economic support for employees who become ill or disabled for reasons unrelated to their employment. All employees in applicable states must pay a percentage of their wages into this program.

Employer's Tax Obligations

As the employer, the producer has certain tax obligations. These are commonly referred to as payroll taxes. They include OASDI or FICA and Medicare and the producer must remit an amount equal to the employee's contribution. Employer's payroll taxes also includes the Federal Unemployment Tax Act, known as FUTA which is calculated as a percentage of all employee earnings. These three taxes are remitted to the IRS. Monies from FUTA subsidizes employee unemployment compensation available in all states. Employer's payroll taxes also include the State Unemployment Insurance known as SUI. Here again the producer must calculate a percentage of all employee earnings and remit them to the proper state department. These monies fund employee unemployment compensation in the applicable state.

Finally, several states have other programs that require employers to remit a percentage of employee earnings. Some of these programs are employer-funded disability, welfare or medical programs.

The budget should reflect an aggregate total of 17 percent for payroll taxes on all gross wages above-the-line. Since a budget is prepared before any personnel is hired it is difficult for the producer to know who will be employed through a loanout situation. Once this is known by the producer, the 17 percent budgeted for those employees (but which won't have to be paid because they are loanouts), will remain in the project's budget and can be moved elsewhere. This is the *second method of providing fiscal security to protect against possible budget overages.*

Finally, the 17 percent payroll taxes and the funds that are deducted for taxes from the employee's wages should be transferred into an interest earning account. At the prescribed time a report of these taxes is made and sent to the appropriate federal and state agencies by the producer's accountant. The interest that these funds accrue while sitting in this account before they are paid out is a *third method of providing fiscal security to protect against possible budget overages.*

If you use a payroll service for paying any of your cast and crew, the payroll service is the employer of record for that portion of the payroll. This will either reduce the interest earned back to your project or prevent you from applying the three methods mentioned in this chapter of providing budget protection to the project.

One last word about actors' salaries. Most actors will work as employees rather than through a loanout company. When an actor works for scale the contract will read *scale plus 10 percent* since agents sanctioned by SAG are not permitted to receive commissions on a scale job. Usually the producer, when issuing payment to the actor includes the 10 percent commission in the total wages for the actor, and the standard practice in the industry is to have the entire payment sent to the actor's agent who deducts 10 percent and gives the balance to the performer. But the actor loses money. The payment the agent received is for *net* payroll and when the agent deducts their percentage (which is based on the gross), the actor has already paid taxes on the agent's commission. And the producer has also paid payroll taxes on the salary plus the agent's commission as a gross amount. For example, a performer works for one day and receives SAG minimum of $596 for wages. Ten percent of that wage (or $59.60) is added to that check for the agent fee.

Employee taxes are then taken out of $655.60, rather than the earned wage of $596 and the net amount is sent to the agent out of which the $59.60 is deducted. The performer has paid taxes on the commission. And the producer has paid employer payroll taxes on $655.60 rather than $596.60. The solution: issue two separate payments; one for the agent and one for the performer. The actor thus avoids needlessly paying taxes on commissions and the producer saves on payroll taxes for a payment that was not payroll. *Every cent counts when producing creatively.*

CHAPTER **6** THE PRODUCTION PERIOD—
PART I

*"The truth of the matter is, most of us in the busi-
ness of "show" are children. And like any child,
what we really need are discipline, structure and
praise; never reward for bad behavior. The creative
producer must hold the bigger picture and budget
in the foreground at all times. Couched in discipline, structure and praise he or she should always
start with an open ear and open mind and the
desire to say, "Yes." This will buy favors and loyalty
that will invariably become a necessity at the 11th
hour. However, the cast and crew should know
from day one that when the creative producer
finally says No it is the last word. And that the "No"
decision was made only after weighing the consequences of saying, "Yes." There's a damn good reason the inmates don't run the asylum."*

—Nancylee Myatt, Writer/Producer,
Night Court, The Five Mrs. Buchanans, Living Single;
the feature film *Burning Liza*, and many plays.

Most above-the-line fees involve components of the project that are
extensive but fixed. Only the cast element will be variable and volatile due to
the flexible nature of the production process. Although there are not many
rules in production, there are a couple of constants that never change.

THERE IS NO SUBSTITUTION FOR PRE-PRODUCTION

Pre-production is everything. As I've already said (and will say again and
again): *What you fail to prepare for in pre-production, will affect production,*

and what you fail to do in production will affect post-production. This is inevitable. One afternoon, while scouting locations for *Hunter's Blood,* the director found a wooded clearing that he wanted to use for the hunters' camp. It was a perfect location with many cotton trees, and located near a stream. The screenplay called for many scenes to be shot in the camp—both by day and night. The first night scene in that location called for a lengthy dialogue scene between the hunters. When everything was set up and ready to go for the first shot, the first assistant director said, "Quiet please, roll camera." Everyone on the set quieted down waiting for the director to call "Action." Almost immediately, silence of the night was broken by the croaking of frogs until there was a cacophony of frog croaking coming from the nearby stream. The soundman was unable to record clean sound, and we had to pay the actors to come back during post-production to ADR the entire scene. If the director had scouted the location in the evening as well as in the daylight, he might have heard the frogs and may have selected another location.

MURPHY'S LAW

"Anything that can go wrong, will." When Edward A. Murphy Jr. uttered these words in 1949, he was not familiar with motion picture production. If he had been, he would have realized that those words were optimistic. Inexplicable things happen during production, and they usually happen below-the-line. The creative producer must be ready when they do. Again on *Hunter's Blood,* we were scheduled to shoot a scene involving seventeen actors in the woods. The weather the day before was pretty good. The evening before the scheduled scene, I received a phone call from Andy LaMarca, our production manager, who informed me that a major rainstorm was coming in and would probably hit our location early in the morning. I recalled the location and told Andy that first thing in the morning he should send people out to purchase rain gear for the crew and plywood planks to use for sidewalks should it get muddy. We were going to shoot! We had to shoot! It was already going to be an expensive day and it was clear to me that to call off the shoot would have been even more expensive (since actors had already received their call times for work and would have to be paid for the day anyway). I counted on the fact that at this time

---

PRODUCERS VOCABULARY

Pre-production—Time before production when the elements needed for making the film, e.g., preparing the script, script breakdown, budget, location scouting, costume design, set construction, are done.

in the schedule the production crew was working together as a team and I believed they could rise above these difficulties and deliver the goods. I was also counting on the fact that the scene was going to take place under a 200 year-old tree whose upper foliage (I hoped) would act as a gigantic umbrella to protect the actors and director while they worked. And it did. In spite of the fact that our dressing rooms were stuck in the mud and couldn't get to the location, and that we had to turn a tin shack near the location into a makeup room, dressing room and eating center—we shot the scheduled day. We got the results onscreen and added sound effects in post-production to account for the wet ground and the rain that was seen onscreen beyond the tree. The audience only knows what you show them onscreen, not how it got there. And what they saw was a fight scene in damp and muddy weather. The dampness and rain actually added to the affect. We were able to carry this off, because we were a team made up of individuals who worked together to make it happen. Andy and I were helping out anyone who needed the help, including the caterer, the gaffer and the key grip. We were putting out fires behind the scenes to keep the camera rolling, allowing the director to be creative. On this particular day, I wasn't the producer and each of them members of my crew. We were all one, working against the odds to finish the day. My job was to make it happen, keep things creatively vibrant, and provide decent conditions in which people could do their jobs and focus on the director's needs.

The structure of a production crew is one of the critical elements in the success of the production. There can be various structures and some are more efficient than others. Each crewmember must respect each other's position, areas of responsibility, and the interconnectivity of function to successfully work together. If there is a weak link anywhere in the structure, the weakness will cause a domino effect during the production process. A basic structure of reporting responsibilities is indicated in Figure #18. Straight dark lines designate a direct working relationship, and dotted lines designate indirect working relationships. The structure may be different from production to production based upon the structure of the pre-production elements, the complexity and requirements for production, and the producer's relationship to the director, the production manager, and other producers who might be involved. When more than one producer is involved on a production, each must communicate with one another, share responsibilities and think as one creatively. They must never be at odds over issues—at least, not publicly. All positions on a production are, in their own way, creative and contribute to the overall nature of the project. A savvy producer allows each to be creative and to recognize that they are expert at what they do to support the whole. You may not understand how they do their jobs, but they don't expect you to. They only expect that you respect them when they work. And that's easy!

The chart in Figure #18 provides a working structure between above, and below-the-line. You will notice that the group of people who report directly to the production manager and the group of people who report directly to the production designer are made up of staff whose jobs are primarily completed before production begins. They are involved in the long term "getting ready" of production. The production designer plans closely with the producer, the director and the cinematographer to create the look of the project that we see onscreen. The staff that reports to the production designer works independently of one another but with one consistent vision to create the look of the project. The production manager is an extension of the producer on the logistics of production from day to day and week to week. The interaction between the production manager and the staff that reports to him or her is important to the final success of the production process. If some of the staff do not do their jobs properly, the rest of the crew are affected and this can cause unnecessary unrest within the production.

On a project I was directing (but not producing) our first day of production was on Western Avenue in Los Angeles. Western Avenue is one of the busiest commercial streets in Los Angeles. Our first shot of the day was planned as a "walk and talk" shot on the street. Tom Denove was our cinematographer. When I arrived at the location, I immediately walked the first shot with Tom so he would know what I had in mind for the camera and could visualize and refine it while I staged the actors. In the middle of the conversation Tom stopped me and said, "Wait a minute, I don't think we can do as you ask." I queried him a moment and he pointed to the street. What we saw made me realize we were in trouble. The trucks that were carrying our equipment were caravaning down the street, circling the block—looking for a place to park. As they passed we waved to them. We soon found out that the producing staff hadn't worked out a place for a base camp at this location or a place for the trucks to park! So Tom and I looked at the production board and rearranged the shooting for the day. We had the grips double-park the trucks and unload enough equipment, props and wardrobe for us to go to an interior location that was planned for later that day, while the producing staff solved the problem of parking the trucks.

Figure #18 shows that the production manager is in communication with the first assistant director who is continually at the side of the director and should know what the director is doing and will do each moment of the day. Through this communication, the production manager has an idea as to the conditions of the schedule, the ongoing requirements on the set, and any problems that may affect the logistics and could possibly affect the creativity or the budget of the project. This information is then communicated to the producer (or line producer) for comment, reaction, intervention or solution. This interplay is important as it provides your support staff with the information needed to keep the production on track, on budget and creatively free.

Finally, Figure #18 also shows the importance of the continuity person. He or she communicates with the Camera Department through the 2nd assistant cameraperson, and with the Sound Department through the sound mixer. Continuity has an indirect relationship with the second assistant director, who reports to the first assistant director, who completes the link back to the production manager. Continuity works closely with the director during production. Once the director has decided on the best take of a shot, he or she says, "*Print.*" Continuity then records that instruction in the continuity log, while the sound mixer records it in the sound log, and the 2nd assistant camera records it in the camera log. At the end of the shooting day, the logs for camera and sound go to continuity who checks that they are all accurate and consistent. This information is forwarded to the 2nd assistant director who copies the information into a daily Production Report. The information then works its way up to the accountant, the producer and the bonding company, all of who are able to determine the fiscal status of the project and if it is on, ahead of, or behind schedule.

HIRING BELOW-THE-LINE

Below-the-line personnel can be hired either on a flat rate for the week, or on an hourly basis. They can be union or nonunion personnel. Most of the below-the-line union crewmembers are represented by the International Alliance of Theatrical Stage Employees, Moving Pictures Technicians, Artists and Allied Crafts of the United States, its Territories and Canada (IATSE), with the exceptions of musicians, production managers and assistant directors. Musicians belong to the American Federation of Musicians (AFM) and production managers and assistant directors belong to the Directors Guild of America (DGA). Only SAG, AFM, IATSE and the WGA are affiliated with the American Federation of Labor and Congress of Industrial Organizations (AFL-CIO). The rate and conditions of employment for each of the artists and crafts people below-the-line can be found in various published labor guides.

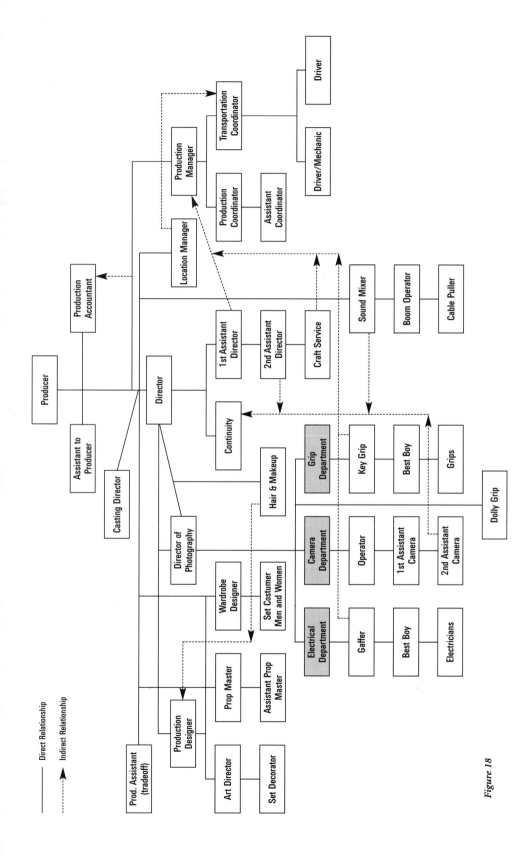

Figure 18

If a project is a signatory to the union (IATSE) then the project is required to use union members. If not, then nonunion members may be employed. It is not uncommon for a project to be a signatory to one or more of the guilds such as SAG, the DGA or WGA, and not be a signatory to IATSE. When you are signatory to one, you do not need to be a signatory to all.

Below-The-Line Overtime

Because the production period is so changeable, overtime work becomes an issue, not only for the producer, but also for the below-the-line crew personnel. Union (IATSE) and guild (DGA) contracts call for different work week minimums, depending on the craft and type of work, and lay out the ground rules that affect overtime status. Thirty-five percent of the budgeted salaries should be added to the budget in each of the production crafts to allow for the payment of union overtime.

Nonunion personnel individually negotiate their own overtime status. It is not uncommon for a nonunion below-the-line crewmember to have the expectation of working a twelve hour day as a maximum normal work day, on either a five or six day week. When paid a flat fee for the week, they will usually ask for a pro rata hourly rate of 1½ times for any work day over twelve hours. This gives them some protection against inexperienced directors or producers. Many inexperienced directors and producers come to the production ill prepared and wind up working fourteen and sixteen hour days (or longer). Overtime fees are a way of letting the inexperienced director and producer know that although the crew is there to support the creative needs of the project, the people in charge shouldn't abuse them in the

---

PRODUCERS VOCABULARY

IATSE—The organization of local unions in the film, television and theater industries in the United States and Canada. The individual local unions include such professions as art directors, broadcast studio employees, cartoonists, costumers, craft service employees, distribution employees, editors, electrical technicians, first-aid employees, grips, hairstylists, illustrators, lab technicians, makeup artists, matte artists, painters, photographers, prop craftsmen, projectionists, publicists, scenic artists, script supervisors, set designers, sound technicians, story analysts, studio mechanics, studio teacher, welfare workers, ticket sellers and wardrobe attendants. The organization typically is referred to as the International Alliance of Theatrical Stage Employees. Founded in 1893 and based in New York City.

NABET—National Alliance of Broadcast Engineers and Technicians, which is the technical craft union for tape television. Affiliated with the AFL-CIO, formed originally for radio technicians and engineers and later expanded to include television technicians and engineers. Recently merged with the Communications Workers of America, now called NABET-CWA. When there was a proliferation of made-for-television movies, an agreement was struck with IATSE (the union for film stagehands and technicians). Now NABET members are typically used for television production while IATSE members are used for film production, though NABET crews are often used on low-budget feature films (especially in New York). It was originally formed when the invention of television was introduced and IATSE, believing that television would be a "fad" and doomed to disappear in a few years, would not permit the technicians in television to join their union.

process. Therefore the budget should reflect an additional 30 percent for overtime on a nonunion production and the producer must make sure that the production is well planned and the director is prepared; this will keep the overtime down to a minimum.

PRODUCTION STAFF—THE ASSIST TEAM
The Line Producer
The concept of a Line Producer is a phenomenon that came into being with the independent movement of the 1980s. The distinguishing difference between a line producer and a producer is seen in the functions of the producing tasks. A line producer is always the person who is involved with the day to day creative and logistical producing decisions that affect the monetary aspects of the production. Some producers only want to be involved with the "dealmaking" aspect of a production and rely on someone else with an understanding of production to make the day to day decisions. Other producers rely on the director to carry the ball once they have provided input into the story and casting. Those producers know that the director needs a front line decision making producer to ensure that a creative atmosphere is prevalent on the shooting set. They will utilize a line producer. On other occasions a production manager may act in that capacity and be given a credit onscreen as a line producer. Whatever the case may be, all scenarios which define the line producer have one thing in common. The line producer is only involved with the production phase of the project. The line producer does not follow the project to its completion, nor provide major creative input to the story, its structure or its characters. The line producer is a hired hand.

The Production Manager (DGA) and Assistant Directors (DGA)
The Production Manager should be an extension of the producer. The production manager is responsible for the planning and execution of the movement and logistical details of the production through the production process. Since the producer must allow the production manager to have specific fiscal responsibilities, the production manager works closely with the accountant on the expenditures that make up the production machinery. The production manager must be on the same wavelength as the producer, since the logistics of the production are in direct correlation to the creative elements.

Although the production manager does not answer to the director, the production manager must always recognize and support the creative needs

Acct. #	Account Name	Units	Rate	Amount	Sub Total	Total
2000	**PRODUCTION STAFF - BELOW**					
01	Line Producer					
02	Production Manager					
	Prep					
	Shoot					
	Wrap					
	Production Fee (DGA)					
	Completion of Assign (DGA)					
03	First Assistant Director					
	Prep					
	Shoot					
	Wrap					
	Production Fee (DGA)					
	Completion of Assign (DGA)					
04	Second Assistant Director					
	Prep					
	Shoot					
	Wrap					
	Production Fee (DGA)					
	Completion of Assign (DGA)					
05	DGA Trainee					
	Prep					
	Shoot					
	Wrap					
	Completion of Assign (DGA)					
06	Continuity (*Script Supervisor*)					
	Prep					
	Shoot					
	Wrap					
07	Production Accountant					
08	Production Coordinator					
09	Assistant Production Coordinator					
10	Payroll Service Company					
11	Production Assistants					
20	Labor Overtime					
50	Other					
	Total 2000					

Figure 19

of the director. At the same time, the production manager should know when the director is making excessive demands that might impact the fiscal limitations, and report those demands to the producer for managing and decision making. The production manager should never be antagonistic to the director, but instead be another pair of eyes and ears for the producer on logistical issues that involve the director and thus the production. Preparation time for a production manager is crucial. You should try to provide as much preparation time as possible since the production manager must be abreast of what is happening on all fronts of below-the-line production.

The First Assistant Director (or 1st AD) is the right hand of the director. The job of the 1st AD is to keep the director (and the crew) successfully moving through a shooting day's schedule. The 1st AD must know what the director is going to do, before he or she does it. Much of preparation consists of logistical planning, so the prep time for a 1st AD begins as soon as certain logistical elements begin to fall into place. A good 1st AD knows exactly what the next shot is going to be and quietly communicates it to the crew before the director gets to it. A great 1st AD will know the shot list (and its order) for the entire day and be sensitive to the director's creativity, allowing for digressions from the shot list if necessary. This way the crew is prepared for the next step and production flows smoothly. The 1st AD must know how to balance the creative needs of the director with the logistics of the day. The better 1st ADs are always gently nudging the director asking, "What's the next shot?" or, "Is this the Martini or the Abby Singer?"[1] Working and preparing at the side of the director means that the 1st AD determines what must happen in each second of the production day. They generally communicate this information to the production manager several times during the day so that what comes next is working in synch with what is happening at the moment of production. The 1st AD will help plan out the production board and the final shooting schedule based on the creative input from the director and the logistical input from the production manager. The production board is then read to see what is needed for preparation or to complete a shooting day.

Directors like to work with the same 1st ADs from project to project, because they develop a solid working relationship and shorthand with their communication. This communication saves time, the most valuable commodity to any production. It is important to note that the first assistant director is also the safety officer on a set: the person given the responsibility of making sure everything happening during production is being done safely.

Second Assistant Directors (or 2nd ADs) are primarily responsible for the caretaking of the actors, performers, and in front of camera talent once they arrive to the set. The 2nd AD makes sure that the actor is ready according to the schedule and the creative needs of the director. It is a difficult and thankless job since actors often take out their personal and creative frustrations on the 2nd AD. A 2nd AD I had on a picture once received the wrath of an actor when the actor came to the location late. Although the actor had a clearly marked map, he blamed the 2nd AD for giving poor directions and

---

[1] The Martini Shot is the last shot of the day. The Abby Singer shot is the second to the last shot named after the producer, Abby Singer, when he was a first assistant director. Towards the end of a production day Abby kept asking his director if the next shot was "the martini shot," until his director said to him, "This is the Abby Singer shot," the shot before the martini shot. It stuck and joined the lexicon of the industry.

making him late. The 2nd AD just took it, knowing that it was part of his job. Because the 2nd AD reports to the 1st AD, they are in continual contact in an effort to make things run smoothly for the director. The 1st AD works with the crew and the 2nd AD with the talent.

A 2nd AD is also responsible for the daily paperwork that must be prepared and passed along to the production manager and the accountant. This includes the daily production report, the daily call sheets and SAG time sheets. It may also include certain SAG actor contracts. Whenever anything happens unexpectedly during production, it is reported to the second assistant director who adds the information to the production report. If a director does not complete the day's work and changes are made in the schedule, the 2nd AD marks the changes on the production board and gets the information to the appropriate people. Second ADs are responsible for preparing and distributing call sheets for each days' work. These are prepared during the second part of a work day for the next day based upon the production board and decisions that might be made during the day.

Second assistant directors are conduits through which information must flow and are extremely important to the producer. The 2nd AD is responsible for reporting accurate and pertinent information reflecting the actors' time each day as each actor must sign in and out with the 2nd AD. Information regarding meal and other penalties are also recorded with the 2nd AD. It is from these time sheets that your accountant issues the payroll and SAG is provided verification. Experienced second assistant directors know that many actors try to build up their overtime if they can, and, knowing the SAG rules, the smart 2nd AD will automatically add fifteen minutes on to the time sheet at the moment the director has excused the actor from the set. In this way they know the time that an actor should be ready to sign out and can follow up with the talent if they haven't reported for sign-out by then.

Production managers and assistant directors may be members of the Directors Guild of America. The DGA provides an intensive training program for training a specific number of people as assistant directors to meet the needs of the motion picture industry. A DGA production manager usually moves through the ranks of assistant directing to production management and so has an extensive background and exhaustive training in the organization, management and logistics of production. There are many nonguild people who work in these capacities also. Many of these people are highly qualified but may not have the extensive training that the DGA provides. Many of these people also have other occupations, such as writing,

02	Production Manager	Unit	rate	amount		
	Prep	6	3227	19362		
	Shoot	8.2	3227	26461.40		
	Wrap	2.5	3227	8067.50		
	Production Fee (DGA)	8.2	699	5731.80		
	Completion of Assign (DGA)			3227.00		

Figure 20

acting or directing, but take jobs as production managers or assistant directors to pay their bills. This does not necessarily mean they are not qualified. What it does mean is that their focus during the time they are working for you may not totally be on their job. They may be thinking about the quality of the script, or the performance of an actor rather than the specific details of their particular job. This is something that you certainly want to think about when hiring your support team. Production management and assisting the director are critical positions in managing the project in relation to its creative needs.

If you are a signatory to the DGA, you must use a DGA production manager and first and second assistant director. They work under the same agreement conditions as the director (See Chapter 5). DGA below-the-line personnel receive payment for prep time, production time and wrap time. In addition they also receive a weekly production fee which is indicated in the published DGA rates. When they have completed their work, the DGA contract calls for each of them to receive a completion of assignment payment, or Completion of Assign Pay. Completion of assign pay is calculated by adding up the total amount earned (not including the production fee) and dividing by the number of weeks worked. In addition to this below-the-line DGA personnel receive 13.5 percent of their final gross salary for Pension, Health and Welfare. *In that case, however, the production fee is considered in the calculation.* The Pension, Health and Welfare would be detailed under "Fringe."

Continuity (IATSE Local 871)

The continuity person is the conduit to the post-production process. He or she is also known as the script supervisor and is considered the left hand of the director. The script supervisor maintains—in writing—all the details relating to the cohesion of the creative and technical elements that take place during the production. This information is kept in a daily continuity log that is given to the editor. The log reflects, through specific markings on the script, the details that took place on each take of a shot. The script supervisor also notes the type of camera shot, the lens size, the camera and sound roll numbers and any comments that the director might have made regarding the shot. A smart script supervisor will even make notations regarding the director's inspirational reaction to a shot and write the comment down in the log. It is not unusual to see such lines as "nice job" or "terrific" written in the margin of a script supervisor's log, since these would be the immediate and instant comments a director might make. These written comments will be used months later during post-production to remind the director of any creative comments that were made at that time. The director relies heavily on the script supervisor for maintaining accuracy in the dialogue of the script, and visual matching of movements and actor eye lines from shot to shot. Since the script supervisor is also the "secretary" of the shooting company, at the end of each production day, the script supervisor must take information from various production departments and correlate it to the notations in the continuity log. Therefore, the production day for continuity does not end when the director says, "It's a wrap!"

Script supervisors need to prepare. They must prepare their logs, go over the script in terms of story continuities and meet with the director ahead of the production date to establish a working relationship for supporting the director's needs. They also need to be given time to wrap up their duties and responsibilities after the production has completed principle photography and spend a little bit of time with the editor and the log. This could require as long as a week, depending on the complexity of the production.

Production Accountant (IATSE Local 717)

The production accountant, sometimes doubling as the location accountant is involved with the myriad details of paperwork regarding the ongoing and projected expenditures of the production budget. After approval from you, the accountant would authorize, write and issue all production payments, including payroll if required. If the project has a completion bond then the bonding company must approve the production accountant. The production accountant must know all contract rules as they pertain to any unions or guilds and be able to calculate on a daily basis the time and payment of payroll accordingly. In addition, this person compiles cost-to-complete reports, statements, quarterly returns, etc. that may be required by the accountancy firm for the production company, the bonding company or

---

PRODUCERS VOCABULARY

Cost to Complete Statement—Daily or weekly form issued by the production accountant indicating how much of the approved budget is left to complete the project.

financing institution. This position is a key position for the producer. If the production manager is your right hand and the producer's assistant is the left hand, the production accountant is yet *another* left hand.

Production Coordinator (IATSE Local 717)

The assistant to the production manager is the production coordinator. Whereas the production manager details what needs to be done for production, the production coordinator carries it out. Coordinators are directly linked to the production manager and they often work with the same production manager on various projects. The speed of decision-making and activity during production requires very quick, very reliable communication between the production manager and the coordinator in order to save time and money. All coordinators have a massive Rolodex of contact numbers, and their own relationships within the production community always come in to play. An experienced coordinator will know what needs to be done just by having the production manager explain any production circumstance that may arise.

Payroll Service Company

A payroll service company is an organization capable of handling all or a portion of the payroll on your project. It acts as the employer of record for the producer, and the project's employees fall under its workers compensation policy. The decision to use a payroll service should be based upon the structure of the project and the needs of the producer. If you are doing a project that has a small cast and crew, you may want to use a payroll service company to avoid paying the premium on a workers compensation policy. Maybe the project you are doing has a complicated payroll both above and below-the-line and you decide that the payroll would be too difficult for one production accountant to handle. Perhaps the project you are doing shoots in various countries, requiring you to hire people under varied circumstances. Under those conditions it might be beneficial to use an outside payroll service organization to take care of the payroll. Whatever the reason may be, the producer needs to make the decision based upon the needs of the project in relationship to time. A payroll service company charges a fee for their services. The fee may be a percentage of the payroll and/or a per check charge. In all instances, however, it is negotiable. A payroll service company will try to work with a producer when its services are sought in the hopes of establishing a long-term relationship.

Other Charges

The word "Other" or "Miscellaneous" always appear in any production budget. You should always make sure that resources are budgeted in this item. It is designed to prepare for the unforeseen in each category, while the contingency on the overall budget is designed to protect not only for the unforeseen but also against Murphy's Law. Therefore, the first place you are able to trim in a budget without affecting the project is in those cost centers that contain "Other" or "Miscellaneous."

VISUAL PREPARATION

Production Designer

The planning of the visual side of the project involves many people. The chart in Figure #18 shows the number of people who report to the production designer, as he or she is responsible for the design and coordination of all of the visual elements seen on the project. This often is referred to as the character and texture of the project.

The production designer works closely with the director of photography and the director in interpreting the vision and creating its "look." In order to do so the production designer works with and guides the creative muses of the wardrobe designer, the art director, the set decorator and the property master for the project.

Production designers also are involved in makeup and hair design, and the minute details that involve the visual layering on the image. The director of photography discusses light, color and the cinematic feel with the production designer. The director, although in those discussions, will be discussing the visual subtleties needed for the character and the story. If there is a visual effects supervisor with the project, then the production designer works closely with him or her on the planning and execution of each element required for the visual effects. Most of the creative work of the production designer is accomplished during the preparation phase of the project. It may also extend into the production phase when there is an ever-evolving schedule.

Many projects do not use a production designer. If you eliminated that position in Figure #18 you will see that the art director, wardrobe designer and property master will report directly to the producer and also work closely with the director and the director of photography. In those cases the

---

PRODUCERS VOCABULARY

Guerilla Filmmaking—Abandoning legalities during production and shooting with little or no regard to clearances, structure or form.

Acct. #	Account Name	Units	Rate	Amount	Sub Total	Total
2100	VISUAL PREPARATION					
01	Production Designer					
02	Art Director					
03	Assistant Art Director					
04	Set Designers					
05	Set Draftsmen					
06	Pre Visualization Model Makers					
07	Pre Visualization Storyboard Artists					
08	Set Estimators					
09	Visual Effects Supervisor					
10	Visual Effects House Bid					
11	Materials Rented					
12	Materials Purchased					
	Total 2100					
2200	SET DRESSING					
01	Set Decorator					
02	Swing Gang Leadman					
03	Swing Crew					
04	Extra Swing Crew					
05	Draperies					
06	Manufacture Labor					
11	Rentals					
12	Purchases					
13	Vehicle Rentals					
14	Repairs and Damage					
50	Other					
	Total 2200					

Figure 21

producer or the director will be involved with the coordination of those elements.

Art Director (IATSE Local 876)

The art director is responsible for creating the sets and scenery for the project. The art director studies the script, speaks with the producer, director and production designer, researches and looks at the project from the perspective of the scenery and its relationship to the story and its characters. Many art directors are trained architects or come from the ranks of set designers or theater designers. They are skilled in creating locations that reflect the fiber of the vision and bring into being the space that gives life to the characters. A talented art director can take a garage, and, with imagination, creativity, some gold mylar paper, a few exhaust hoses and dry ice, can turn it into the frightening clone room set in *The Clonus Horror*. They can take an exterior of a house on location and match a suitable interior of that same house on a soundstage. Can anyone ever forget the art direction for *Crouching Tiger, Hidden Dragon; Gladiator, The Matrix, My Fair Lady* or *Gone With the Wind*?

The art director, like the production designer, must be up on all the various techniques of creating the scenic visual look. This includes any current methods of creating set environments either partially or entirely with the computer. In these instances, art directors work with visual effects supervisors and artists who specialize in digital designs. It is what helped the look of the sets in *Gladiator*, where the Coliseum and its crowds were created digitally. A faithful recreation of the original in Rome, the designers' construction team built a fragment of one of the first tiers of the Coliseum; the remainder was achieved using state-of-the-art computer graphic imaging (CGI). Utilizing models programmed into a computer, the circumference of the first tier, and the second and third tiers of the structure were created electronically—replete with statuary. CGI was also utilized to produce the

———— • • • ————

I have been in many strange situations that were required by producers who always thought they were creative. From painting flowers on an actress' panties—while she was wearing them! — to designing a set strong enough to support an elephant who weighed in at four tons. One of the producers on the Disney movie, George of the Jungle, *called me up one day and asked me if I knew where a four ton elephant walks. Since I was the art director on the picture, I innocently answered, "in the jungle." He told me, "No, anywhere he wants to." Then he told me that they had just cast a supporting actor who weighed four tons: an elephant named Tai. He told me that they had to take insurance out on Tai and wanted to make sure that with the building of the enormous jungle set (measuring 120' by 300' inside the Hughes Aircraft Spruce Goose hanger in Culver City, California), the elephant would always be safe from injury. We did not know how safe things were in this old space and since the producers were concerned about the safety of the elephant (and the cast and crew), I had to consult with a structural engineering firm to design a gigantic structurally sound platform to hold the jungle, the cast and crew, and a four ton elephant named Tai. In the end, she performed her acting assignment beautifully and safely, and when the director said, "That's a wrap," the producers gave a great sigh of relief. And so did I!*

—David Haber, Production Designer and Art Director,
*Pretty Woman, The Two Jakes, Lady Sings the Blues,
Ice Pirates, The Beast Within, Under Siege II*

———— • • • ————

velarium, the ingenious retractable canvas roof that was used to shade the arena's spectators from the glaring sun. In the Coliseum scenes, 33,000 extras were computer generated. They were created by filming real extras performing a variety of motions and then mapping them into two-dimensional cards positioned in each seat in the computer-generated Coliseum. By replicating them in the computer, the visual effects team (working with the production designer and art director) gave the arena a "virtual" sell-out crowd. The CGI elements were so seamlessly blended with the real sets and people, that the director, Ridley Scott, could do sweeping 360-degree panoramic shots and overhead views in which actual and visual effects elements are indistinguishable.

Any work on the project in the digital or effects field may impact the performance of the talent *unless* your director does his or her homework and understands the process.

Set Designers, Model Makers and Storyboard Artists
(IATSE Local 847, 839, 790)

Set designers work for the art director and are assigned individual sets to design. There may be several set designers working on one project, each designing one or more individual sets under the supervision of the art director. The designs may be drafted through traditional methods or generated through computer software programs. Sometimes the director may require assistance visualizing a sequence and a production designer or an art director may employ a model maker to build a model of a set that the director can work with to better see his or her ideas. 3D modeling software programs are used to render drawings of a set which directors and cinematographers use to walk through specific camera and lighting angles. James Cameron had a model built of the Titanic to help his visualization of some of the intricacies of that film. Sometimes a storyboard artist is employed to sketch out shots that are complex in production techniques.

3D animated storyboards are also used as in the case of the fight sequence on top of the Statue of Liberty in *X-Men*. These tactics are all designed to assist in the creative collaborative process during pre-production in an attempt to reduce the effect of Murphy's Law on production.

PRODUCERS VOCABULARY

Practical—Any prop or part of a set that actually works, such as an electrical fan; a practical prop. The opposite is a dummy prop. Also called a prac or functioning prop. Practicals are often discussed at both lox and bagel meetings.

———— • • • ————

In The Girl, the Gold Watch and Everything *we created the fantasy world of stopped time through the marriage of original picture negative and 24-frame tape to film negative. I hired a storyboard artist to visualize each of the frames of the unique (at the time) special effects we were doing. Once we had the storyboards the director and myself were able to determine the shots to be blue screened and those that could be done during production. We also determined what images needed to be done during production that were to be used for the bluescreen video process.*

———— • • • ————

Visual Effects Supervisor

Many projects today require a visual effects supervisor, someone who is creatively responsible for creating and achieving specific visual effects that might be required in the project. Those people work closely with the director and the producer in designing the effects, and then with many different people, such as the art director, cinematographer, production designer, mechanical and makeup specialists and the editor in achieving the final result onscreen. They often work on the set during production, assisting the director in shooting the elements for the visual effects. Their work begins in the pre-production phase and continues through production and post-production.

The script may be as simple as:

    44. EXT. SPACE
        A space battle ensues between the Galactic
        Patrol Cruiser and the Interstellar Saturn
        Space Voyager.

But the director may have no idea how to create that battle, so a visual effects supervisor is hired to create the battle with the director. Visual effects supervisors find their motivation in the story and its characters, and the challenge to make the visual effects invisible. If the audience is aware of the visual effects then they are pulled out of the story and the supervisor has not succeeded with the job.

The visual effects supervisor must be familiar with the latest technology available for creating digital effects and combining them with live action.

Studios have entire departments devoted to these images. There are also boutique effect houses that can, by bid, be employed to do the effects under the supervision of the visual effects supervisor. (But keep in mind that there may be hidden costs associated with these visual effects that are not covered by the bid, such as additional lab processing fees.) What is most important here is that the visual effects must enhance and work with the story, not detract or stand out from it. Good storytelling should be the primary goal for you, the director, the visual effects supervisor, the production designer, the editor, the cinematographer and the entire creative team.

Set Decorator (IATSE Local 44)

Set decorators are responsible for adorning or "dressing" the set for each scene. They report to the art director or production designer. They are often thought of as interior designers although their job includes exterior locations as well as interiors. This is not as simple as it sounds. A good decorator creates and defines the characters' relationship to the set, and provides the subtle touches that create the physical existence of the set or location for the audience. The ego of a creative and talented set decorator should be a guiding force in terms of realizing the final visual details and the quality of the project. The crew for the set decorator is called the swing gang and the head of that crew is the leadman or leadperson, sometimes called just the lead.

Since the Set Department is responsible for getting a set ready for production, you will need to make sure that you arrange an appropriate vehicle for their use, as it will not be possible to use any of the production vehicles for this purpose. A cube van or small truck always seems to do the job when it comes to hauling furniture or other set dressing materials to and from a set or location.

It is the creative egos of set decorators, art directors and production designers that fuel their relationships with set and prop houses, vendors and interior designers who will work with them to provide the visual look of the project even if there is a legitimate shortage of funds in your budget. Choose these people carefully and consider not only their creative abilities, but their ingenuity, relationships, integrity and ability to work with other creative people. Listen to them when they discuss the project with you creatively and hear what they *see*. Their perspective is specific and their basic motivation is to do a good job, because when they sit at the premiere of the project they see the results of their work on the screen.

It is in this preplanning stage of the visual side of the production that you will begin to create a philosophy towards your production that will deter-

Acct. #	Account Name	Units	Rate	Amount	Sub Total	Total
2300	**SET CONSTRUCTION**					
01	Foreman					
02	Crew					
03	Materials Purchased					
04	Materials Rented					
05	Outside Set Construction Bid					
06	Set Load – In Studio Crew					
07	Electric Scaffold					
08	Set Striking					
09	Other					
	Total 2300					

Figure 22

mine the direction the production and its budget will take. If you decide that you wish to budget for the construction of a set or sets for the project (Figure #22) then you must also budget later for somewhere to put the set, such as a soundstage. You will also have to budget for setting it up and striking it (or tearing it down). You may decide that you want to avoid the problems associated with buying materials and having your own construction crew, so you might put the set design out to bid by scenery construction companies that will provide you with a set for a flat fee for everything, including delivery and set up. You may be able to find an existing set somewhere that you can use, or you may find some scenery in storage that you can rent. You may decide that you will build only certain scenery units and digitize the rest of the set via computer software, or you may decide that your budget cannot afford any construction at all and rework the screenplay to take advantage of practical locations already available to you. Whatever your decision, it should be motivated by the shoe fit the foot theory or you need to be ready to increase your budget to accommodate the rest of your creative team.

When we shot *The Girl, the Gold Watch and Everything* for Paramount Studios, we had many interior and exterior locations and I wanted to spend at least two weeks in San Diego capturing the exterior feeling necessary to the story. A difficult task on the small budget for the project, since this was an IATSE project. In order to shoot the two weeks on a distant location, I needed to find a way to economize on either the locations or the art direction. I knew I had the existing resources of the entire studio at my disposal so I walked the stages to see what sets for other movies and television shows were already standing which, with a little persuasion and a little ingenuity might be used for *Gold Watch*. I knew if I could convince the studio brass to keep the sets after they were used for their original projects, all we would have to do was repaint and redress the sets and try to match them to the location exteriors of San Diego. Much to the creative consternation of my art director, it worked and I wound up using the very expensive and beautifully detailed sets built for a cop movie, an action picture and a television series, all while saving a lot of money. I only had to build the interior cabins of a yacht, because we had to create a fire in one cabin and I wanted a Jacuzzi in the other cabin to show the luxurious decadence of the characters.

In Figure #18 art direction, set dressing and ultimately set construction all fall under one area. Although they are specific areas they also have an interrelationship and co-dependency with one another and, to some degree, with the Property Department (Figure #23). So therefore you should think of the funds you allocate for rental and purchases in those cost centers as interchangeable. That is because it is sometimes difficult to determine what should actually fall under which category depending upon the structure of the production. Keeping that fact in mind, you should consider an aggregate amount you may want to appropriate towards the materials of the visual production and extend it within those various cost centers. In that way, one cost center will not appear to have too much money for rental and purchases while another not have enough. And the question of having enough resources allocated to the visual production will not be raised by the bonding company. As an example, if you wish to allocate $100,000; perhaps you allocate $20,000 to 2111 and 2112 (Visual Preparation), another $20,000 to 2211 and 2212 (Set Dressing), in Figure #21 and the balance as part of 2411 and 2412 (Properties) in Figure #23.

PROPERTY DEPARTMENT
Property Master (IATSE Local 44)
The property master, although responsible to the production designer, also reports to the director, and is responsible for the acquisition, creation, organization and management of all the props handled by actors. In some instances these props can be quite complicated (as in a James Bond movie), so the property master must interface with other departments such as special effects, art direction or set dressing depending on the specifics of the project. The property master must be given time to prepare before the start of principle photography for the huge task of propping the project.

The property master must be ready not only for the expected and required, but also the on-set inspiration of the director or actor. It is a cre-

Acct. #	Account Name	Units	Rate	Amount	Sub Total	Total
2400	**PROPERTY DEPARTMENT**					
01	Property Master Shooting Company					
	Prep					
	Shoot					
	Wrap					
	Assistant Property Master					
	Prep					
	Shoot					
	Wrap					
	2nd and 3rd Assistant Property Master					
02	Labor Overtime					
03	Prop (Kit)Box Rental					
04	Animal Wrangler - Trainer					
05	Animals					
06	Ammunition and Explosives					
	Picture Vehicle Rentals					
08	Picture Vehicle Purchases					
11	Prop Rental					
12	Prop Purchases					
13	Property Vehicle Rental					
14	Repairs and Damage					
50	Other					
	Total 2400					

Figure 23

ative position and one that is tough to do well. The property master reads the script and breaks it down for all the hand props that are required. A good property master also thinks through the unrequired, based upon their interpretation of the script. For instance, if a scene calls for a character, to carry a tray of food, the property master should know that the character will also need a note pad to take food orders. A creative property master recognizes that *the director may also use any prop in a close up at any time* and cheating the look of a prop will limit the director's creative ability. The property master for *Gold Watch* was a genius. The story centered on a gold pocketwatch that could stop time, invented by the hero's eccentric uncle. The watch had the ability to stop time for the person holding it. Attached to the pocketwatch chain was a watch fob designed to be a distraction from the watch. The fob was to be a miniature spyglass containing a naughty photograph. Our property master had a heck of a time finding a real watch fob that would work. He scoured antique and junk shops, searching everywhere for something he could use. One day he walked into my office and put a small cylindrical object on my desk. Fashioned of shiny brass and with a lens at both ends, it was about the size of my little finger. I picked it up, fascinated by the object and thinking it was a fob as described in the script, I looked through the lens expecting to see a scantily clad woman. What I saw was a distorted image of the other side of my office. But it looked perfect. I asked him what it was, and he told me that he had purchased a door peephole from a hardware store and welded brass rings around the shaft, making it appear to be a gold watch fob good enough for the director to shoot in a close up. And he had made three of them in case any got lost or damaged during the production.

The property master should not only determine the props that are necessary for the project but also try to determine, during preparation, how the director may think or work on a set. The property master visits locations and discusses specific props and character issues with the director before the project starts shooting. The more informed the property master is about production issues, the better he or she is able to plan. A creative property master should also know the details of the production process and the impact Murphy's Law can have on a project. One day I was visited the location of a film I was producing which was shooting in a small boat marina. I noticed the property master flying two kites about thirty yards away from where the director was shooting. I thought this to be unusual, so I went over to him and asked him why he was flying the kites. He pointed up towards the sky and said, "Look!" When I looked up I saw three small propeller aircraft some distance away from the location. As one of them started to come in our direction, the property master would let out more string allowing the kites to go higher—keeping the planes away. He then turned to me and said, "You want clean sound don't you?" I was flabbergasted. He had noticed during his scout that the marina was located near a small craft airport. He was ready with the means so that the director did not have to wait for airplane noise to subside during shooting.

Some projects may be so complex that they may require more than one property master, or perhaps more than one property master may be needed

———— • • • ————

Author's note: While the unions (DGA, WGA, SAG, IATSE and AFTRA) enforce strict wage ranges for their members, nonunion labor rates will vary widely from state to state or country to country. Because they are not tied to union minimums, all nonunion labor rates are negotiable. As a creative producer, it is always worth your energy to negotiate for the best rate.

———— • • • ————

only on specific days of production. Since the production board shows you the relationship of production to time, the information on the production board will help provide you with the solution. You may notice days when you have a lot of props to be handled by actors, or a lot of actors who might handle many props. You may realize that on those days it might be more cost effective to have a second prop person on set. Or it might be that the project is a difficult show to prop and you want to have two prop people on the entire project. Once again, the thought you put in regarding this issue will impact elsewhere in the budget and will further affect the philosophy of your producing.

Prop Boxes or Kit Rentals

In Figure #23 account #2400-03 indicates an item called *prop boxes*. Similar items show up as "kit rentals" in the Grip, Electric, Makeup, Wardrobe and Camera Departments. This grants a rental fee for the small personal tools and equipment used by the heads of those departments as they do their jobs. Even though the grip, camera, electrical equipment and wardrobe are all rented from rental houses, the smaller items needed for those jobs are customarily rented to the production by the heads of those departments. In the case of the prop box, it usually is a rolling chest with many drawers similar to the tall tool box you might see in your mechanic's shop. In each of these drawers, the property master has items that are either used on the project, or items that might be used if the director decides, during production, that they might be called for. The director may be directing a scene in a bar and at the last minute decide to have one of the characters smoke a Cuban cigar. The property master can go to the prop box and pull out a cigar that would be suitable in the scene.

Although funds to replenish these kits come from your budget, it is still customary for you to rent the box or kits. However, you can use this to your advantage. Let's assume that you decide you will budget the property master on a flat rate of $1200 a week. You have also budgeted a box rental at $300 a week. The production has a shooting schedule of six weeks. Using these figures as a calculation, the property master is budgeted at $7200 as a taxable wage during production and an additional $1800 as a rental fee for the use of the prop box. (A total of $9000 to the property master.) Besides the property master being taxed on $7200, you would be paying the payroll tax on the same amount. Through your production manager, you might try offering a wage of $1050 with a box rental of $350 a week. Using these figures, the taxable wage would be $6300, and the box rental would be $2100.

The property master would be paying less in taxes and gaining more in the rental. If the property master agrees you pick up an additional $600 on the overall and save on the payroll taxes. Of course the property master must have a qualified company through which a rental invoice is issued. Your accountant will be able to assist with this. If not, and if the rental for the project is over $600, you will be required to file a Federal 1099 form reporting the property master's additional income to the IRS.

Animals

Perhaps your project calls for an animal. When renting an animal, you are also paying for the trainer who handles the animal. Sometimes the project may call for an animal to do something onscreen that is not endemic to the story. For example, perhaps the scene calls for a dog to play a pipe organ and a group of children to react to the weirdness of the dog. It may cost you quite a bit to have a trainer teach a dog to play a pipe organ. It might be simpler (and less expensive) if you have the shoe fit the foot by asking the animal trainer about any dog he or she might already have that is already trained in some peculiar skill or trick and adjust the scene to accommodate for the new trick.

Firearms and Explosives

Many projects use ammunition or minor explosives. Other projects require firearms to shoot blanks. It is not true that when firing a blank nothing comes out of the barrel; the blank does. There is always some substance that comes out that could possibly hurt someone if precautions are not taken during production. A property master licensed by the ATF as Class #1 is the only property master who is legally allowed to handle ammunition and explosives. It is not something that you want to trust to a beginner.

Picture Vehicles

Vehicles that are used by actors and seen in the project are considered props. Thinking through the use of vehicles will determine whether you will need to purchase or rent a vehicle. (Or both!) If the story requires a character to drive a vehicle and then crash it, you may want to see if you can get an automobile body from a junkyard and paint it to match a similar one you rent.

The Property Department is quite important to the project. It encompasses many of the minute details that are so important to storytelling. Don't cut yourself short but make yourself think through the use of props.

Props makes a difference to the look of the project. As a producer, one of your tasks is to make sure you maintain the integrity and quality of the storytelling, while making sure the story you are telling is a worthwhile tale.

Special Effects

Today, special effects take on many forms. As digital effects software improves, the imagination pushes it further and further. Many effects use a blue- or greenscreen process. Although conceived during pre-production with a visual effects supervisor, most effects are usually put together in post-production. The production process may include the creation of certain effects which are incorporated with these other effects or that may stand alone.

Special effects done solely during the production process as real time effects are classified as either mechanical effects or makeup effects. A mechanical effect can be a bullet hit or an explosion. It can be steam, rain, snow, fog, fire or wind. Motivated by the story, the effect is planned and created mechanically during the process of principle or second unit production. A makeup effect is an effect that modifies the appearance of an actor. It can be an arm that has been blown to shreds or a torso that has been distorted. It can be a face that is very weathered or heavily scarred, or bullet holes that have ripped through a leg. Remember when Giovanni Ribisi was shot in *Saving Private Ryan*? His upper torso, oozing blood from bullet wounds, was a makeup effect. In some instances, mechanical and makeup effects work together. In other instances mechanical or makeup effects are produced during the production period and are then manipulated digitally in post-production. Whatever the situation, it is important that you, the director and the creative visual team think through their execution. Special effects people work closely with the director, the production designer, visual effects supervisors and art directors. Unless the story is based upon

Acct. #	Account Name	Units	Rate	Amount	Sub Total	Total
2500	**SPECIAL EFFECTS**					
01	On set Special Effects Person					
02	Mechanical Effects Contractor					
03	Makeup Effects Contractor					
04	Additional Production Effects					
	Total 2500					

Figure 24

effects, you should be involved with some of the creative discussions surrounding the effects. If you rely entirely on the team's collaborative notions, you may find that the last thing they consider are the fiscal restraints. In *Hunter's Blood* there is a scene where the character of Purty Boy is supposed to have his head blown off by Sam Bottoms' shotgun. During the creative meetings, the director said that he wanted to see the head explode from the blast. However, I thought that the focus of that moment needed to be on Sam's character and his struggle to escape the terrors of the forest. I thought that the image of a characters' head blasting open would be inappropriate— and also quite expensive and I was not convinced it was money well spent. The cinematographer agreed with me. I asked the special effects people what it would cost to show the results of the head being blown off once the body was on the ground. They indicated it would be very inexpensive since they could do it with mechanisms that they had sitting around their shop. The director was adamant about the blasting head effect and I had to tell him that our budget just couldn't afford it. We went with the results of the blast rather than seeing the blast itself. When the picture was finally edited we employed Hitchcock's technique of diverting the audiences mind from the incident and then bringing them back to it with subtlety. Sam takes aim at Purty Boy as he approaches. He shoots his rifle. The image then goes to another character who sights Sam and runs after him. Sam then runs past the body of Purty Boy, and the audience for a brief moment sees an open head cavity attached to a body lying on the ground with the arms of the body still twitching in shock. It is an effect that the audience always reacts to and one that sets the horror and reality of the violence in the clash of cultures in the film.

Mechanical and makeup effects can be contracted out to either a special effects company or a makeup effects company through a bid process. If you give the screenplay to effects companies during the development phase of the project, they will read the script and break it down in terms of their creative contribution. Remember *ego* plays a big role in their bid. Although they are in the business of making money, they are also in a creative business and at least partially motivated by the opportunity to be involved in a creative project and by seeing their credit onscreen. You should expect the bid from the effects house to include effects that are not necessarily written in the script but are envisioned by the effects supervisor as the script was read. They would be motivated by the story and characters and add to the details of the project. As an example, if a scene takes place in a haunted house, the bid might include the creation of spiderwebs and bird droppings. Bids are always based on the amount of work required in preparing and delivering the effects. Bids of any sort are also impacted by supply and demand. If the effects house is not overwhelmed with projects, their bid may be lower than it will be at the height of a busy season. A final important issue to remember is that special effects take extra time to shoot. You must allow for this when preparing the production board and schedule.

CAMERA DEPARTMENT
Director Of Photography (IATSE Local 600)
It was pointed out earlier in this chapter that the moment-to-moment shooting activities of the production company are not only in the hands of the director and the first assistant director but also in the hands of the director of photography and the crew reporting to that position. (See Figure #18)

The director of photography (or cinematographer, as it is sometimes referred to) is a key ingredient towards the quality of the project. In some arenas, the cinematographer is looked at as a lighting director, or someone who creates the mood, texture and feeling of the image with light. In other arenas, the cinematographer also works with the dramatics of the shot and the interpretive use of the camera in telling the story. This clearly depends on the working relationship between the director and the cinematographer and it is *absolutely* critical that they be in synch about the creative concept and the telling of the story. Not only should you have a cinematographer who is creative and knowledgeable, but also one who knows how to balance the crucial relationships of time to production. The cinematographer's crew can slow a project down. The cinematographer must have a close working relationship with the key components of the crewmembers who report to him or her. When a director works with actors during production, time is very precious and experienced cinematographers recognize that the bottom line is the performance in front of the camera. They try to work within the director's schedule, getting the actor ready to perform so at the precise moment the camera roles, the actor is giving the best performance possible. Cinematographers are very motivated by performances and their enthusiasm increases when they have a sense that something special is happening with the project.

You must consider the cinematographer very carefully when planning your project. It is not a position that you want to trust to someone without the proper experience; too much of the responsibility for the success of the project rides on the shoulders of the cinematographer.

Acct. #	Account Name	Units	Rate	Amount	Sub Total	Total
2600	**CAMERA DEPARTMENT**					
01	Director of Photography/ Cinematographer					
	Prepare					
	Shoot					
02	Camera Operator					
	Shoot					
	1st Assistant Camera/Focus					
	Prepare					
	Shoot					
	Wrap					
	2nd Assistant Camera / Loader/Clapper					
	Prepare					
	Shoot					
	Wrap					
03	Extra Operators					
	Extra Assistants					
04	Still Photographer					
12	Labor Overtime					
13	Camera Package Rental					
	Camera Dolly Rental					
	Camera Crane Rental					
	Steadicam Rental/ w operator					
	Camera Car Rental					
14	Still Equipment Rental					
15	Box Rental					
16	Special Equipment Rental					
50	Other					
	Total 2600					

Figure 25

If you have a first-time director, you *must* have an experienced cinematographer, someone who knows the ropes of production. An experienced cinematographer will help a new director get over the hurdles inherent to working with the specific limitations and restrictions that will surround the project. In addition, the experienced cinematographer will provide assurance for a bonding company and potential distributors.

When considering a cinematographer, don't be fooled by the cinematographers' demo reel. They can be very slick these days, and it is always difficult to know what their total contribution was to the various examples on the reel. Try to watch it without sound, and this will help you focus on the images. If you see a clip in their demo reel that shows promise, ask to see the completed film to see if they are able to visually tell and support a story because the demo reel will only have the better images from the project. It is also a good idea to check out their previous experience and speak with people with whom they have worked, or the laboratories they have used. Finally, ask your bonding company for advice. They should be able to dig and find information for you that you might not be able to access.

Once hired, the cinematographer must prepare with the director. Try to give the cinematographer as much preparation time as you can. The cinematographer and director will need to continually talk about image, style, narrative and character. They select locations both from a cinematic point of view and a practical point of view. If you want to reduce the results of Murphy's Law, give your director and cinematographer plenty of quality preparation time.

Camera Operator (IATSE Local 600)

Some cinematographers prefer to also operate the camera. You must, however, use a camera operator if the project you are doing is signatory to the IATSE. One of the reasons that some cinematographers like to operate the camera, if possible, is that they like to have their eye in the eyepiece of the camera to actually see the shot. Tom Denove is an Academy Award® winning cinematographer with whom I have worked for over fifteen years. His credit list is lengthy and includes both union and nonunion projects. Many times when we were working together I would look at his face when he took his eye away from the camera eyepiece at the end of a camera take. While my instinct might tell me it was a good performance, his face would tell me it was a *great* performance and I knew I had to yell, "Print," on that particular roll of the camera. We established a shorthand that we continue to use whenever we work together, in either the academic or professional environment. This is rare but it happens from time to time. I recently worked with cinematographer Johnny Simmons and we quickly established a similar working relationship. When it occurs, the working experience between director and cinematographer becomes more creative.

When a cinematographer works with a camera operator it is crucial that the operator understands exactly what the director and cinematographer want in the framing of the shot. The operator attempts to find appropriate framing of the image and looks for creative motivation when movement is involved. The better operators listen carefully to the actors' dialogue, watch carefully the director's staging and quickly and efficiently execute the desired shot. Camera operators should try to become one with the talent, and use the invisible creative thread between the talent and the camera as their focus.

First Assistant Camera (IATSE Local 600)

The first assistant camera (1st AC) is responsible for changing the lenses and filters, keeping the gate of the camera clean, loading the film in the camera and measuring and following focus with the main action as decided by the cinematographer (or director).

An experienced 1st AC pays attention to the action as it is being staged by the director and, at the appropriate rehearsal moments, makes all the notations for the focus in relation to the camera and its position to the actor. This is an extremely difficult and very important job because it is sometimes hard to know exactly when the lens is in precise focus. You must wait until after the film has been developed in the laboratory to see the results of the image (unless you are shooting video or digital video) to verify the accuracy of the focus.

Second Assistant Camera (IATSE Local 600)

The second assistant camera person (2nd AC), loads and unloads the film in the camera magazine before it reaches the 1st AC, maintains accurate information on the slate (commonly known as the clapper), and keeps track of the paperwork through the camera reports required for film developing and the post-production process. Camera reports are critical to noting the exact takes the director wishes printed by the laboratory, as well as the amount and use of footage from take to take. These camera reports are then given to the continuity person who checks them for accuracy before copies are provided to the laboratory and the editor. Both the 1st and 2nd AC may be involved with preparing the camera for production and wrapping the camera for return to the rental house. This preparation should consist of all appropriate camera tests.

The cinematographer ordinarily recommends the camera crew. They are generally a strange lot. They have their own quiet methods of communication, which only they understand. They are attuned to the body language of the cinematographer in order to anticipate his or her needs. They keep to themselves and rarely communicate with other members of the production crew while working. They may not respond to you if you speak with them, or notice any of the other activity going on during the production. Don't worry. They are normal. There is a reason for this learned and planned behavior. The Camera Department has no margin for error and must be completely focused. If the 1st AC fails to remove a microscopic hair from the camera gate, the negative can be scratched and the day's work is ruined. If the film is loaded in the magazine incorrectly it can get clogged in the camera and no image will be recorded ... again the day's work is ruined. If there is a continual microphone boom in a printed take, or scenes that are continually out of focus, the image is unusable ... and the day's work is ruined. The work the Camera Department does is so critical that it has far reaching and irreparable consequences. So it's okay if they seem quiet or segregate themselves from the rest of the production company. They do it to maintain their creative and technical focus.

Additional Camera Crews

When the director and cinematographer look over the production board they may decide that certain sequences would be better handled by shooting multiple cameras. These may be stunts or fight sequences or scenes in which the director wants to take a specific approach to the performance. Whenever this is decided, additional camera crews are hired to assist.

Still Photography—Distribution Delivery Requirement

You must employ a still photographer during the production phase of the project. One of the delivery items for distribution will be production photographs. These are stills that are used for publicity and promotion. If you don't have these photographs it may affect the amount of money you can get during the end use of the project. When no photographs have been taken, the distributor will go to the outtakes from the picture negative and try to manufacture publicity stills. They are never quite as good as having the actual stills. This does not mean that you need a photographer every day of the shoot. The production board will tell you when and where there will be a likelihood of exciting or interesting possibilities for publicity photographs. Schedule your photographer for those days. Please make sure it is a photographer and not someone's brother or sister who has just purchased a new 35mm still camera and wants to try it out. Choose your photographer with the same selective creative care as you do anything else on the project. You will only have one chance at doing it right, so you should do it right to begin with and employ the tenets of ego and relationships in finding the right photographer.

The Camera Package

A basic film camera package should consist of a synchronous camera and a non synch camera, both of which have a complete set of the appropriate normal and high speed lenses. The package should also include an additional second camera body for the synchronous camera since you must make sure that your camera is always able to work. A second synchronous camera body as part of the package guarantees you have a backup available should the first synchronous camera break down and go in for repairs. The non-synch camera will provide the director the opportunity to quickly shoot a sequence (when it is not necessary to record sound) without breaking down the primary synchronous camera from its fixed tripod or camera dolly. This will save time. Also, having three camera possibilities provides the director with the opportunity to shoot with multiple cameras when needed.

It is common today for there to be a video assist as part of the camera package. Video assist is a video camera attached alongside the film camera that instantly provides an image for the director and cinematographer to see in a small television monitor. You do not see the exact quality of the cinematography, but you do instantly see the performance of the actor in relationship to the camera. This is helpful and directors use it quite often. It is not absolutely necessary, however, and is something that can be eliminated from the package if it is cost prohibitive. Also, a director can get too dependent on the video assist image and focus on the monitor and not the actor. Psychologically, this can have an impact since actors often perform for the director and they like the idea of the director watching their performance and not off somewhere staring into a monitor.

When you are renting a camera package from a camera rental company, have your production manager ask if there is a camera that no one else wants to rent. (There always is.) It may be an older model, or one that is not generally in favor. Ask them to throw it into your package at no charge. You will be surprised to find that in most cases they actually will. They would rather have a camera used than not used and it lets them tell their other clients that the camera was used on a project. You will have fully protected the ability of your project to keep shooting should there be camera failure during production and you have done it cost effectively. Once again you are minimizing the effect of Murphy's Law.

Your cinematographer should have longstanding relationships with camera, grip, and electric rental houses and those relationships will come in handy when you are limited with your budget. These relationships can be used to make the shoe fit the foot provided your cinematographer is doing the project because of the quality of the script, its story and its characters. Ego becomes a great motivator for relationships to work.

Rental Houses

I need to add a word about dealing with rental houses for camera, grip and electrical equipment. This is a business of supply and demand. If you rent the equipment on a daily rental you will be paying the listed rate. You can also rent equipment on a weekly rate and negotiate for the rate as a percentage of the week, such as a three-day week, or two-day week. This negotiation is generally done by your production manager and is based upon supply and demand. If there is a great demand for equipment you will be paying the higher weekly rate. If the demand is less, you are in a stronger position for getting a better deal. Therefore, when it is the television production season in Los Angeles and New York, the equipment rental fee for your independent theatrical feature will not be as favorable as it might be if you rented your equipment during the normal television hiatus period.

Camera Dolly, Crane, Steadicam and Helicopter

The camera dolly is an essential part of your package. Your cinematographer and director will determine the type of camera dolly (or dollies) you will need. This will depend on the logistics and complexity of production. Different kinds of camera dollies have different types of wheels to allow them to move on a track or on a smooth flat surface. Dolly shots are not easy shots to perform and are not always cost effective, as they invariably use up a lot of film or tape stock. When you have multiple takes this can be problematic. Dolly shots also require the coordination of several people, including the actors, and will take a lot of time in production. So be sure to encourage your director to use dolly shots effectively.

The camera crane is one of three cost effective technical devices that, when planned for, can provide your project with the visual look of a large-scale project. Camera cranes are rented by the day and the normal rental should include extension pieces. Make sure that the production coordinator or production manager asks for the extensions, as they are not always delivered with the crane. Having the options to use the extensions will give the director and cinematographer more creative latitude when they plan sequences on the production set. Crane shots require coordination between different people and there are specific safety issues surrounding the use of the crane that the crane operator will be able to explain. Planning with the production board will help you in scheduling the crane. Just make sure that your director uses the crane effectively. When planned for and used well, it can be spectacular. Think of the last shot of the film *Pay It Forward*, when the camera cranes up and the image of cars coming from a great distance to the front gate of the boy's house causes every eye in the audience to tear up, or the magnificent ten minute crane shot in a studio parking lot that opens Robert Altman's *The Player*.

A second cost effective device is the Steadicam. The Steadicam on larger projects is part of the normal camera package and is always available to the director. However, on smaller independent projects, you may only be able to budget for a Steadicam and its owner/operator on a daily basis. Sometimes, a

Steadicam owner/operator's ego will motivate a free or discounted use of the device. Here again, it is a matter of supply and demand, ego and relationships.

The main issue to remember with using the Steadicam is that it, too, takes time. Since it is a device that provides for a smooth floating-like mobility of the camera through a series of locations, setting up the lighting and the rehearsal to do the shot takes a lot of time. Like the crane and the dolly, the Steadicam uses up film (or tape) quickly. So planning for its use should be done carefully and effectively. Its use can provide a small project with great production value. Remember the Steadicam shot in *Goodfellas* that starts when Ray Liotta gets out of his car and goes through the back door of a nightclub, down its stairs, through a series of hallways, then through the kitchen and into the main showroom of the Copacabana? How about the point of view Steadicam shot in *The Untouchables* that starts outside on a ledge of a second floor building, goes through a window into an apartment and then searches every room for Sean Connery to set him up to be murdered? These are brilliant uses of the Steadicam.

The third cost effective device is the use of a helicopter for photographic sequences. Helicopters are rented by the hour and you pay for it under a "portal to portal" arrangement. The rental begins the moment the helicopter has left its home helicopter pad and ends when it returns. So you want to make sure that you find a helicopter service as close as possible to where you are shooting. They also have limited flying time and require refueling near the shooting site. Also, not just any helicopter will do. The helicopter has to be rigged with a specific mount for the camera and the pilot must know how to fly for the image. Again, the production of a helicopter shot takes time but its value can be great. *Thelma & Louise* had amazing helicopter shots that established the journey of the characters.

None of this equipment means anything unless their use is motivated and necessary to tell the story. It is too easy to give a director the tools and not

PRODUCERS VOCABULARY

Tracking Shot—Also known as a dolly shot that follows the movement in a scene. It can be accomplished on a camera dolly or from a camera car or other moving vehicle.

Video Assist—A system in which videotape is shot simultaneously with film through the lens of the principal camera. It allows the director and others to view the shot during and immediately after a take. When video assist is used the grip department sets up a "video village viewing area" set away from the camera. Many directors decline the use of video assist since it can extend the time it takes to do a sequence and actors generally prefer to have their directors watch their performance from the viewpoint of the camera and not the video village. In recognition of video assist's contribution to filmmaking, the developer of the technique, Paul A. Roos, was honored by the Academy of Motion Picture Arts and Sciences with a 1988 Technical Achievement Award.

——— • • • ———

The creative producer is a blessing to any cinematographer or director that is passionate about their work. The needs of the script come first and a creative producer is there to answer those needs.

—John Simmons, Cinematographer, *Once Upon a Time . . . When We Were Colored; Cool Women, Selma Lord Selma, 3 Strikes*

——— • • • ———

have them used effectively. As a creative producer you must make sure that the story and its vision motivate the production.

The Camera Car

Road pictures and projects that involve scenes which take place in moving cars require the use of a camera car. This is a specially designed vehicle which is designed to push or pull the picture vehicle while the cameras and lights are focused on the actors inside the vehicle. There are many different ways of using a camera car, but they are all complex and take time to set up and rehearse in a production environment. Working with camera cars can be hazardous, so safety is paramount. Continuity is also an issue. In order to maintain continuity, the background behind the picture vehicle should be controlled with other picture vehicles to help maintain consistency. This relates to another issue: coordination. In order for the camera to roll, many different people, all doing different jobs, must all communicate through walkie talkies. A final issue is the potential difficulty the director may have forming a strong creative link with the actors while the shot is being done.

ELECTRICAL DEPARTMENT

Sometimes a production schedule will require the cinematographer to pre-light a location or a set. In those instances, you will have to hire a separate crew to do the work since it is usually done while the shooting company is working. But it is often more cost effective to have a fresh crew pre-rig a set or location than have your tired production crew work overtime to do it. Again, by examining the production board and its relationship to the work schedule, you can determine when this will be necessary.

A shooting company will sometimes work more than twelve hours a day to complete the day's schedule. Maybe it's the last day at the location, or the

Acct. #	Account Name	Units	Rate	Amount	Sub Total	Total
2700	**ELECTRICAL DEPARTMENT**					
01	Pre-Rigging Set or Location					
	Striking Set or Location					
02	Electrical Equipment Rental Set or Location					
03	Electrical Department Shooting Company					
	Gaffer					
	Prepare					
	Shoot					
	Best Boy (Person)					
	Prepare					
	Shoot					
	Wrap					
	Electricians (Operators)					
	Shoot					
	Generator Operator					
	Shoot					
	Ritter Operator					
	Shoot					
	Extra Electrical Operator(s)					
	Shoot					
12	Labor Overtime					
13	Electrical Equipment Rental Shooting Company					
	Generator Rental					
	Miscellaneous Rentals					
14	Box Rental					
15	Expendables					
	Globe Burn Outs					
	Generator Fuel					
	Miscellaneous Purchases					
16	Repairs					
50	Other					
	Total 2700					

Figure 26

last day an actor is scheduled to work. Maybe the director is behind and needs to get caught up. Whatever the reason, this is why you budget for labor overtime and for a second crew to come to the location to strike the grip and electric equipment. There are companies that provide this service to the producer. They have names like Strike Force or the Wrap Pack and are made up of electrical and grip personnel who move like a military battalion when doing the job. If used for a strike, the production manager would give them as early a notification as possible and on the day of work the crew shows up at the set at a specific time, usually in fatigues. They stand at military attention until the director completes the martini shot and the 1st AD announces the wrap. The production's electricians and grips pick up their personal items and leave. The strike crew immediately and methodically performs the strike, instructed by one crewmember as to where to put the equipment once it is struck. This is usually one of the electricians who sits, drinks a much deserved beer, watches the strike and is given a later call time the next day. This service is always a major morale booster for production. You pay these strike companies one flat fee depending on the number of people you need for the strike.

Gaffer (IATSE Local 728)

The lighting crew reports to the cinematographer. The head of the production lighting crew is the gaffer whose main responsibility is to make sure that the set, location or shot is lit according to the creative judgment of the cinematographer. You may think of this person as an assistant lighting director or in some instances as the lighting director executing the light plot of the lighting designer or cinematographer.

Cinematographers have longstanding relationships with gaffers since they rely heavily on the gaffer knowing their idiosyncrasies and the details of how they prefer to light a scene or sequence. The gaffer role is also creative, so it is important that the gaffer have a sense of the texture of the image and how to achieve it with light. The gaffer must have knowledge of electricity and be creative in finding a source of power in any situation. This might mean bringing a generator to the location or tying in to existing power. It is therefore important for the gaffer to visit all the locations before shooting once the director and cinematographer have selected them. Sometimes a cinematographer will take the gaffer along on a location scout to get an opinion of the location in terms of the potential logistical problems. This opinion may enter into the final decision concerning the use of the location.

It is not unusual for gaffers to approach producers and offer the use of their own electrical (and grip) equipment on the condition that the producer employs the gaffer on the project. In such cases the gaffer may offer the producer a rental deal that is hard to refuse. Being forewarned is being forearmed! The speed of the gaffer and the crew will affect the ability of the director to complete the daily schedule. Unless your cinematographer knows or has worked with the gaffer previously, be careful. The gaffer who offers this kind of deal may not be very creative or very fast, or the equipment may be old or unsuitably maintained. There are, however, professional gaffers who do have excellent equipment and are good at what they do. The cinematographer will recommend them to you and, if you have established a relationship with them, or if your cinematographer has a relationship with them, they may offer you an excellent deal on the equipment. Sometimes a professional gaffer with excellent equipment will want to make you an excellent deal just to work with your cinematographer and establish the relationship. If you use a gaffer with his or her own equipment, adjust the rental of the equipment with the salary of the gaffer in the same way you adjust for kit or box rentals. Of course, you can always rent the equipment from a qualified grip electric rental company and employ a gaffer with the skills necessary for the cinematographer and the project.

Best Boy (IATSE Local 728)

The best boy is the assistant to the gaffer. The primary responsibility for the best boy is the care, inventory and maintenance of the electrical equipment and handling the schedules and work times for the electricians with the shooting company. Once the cinematographer and gaffer have determined the electrical equipment required for the project and the rental house has been secured, they turn to the best boy to pick up and organize the equipment for easy accessibility during production. The best boy, being responsible for the inventory, is also responsible for making sure that everything rented is returned and in appropriate condition. If there are any problems or variables, they are worked through your production manager.

Make sure that the best boy works for the production company and not for himself. I have seen situations where rental equipment was on the inventory but was never used or was never even considered for use. The rental company was getting paid a few bucks extra for unnecessary or unordered equipment. Perhaps there was a kickback to the best boy for that service. Your cinematographer and production manager will be helpful in assuring this doesn't happen. If it does, do not be afraid to immediately replace the best boy.

Electricians (IATSE Local 728)

Electricians are also called "juicers." They are the crewmembers who set the lights in place under the direction of the gaffer. Electricians should have a thorough knowledge of the type of equipment that is being used on the production and, although not critical to their job, a creative sense as well. When they position a light, they should know how the light is being used and what it does to the image. The more informed an electrician is, the more likely he or she is to be creative. It is important to the production process that electricians, like grips, become part of the family of production so each will have pride in their contribution to the final product.

Generator and Ritter Operators (IATSE Local 728)

You may need a generator operator depending on the size of the generator you are renting. The gaffer will be helpful in this determination. You may only need a generator that requires a separate operator on an occasional daily basis since it is common to carry a small generator with the basic electrical rental package. The choice of location and the production schedule will help you with this decision.

A Ritter is a wind machine. Some Ritters are so large that they require a separate operator. If the project calls for a hurricane or a windstorm, you will have to rent one or more very large Ritters, which will require people to operate and monitor them. If a generator is used, you will have to buy fuel for its operation. Perhaps you need a generator to operate the Ritters, or a generator to heat the actors. Thinking through the logistics and choreography of production will assist with these decisions. I know of a project shot in Chicago in the dead of winter that required generators to heat the generators being used to light the set.

Your production is responsible for expendable items, such as the gels of various colors used in front of the lights. Bulbs that burn out during production are replaced with spare bulbs that come with the rental package. Keep the burnt out bulbs to return with the equipment, as you need to show proof of the burn out to the rental company or you will be charged for any missing replacement bulbs.

SET OPERATIONS
Grip Department
Electrical is only one support side for the cinematographers creativity. The other side is the Grip Department which provides further on set operations during production.

Key Grip (IATSE Local 80)
Grips are the people who support the needs of the Camera Department and the production by moving things that need to be moved. In the theater, the grips would be equivalent to the stagehands, which are the spine of a theater production. Grips also work hand in glove with the electricians in supporting the immediate needs of the cinematographer. This can be something as simple as erecting a parachute to provide shade for the shooting company on a scorching hot day, or rigging a light on a scissors lift and hoisting it in the air. It can also be as complex as rigging a mount for the camera on the side of a bus. Whatever it is, the Grip Department is there to do it.

The head of the Grip Department is the key grip who is often equated to the gaffer. Key grips prepare in much the same way as gaffers. They scout locations with the cinematographer and gaffer and assist in determining the needs of the moment to moment move of the shooting company. Key grips also help the cinematographer decide on the grip equipment for the production after consultation with the gaffer. They must anticipate the creative needs of the cinematographer (and director) and be ready for the unexpected. They are the one closest to circumstances when Murphy's Law takes place and the crewmember to whom people turn to resolve the problem. A good key grip thinks ahead of the production on a moment to moment basis and manages the grip crew in such a way that is unnoticed by all but the cinematographer. The key grip sets the tone and tempo of the grip crew and—through creative thinking and action—works in harmony with the gaffer and the electrical crew. When the harmony does not happen, when key grips believe that the center of production revolves around their position, the effectiveness of the cinematographer tumbles, adversely affecting the needs of the director and resulting in a project that eventually crashes. An experienced cinematographer, production manager, line producer or 1st assistant director will see it coming. On the first day of shooting of *Hunter's Blood*, my production manager, Andy LaMarca, told me that Tom Denove, the cinematographer, was having trouble with the grip crew. The key grip was being stubborn and argumentative and most of his crew had the same attitude. And it was this attitude that had caused accidents to happen that day. They were not paying attention to the needs of the project. Tom wanted to fire all but the one member of the grip crew who was paying attention, and he wanted to promote him to key grip and bring on a new crew. Andy told me he could have a new crew ready the following morning. I gave the

Acct. #	Account Name	Units	Rate	Amount	Sub Total	Total
2800	**SET OPERATIONS**					
01	Key Grip					
	Prepare					
	Shoot					
02	Best Boy (Person)					
	Prepare					
	Shoot					
	Wrap					
03	Production Grips					
	Shoot					
04	Dolly Grip					
	Prepare					
	Shoot					
05	On set Greensman (IATSE function)					
06	On set Painters (IATSE function)					
07	Craft Service					
	Prepare					
	Shoot					
	Wrap					
08	Police					
09	Security					
10	Production Assistants					
11	Medical (First Aid, Doctor, Nurse)					
12	Labor Overtime					
13	Medical Equipment					
14	Craft Service Rentals					
15	Craft Service Purchases					
16	Grip Package Rental					
17	Grip Puchases					
18	Grip Boxes					
19	Motion Equipment Package					
20	Repairs and Damage					
50	Other					
	Total 2800					

Figure 27

okay, and at the end of the day, all but the grip who was promoted to key grip were unemployed.

Best Boy (IATSE Local 80)

Like the best boy in the Electrical Department, best boys in the Grip Department are the assistants to the keys and are responsible for the maintenance and inventory of the rented grip equipment. They also handle the scheduling and time reports of the grips on the production, working closely with the best boy of the Electric Department and with the production manager. They, along with the best boy electric, are involved with the pickup and return of the equipment, including the camera dolly used in the production.

Dolly Grip (IATSE Local 80)

Dolly grips are responsible for the "care and feeding" of the camera dolly. This is their only function on the production. The dolly grip lives, breathes and sleeps with the camera dolly to ensure that it is always operational and at the ready for the director.

The dolly grip position, like all positions, is a creative position. But it is especially true with the dolly grip since he or she operates the dolly on which the camera sits and camera movement has motivation of its own. Its speed and direction are often used to imply character intent and this intent must be "felt" by the dolly grip. This is not an easy task, but a task to which many grips aspire.

Grips (IATSE Local 80)

Although grips are like stagehands on a shooting set, if the project is a signatory project with the IATSE, the production will also need to have a separate stagehand called a greensman (IATSE Local 729) whose job it is to take care of and move any live plants that are being used as set dressing. Also, under the same signatory conditions, it may be necessary to employ a standby painter (IATSE Local 44) who performs necessary paint touchups that might be required from time to time. Of course, if the project is not an IATSE signatory project, these jobs can be done by any grip other than the dolly grip.

A standard relationship of a basic grip and electric crew, everything being equal on a medium to low budget project, is usually four grips and four electricians—including gaffer, key grip, best boy electric, best boy grip and two electricians and two grips. The complexity of the logistics of production indicated by the production board may adjust, the ratio of the grip crew to the electrical crew slightly. The dolly grip is not included in the count.

The production board will also help determine when it is necessary to pick up additional electricians or grips. For example, night exteriors will probably require a larger grip and electrical crew than day exteriors. The balance of the grip and electric crew on the production affects the production schedule and the overall relationship of time to do the production to its fiscal limitations. Make sure you discuss these needs carefully with your production manager, director and cinematographer to ensure maximum efficiency.

Although grip equipment usually comes from a grip and electric rental company there may be other materials and equipment used by grips such as the dolly, lumber, nails, screws and rope that may need to be rented or purchased from other sources. As an example, the project may call for a specific type of picture car camera mount, such as a hostess tray[2], which must be either rented or created by the Grip Department. This is called a motion equipment package and many grips specialize in this area. So make sure that the Grip Department is ready for anything: the planned and the unplanned will both affect your project!

Craft Service (IATSE Local 727)

The position of craft service on a production crew is someone who "services the craft" members or the crew. Their primary task is to make sure that the crew has available to them certain comforts that improve their working conditions. Craft services also takes care of the set, making sure that the area in which people are working is clean and orderly. Craft service people provide the food that is continuously available to the company throughout the production day. They prepare and arrange for such things as coffee, donuts, bagels, juices and other such items that any member of the production company might want to "nosh" on during the long working day. Experienced craft service people cater to the needs of the director, the cinematographer and the actors on the project. They will know when the company needs a lift and provide treats that are unique and different. It is not unheard of for an experienced craft service person to prepare omelets or freshly popped popcorn, special sandwiches or freshly baked cookies to lift

---

[2] A hostess tray is a platform that is mounted by the side window of a vehicle The camera is mounted on the platform for a side angle shot inside the vehicle. It is given its name from the days of drive-in restaurants when the hostess brought the meal on a tray and put it into position over the open window of a car.

the spirits of a tired crew. (Health Departments in certain cities, however, may require craft services to handle only prepared or prepackaged food.) The preparation for a craft serviceperson will consist of researching the needs of the company and shopping for the materials. You must make sure that the person has the experience to know how to buy frugally. They should have membership cards at wholesale food supply houses, or envelopes full of newspaper discount grocery coupons. Many times they will come with their own coffeepots, coolers, electric pans and serving trays to do their job thoroughly. The more creative a craft service person is, the happier the production crew. You should try to find a craft service person who is not only inventive, but also uplifting in spirit as it is often the craft service person who becomes the "cheerleader" for company morale. Make sure they set up craft service *before* anyone reports to work. Few things bog down the day like starting work in the morning and not having fresh coffee or tea available upon arrival. If your production company knows they can depend on craft service being ready at the beginning of the work day, you will have a more enthusiastic crew, since it sends the signal to them that someone (the producer) cares about their needs.

Police, Security and First Aid (IATSE Local 767)

Police and security are involved in set operations and are directly involved with the protection and security of the shooting company. An uniformed motorcycle policeman may be needed if you are using a camera car on city streets. If you are using a famous actor and shooting in a public place, it may be necessary to employ security guards to protect the privacy of the actor and to allow the production to work unmolested.

First aid is critically important for the safety of your project. Some projects have a permanent nurse or doctor with the production company. Whenever the production schedule shows a possibility of an accident, a doctor and first aid person is highly recommended. These could be days that involve stunts or special explosive effects. At the very least you should have a *complete* first aid kit available at all times and a procedure in place in case anyone needs serious medical attention during the course of production. You must make sure that your production manager and 1st AD (the safety officer) have the phone number for the nearest hospital and ambulance service. It's also not a bad idea to have at least one person on the permanent crew trained in CPR. Murphy's Law often results in accidents and injury. So it is wise to be prepared.

——— • • • ———

In Hunter's Blood, *the poachers leave a visual message for the hunters: a dead man who they had skinned and hung on a tree. The actor portraying the dead man had to report to the makeup studio at 5:00 A.M. to get into the special effects makeup that took three hours to apply. He was then transported by van, lying prone, to the exterior location while being kept as comfortable as possible. Once on the location, the actor had to be carried by gurney to the tree that had been rigged for safety by the stunt coordinator and the mechanical effects supervisor. Further, because he was virtually naked, it was planned for the director to have the shot already rehearsed and ready to go once the actor was in place. This sequence was planned weeks in advance. The day of the scheduled scene was very cold. The production manager, Andy LaMarca, and I decided to have portable space heaters brought in and placed near the tree (but out of camera range) so the actor would be as comfortable as possible during the shot. All was carefully planned to create the shot safely and effectively. The cost versus the effect in telling the story was too important for there to be any mistakes. That day the director decided to do a dolly shot when the hunters discover the body before doing the scene at the tree with the hanging body. While the shot was creative, I thought it was a mistake because it was unplanned. I thought it was probably wiser to do the scene first, then go for the establishing of the location later, since in a long shot you can cheat certain things if need be. But a producer must never interfere with the director's work on the set so I stood by trying to make sure that everything was being done safely and that the scene (which was expensive) was getting the necessary camera coverage. When we went to do the shot and just after the camera started rolling the director yelled to the actor to hold his breath just before he called "Action." My heart began to beat quickly as I knew that he should not have said this. As the camera rolled I was standing directly behind the actor (out of camera range) and noticed that the back of his ear was turning blue—he was close to losing consciousness. I yelled, "Cut!" and ordered the actor off the tree and taken immediately to a medical facility nearby. When the actor had held his breath, he lost oxygen to his brain causing him to pass out. Safety must be considered first. The special effects people had put the actor in a special "nude" harness that would safely constrict his breathing. The fainting was caused by asking the actor to unnecessarily hold his breath.*

——— • • • ———

CHAPTER 7 THE PRODUCTION PERIOD— PART 2

"Most producers are creative in a deal making or financial sense, so to find a producer who is also creative in the art of filmmaking is a unique pleasure. In developing a recent Dimension project, Kevin Messick proved to be that kind of producer. He is inspiring, enthusiastic, loyal, and always protects, defends and supports a director in a way that I have never previously experienced."

—Penelope Spheeris, Director, *Senseless, The Beverly Hillbillies, Wayne's World, The Decline of Western Civilization*

The previous chapter included areas of production affecting the image and the process of production. This chapter will continue that dialogue but will begin with two areas that closely work with the onscreen talent.

WARDROBE DEPARTMENT—CLOTHING THE ACTORS
Costume (Wardrobe) Designer (IATSE Local 892 *Los Angeles,* Local 829 *New York*)

Costume design (sometimes called wardrobe design) is important to the nature of the story. Designers are always thinking of the character as opposed to the actor. They are always asking the question, "Who are these people and where do they come from?" Their answer lies in the clothing. Costume designers determine the wardrobe for the project. They begin their task by reading the screenplay. They refine it by speaking with you, the director and the production designer to try to define the characters or the creative vision of the project. They continue by researching the historical, regional, cultural, and social texture of the characters. Finally, they complete their planning and sketch wardrobe design details for the look of each of the characters and present it to you, the director, and to the production designer for discussion and approval. Wardrobe designers must consider the budget and determine what wardrobe needs to be purchased, manufactured or, in some cases, pulled from the actors' own closets. You should find a costume designer who has trade-off relationships with clothing manufacturers or businesses that may be helpful to your project. In most cases, the trade-off will be a screen credit at the end of the project or seeing a trademark logo on the wardrobe worn by one of the principle actors. Costume designers should also have relationships with wardrobe rental companies for discounts and with wardrobe construction companies for lower than quoted rates should any wardrobe need to be constructed. Producers and directors often forget some of the major issues costume designers must consider. Each character's wardrobe must be broken down in terms of the screen time in the story and the wardrobe must be detailed out by days and nights. A wardrobe breakdown will show the number of days and nights covered in the story. They must also consider duplicates and triplicates of certain wardrobe items as necessary for the shooting schedule. They must consider stunt people doubling for actors and provide wardrobe accordingly. They must consider the color and texture of the setting when they determine the color and texture of the wardrobe. Finally, they must know who has been cast for specific roles as quickly as possible since the wardrobe designer and eventually the production wardrobe supervisor (which can often be one and the same) must establish a positive working relationship with each actor. The longer it takes to cast an actor, the more difficult it becomes to wardrobe the actor—and this delay can cost the producer time and money.

It is imperative that your costume designer has a good rapport with the actors. The wardrobe designer becomes a confidante for actors and will be aware of every body flaw or feature (real or imagined) that the actor is convinced is hideous. (Actors will often swear the costume designer to secrecy, threatening excruciating pain if news of their "flaws" ever become public knowledge.) Actors, like children, are very concerned with how they look. Even though you, the designer and the director have determined very specific ideas about the actors' wardrobe, the actors may have specific ideas of their own. A good designer will listen to actors, recognizing that sometimes they know themselves better than anyone else. If an actress considers herself to be thick-waisted, the designer will know it would be foolish to force her into midriff revealing outfits. A creative wardrobe designer often has the task of negotiating with the producer or actor in deciding the final wardrobe. Emmy Award winning designer and University of California at Irvine Professor Madeline Kazlowski first meets with the producer or director and asks them to look at magazines and tear out photographs of the look they think they want. She does the same in order to communicate ideas to producers. After these initial meetings she then begins to sketch out the wardrobe for final approval.

Sometimes this has to be taken further. When Madeline was designing *The Return of Hunter,* a television movie that was a follow-up to the *Hunter* police series starring Fred Dryer, she was faced with a problem in the story. The movie takes place several years after the series aired and Dryer's character had moved up the ranks from sergeant to lieutenant. As a sergeant, he wore a tie and sport coat with blue jeans, which was a look of the day when *Hunter* first aired. Dryer wanted to continue to look that way, or so he thought. The producers and Madeline knew times and styles had changed, and that now that look was too dated to be effective. They wanted him to look "cool," but with a new appearance for a familiar character. Madeline designed the look they wanted but she needed to get Fred convinced that it was right. So she brought him samples of Italian cut trousers. Fred tried them on, liked the fit and the way they were cut and saw that they kept the youthful but sophisticated feel that he needed for the character. Once he understood the direction they were headed, he and Madeline went shopping and together they selected stylish shirts in great colors to go with this new look. This gave him the "cool" factor that he was seeking as the foundation of his character.

Costume designers may be involved with the onset of production, or they may have completed their task by the start of the project and hand over the actual wardrobe work of the project to the supervisor. Many independent productions employ the supervisor as the designer. Whatever the case may be, the wardrobe person is the first person actors see when they report to work each day, so that person will know how actors feel when they come to the set. Did they have a difficult night? Were they in a rush getting to work? Are they nervous about the scenes they are doing? Any scenario can impact a performance. This information will be important for the director since the creative performance is what it is all about.

I was directing a feature a few years ago with a well-known actor who had to play a scene in which he was breaking up with his girlfriend. He is a reliable actor who always remembers his dialogue, so I decided to shoot the scene as continuous action between the two characters. When we rehearsed the scene I was surprised that he was having a difficult time remembering his lines. The actors were both very experienced, so at one point I told the actors to improvise the intent of the scene and decided to try to shoot the scene differently than originally planned so the actor could take his time with the dialogue. It wasn't until the next day that I was told by my 1st AD (who had been told by the wardrobe supervisor), that the actor was breaking up with his real life girlfriend of ten years. I immediately understood that the scene had hit home. At the time I wished I had known about it sooner, saving the crew time and saving the actor unnecessary anguish.

Wardrobe Supervisor (IATSE Local 705)

On an IATSE project, a wardrobe supervisor (costumer) is not permitted to take pen to paper to design even one scrap of a costume. Of course, on a nonunion project no such rule exists and it is not uncommon to find the onset wardrobe person is also the designer and faced with such tasks as supervising the manufacture of wardrobe, or shopping for specific wardrobe for actors during production. This will require the hiring of several onset assistants. The wardrobe supervisor must also handle wardrobe for atmosphere when it is applicable to the story, although atmosphere are generally asked to come in wearing their own wardrobe. If it is a period or historical project the wardrobe for atmosphere can get quite complex. The wardrobe supervisor must also consider the bit roles since this department must make sure that all people who populate a scene are appropriately dressed.

It is imperative that set wardrobe people have certain creative skills—which include the ability to research atmosphere wardrobe along the lines of the designer's vision—and certain organizational skills required to maintain continuity of clothing from one scene to the next. A big budget item in wardrobe is for Polaroid film and cameras, which allow the Wardrobe Department to constantly photograph actors and keep a record of what and how they are wearing the clothes in the production. Some onset wardrobe supervisors use a digital still camera and a laptop computer to maintain this information. This saves the expense of Polaroids and makes the whole process more manageable. Onset wardrobe people must also have fitting and stitching skills, because most of the time they are working out of a wardrobe truck and a seamstress and shop crew are not available. The wardrobe truck must contain clothing racks for the wardrobe, ironing boards, sewing machines, steamer machines and possibly even a small generator. On smaller projects, the wardrobe vehicle is also used for props. Since the wardrobe crew works with the actors on a day-to-day basis it is some-

Acct. #	Account Name	Units	Rate	Amount	Sub Total	Total
2900	WARDROBE					
01	Costume Designer					
	Prepare					
	Shoot					
02	Mens Wardrobe Supervisor					
	Prepare					
	Shoot					
	Wrap					
03	Womens Wardrobe Supervisor					
	Prepare					
	Shoot					
	Wrap					
04	Wardrobe Assistants					
	Prepare					
	Shoot					
	Wrap					
05	Labor Overtime					
06	Mens Wardrobe Manufacture	Allow				
07	Womens Wardrobe Manufacture	Allow				
08	Mens Wardrobe Purchase	Allow				
09	Womens Wardrobe Purchase	Allow				
10	Mens Wardrobe Rentals	Allow				
11	Womens Wardrobe Rentals	Allow				
12	**Wardrobe Cleaning**	Allow				
13	**Wardrobe Damages**	Allow				
14	**Kit Rental**					
15	Wardrobe Vehicle Rental					
50	Other					
	Total 2900					

Figure 28

what like going to camp. They are the camp counselors who have to be with the actors the entire time making them look as right as possible whether they are playing heroes or homeless people. It is up to the Wardrobe Department to ensure that the actors are true to the designers' big picture because that is developed from the producer's and the director's creative vision.

The Wardrobe Department continues to work after the production has wrapped each production day. It must prepare for the next day's schedule, which might include doing laundry or running to the dry cleaners to get the wardrobe back in time. This must be taken into consideration when planning the project. Like the Property Department, the Wardrobe Department must have more wardrobe than necessary in case the director wants something different, or something irreparable happens to an item. Wardrobe is a critical element on a project. Some independent producers may believe that on smaller projects it is unnecessary to use wardrobe people. This is a massive blunder. Wardrobe is so critical to the texture of a project that it takes a designer, supervisor or onset wardrobe person to clearly focus on the details of this aspect of the story.

This does not necessarily mean that you need to spend a lot of money to hire someone to do the job. Ego can be a stronger motivation than remuneration. You may want to look for a person from the ranks of college theater departments, or contact local film commissions for recommendations of people in certain areas. You may find people who have been doing commercials or industrials and want the creative opportunity of doing a longer narrative piece, or you may find someone ready to use the knowledge and skills they have been practicing in an educational environment. You might try local costume rental houses and find someone who wants the opportunity to do something more. Wherever you look, remember that it is an important creative position that is directly impacting your vision.

MAKEUP AND HAIR DEPARTMENT
Makeup and Hair Artists (IATSE Local 706)
The question often arises as to whether you need to have both a makeup person and a hair person on the project. If it is an IATSE signatory project, then the answer is yes. If it is nonunion, one person often does both. Makeup for the camera is significantly different than makeup for the theater, so it is important that you find a makeup artist who knows the subtleties of on-camera makeup. The cinematographer will be very attuned to those subtleties and may often provide specific instructions to makeup people regarding the look. Makeup people usually have a confidential relationship with the actors. It is the nature of the job that actors confide personal issues with the makeup artist. The relationship between a makeup artist and the actor can be quite strong and may be a possible problem for the production especially if the actor is the "star" of the project. The makeup artist may use the relationship with the actor as leverage if the cinematographer or director is not pleased with the work the makeup artist is doing. You do not want to have any contentiousness between the talent and the creative team as it will only lead to trouble.

Many actors insist that the production hire their own makeup artist as a condition of their employment. This can present problems because it sends out the signal that the makeup artist works for the actor and not for the pro-

Acct. #	Account Name	Units	Rate	Amount	Sub Total	Total
3000	MAKEUP AND HAIR DEPARTMENT					
01	Makeup Supervisor (Makeup Artist)					
	Prepare					
	Shoot					
02	Assistant Makeup Artist					
03	Body Makeup Artist (IATSE)					
04	Additional Makeup Labor					
05	Hair Stylist Designer					
06	Hairdresser Supervisor					
	Prepare					
	Shoot					
07	Assistant Hairstylist					
08	Additional Hair Labor					
09	Labor Overtime					
10	Makeup Purchases	Allow				
11	Hair Purchases	Allow				
12	Makeup Appliance Manufacture	Allow				
13	Wigs and Hairpieces Manufacture	Allow				
14	Rentals	Allow				
15	Box Rental - Makeup					
16	Box Rental - Hair					
50	Other					
	Total 3000					

Figure 29

duction. On one project I produced, one of the starring actresses required that I hire her makeup artist as a condition of her employment. After long consideration (and because I wanted the actress to be comfortable), I agreed to the hiring on the condition that whenever the actress worked the makeup artist would do makeup for the other actors as well. The actress was happy because she had her own makeup artist, and I was pleased that our makeup artist did not feel slighted and the other actors did not think that this particular actress was receiving special treatment. (The only one who might have been unhappy was the actress' makeup artist —because of his relationship to her, he was coerced in doing makeup for other actors as well.)

There is little pre-production preparation time required for makeup and hair other than checking with the principle actors concerning any special personal makeup requirements. In some instances makeup may be designed by a professional makeup artist who then teaches a trainee how to maintain the look. This is often done when there is not much complexity to the makeup. It allows the producer to hire someone at a low rate and either pay a professional makeup artist a flat fee for the design, or provide the designer a specific onscreen credit acknowledging the makeup design.

You may also want to use the same tenet with a hair stylist. On many films I have produced, the look of the hair design was created by the late Michael Mariani, a well-known hair stylist for men and women. Michael would read the script, then discuss his ideas for the characters with the actors and me. The actors would go to his salon for the styling and he would either teach the makeup artist how to keep the hairstyle, or assign a hair stylist from his shop to work on the project. This worked well for all concerned. Michael was given a "hair designed by" credit, the actors were pleased because they were all given special treatment, and one of his shop hair stylists got a brief change of pace by working on the production set.

THE SOUND DEPARTMENT
Sound Mixer (IATSE Local 695)

The Sound Department is often overlooked. Producers and directors always seem to think of the picture first and fail to consider the importance of sound people to the process of production. All other crafts on a production are concerned with the picture, and people sometimes forget that what they do may have an impact upon sound. You need to instill the notion that sound is as important to the project as the image and that sound is an integral part of the production process.

The best sound people are silent. That is to say that they go about their work preparing to record production sound quietly and effectively. Excellent sound mixers will watch the director's staging very carefully before determining how to "mike" the scene. They will then discuss the staging with their boom operator and together the two will determine the most time effective way to record sound skillfully. It might require the placement of

Acct. #	Account Name	Units	Rate	Amount	Sub Total	Total
3100	SOUND DEPARTMENT					
01	Sound Mixer					
	Prepare					
	Shoot					
02	Boom Operator					
	Shoot					
03	3rd Soundman (Cableman)					
	Shoot					
05	Labor Overtime					
10	Purchases					
	¼" Magnetic Tape (Nagra)					
	Dat Tape					
	Batteries and Miscellaneous					
11	Rentals – Sound Package	Allow				
	Wireless Microphones	Allow				
	Special Equipment	Allow				
	Walkie-talkies	Allow				
	Playback Equipment	Allow				
12	Equipment Repairs	Allow				
50	Other					
	Total 3100					

Figure 30

microphones hidden in the set whose cables are attached to the sound mixing console, or actors wearing hidden wireless microphones. It might mean using a traveling microphone boom or a combination of methods. Sometimes a sound mixer may have a suggestion for the director to ensure that sound in a specific scene will record well. Whatever the solution, the Sound Department does it without disturbing the director, the actors, or the set up of the camera. Professional sound mixers try not to ask for a specific rehearsal for sound unless there is a good reason for it (such as a scene in which an actor might need to whisper and then suddenly scream). The ability to record excellent sound in this case will require a rehearsal for both the sound mixer and the boom operator. Recording clean production sound is a priority for the Production Sound Department as it will reduce the need for post-production automatic dialogue replacement (ADR) or "looping." Sound mixers should position their sound cart where they are able to watch the action of the scene. They must also know the image being recorded by the camera and be aware of where the focus of the production sound should be for that image. Production sound mixing is a difficult and creative job requiring both experience and skill since sound mixers are the only people on the project protecting your sound tracks. During pre-production you should make sure that your production sound mixer meets with the post-production sound house that will be working with the production tracks during the final sound mix phase of the project. The technical sound information that is required in the mixing phase may have an impact upon how the sound needs to be originally recorded. The end use of the production sound and the needs of the post-production mixer should dictate the original recording of sound *(End Result Theory)*. Your production sound mixer should visit locations to hear their natural ambience, and listen for a potential of echo or other problematic sounds.

During production, the sound mixer should periodically listen to the production tracks with the post-production sound mixer (if he or she has been

---

PRODUCERS VOCABULARY

Looping—A length of film or audiotape that is spliced end to end so that it can be machine-played repetitively. In a special sound studio, an actor or voiceover artist would watch a "looped" scene on a screen and, using a microphone and single or dual headphones that are worn on the head or held close to one ear, respeak or resing those words or lyrics that need to be improved or changed. This process is called looping or dubbing. Another way is through the use of an automatic dialogue replacement system (ADR). In this more advanced and popular system, the picture and soundtrack of the scene in question are played forward at normal speed without the use of a physical loop connection. For each new try at recording, the picture and track are rewound at high speed to the beginning of the scene and then played forward again at normal speed.

hired) in order to catch and correct any unforeseen production sound problems that could show up later or need to be fixed before the final mix.

Many production sound mixers will come to the job with their own equipment. In those instances, the production sound mixer rents the equipment to the production on a weekly basis and you adjust the mixers' salary and the rental fee for additional savings using the same method as discussed in the section in Chapter Six on "box rentals." Equipment owned by production sound mixers may only include basic microphones, cabling and a Nagra tape recorder. It may not include wireless microphones, a time code Nagra recorder or a DAT (Digital Audio Tape) recorder. You may have to add this equipment through an outside sound rental house once you determine the path your project will take in post-production. Although digital sound is the state of the art, sound mixers have found that digital recording has proven to be less than satisfactory, while analog recording through the tried and true method of using a Nagra has had 100 percent reliability. So it is common practice for sound mixers to record production sound with both a Nagra and DAT recorder.

In most cases, if you decide that your post-production process will employ digital nonlinear picture editing and/or digital post-production sound editing you will need to record your production sound using a time code Nagra or DAT recorder. This is quickly becoming the norm in production today. However, please be aware that digital recording is in a state of flux and there are new recording systems coming rapidly into the market. So it is important for your sound mixer to know what equipment the post-production sound house is using as their standard. If you are shooting your project using a digital video camera, the production sound mixer's console will plug directly into the camera and the sound will be recorded on the videotape. It is a wise idea to simultaneously record with a time code recorder to ensure a protective backup production track.

Wireless microphones are now a standard part of a sound package. They allow the director creative mobility to stage the actors, therefore wireless microphones have become a cost-effective piece of equipment. On lower budget projects you may want to consider renting wireless microphones just for certain sequences rather than for the entire production. Close collaboration by the production sound mixer with the director and production manager during pre-production will help determine that decision. Also, wardrobe must be informed when there is an intention of using wireless microphones. Wardrobe must make sure that the actors' costumes are suitable to hide the battery pack powering the microphone. For example, it would be tough to use wireless microphones on actors in bathing suits. It is also difficult to use wireless microphones on wardrobe that makes a lot of noise, like taffeta or leather.

Boom Operator (IATSE Local 695)

Boom operators are very important to the creative recording of sound. They are always on the set watching and observing to make sure that the Sound Department accomplishes its goals. The boom operator should be strong, agile and probably tall; since it has been my observation that the taller the boom operator the easier it is to get the mike in the scene and not in the shot. The relationship between the boom operator and the sound mixer is very important since the creative recording of production sound has a lot to do with microphone placement. Boom operators who have a close relationship with their production sound mixer will know where to set the microphone without being instructed. The boom operator will have to have a working relationship with other crewmembers since the actions of other crew personnel may affect the work of the boom. Boom operators must also know how to work diplomatically with talent. The better operators have a pleasant demeanor, since they often have to attach battery packs and hide wireless microphones on actors. (This can be a very delicate art form unto itself.) They will work quickly and silently, reporting any problems to the sound mixer or first assistant. They want to make sure that the director never has to wait while the Sound Department does its job. On more complex production days it might be necessary to hire a second boom (or cable) operator. Once again, this is where the production board will come in handy as this is one of the choreographic needs of the production period.

The Sound Department has the responsibility of purchasing DAT cassette tape for the DAT recorder or 1/4" audio tape (3" reels) for the Nagra. To determine the amount of tape stock to budget, you must first determine the amount of picture stock that will be required for the camera. Although this will be discussed later in this chapter, the determination of audio stock correlates to the shooting ratio of the project. You should purchase the exact amount of tape stock as you do picture (camera) stock. While there are times when it will not be necessary to record sound with the picture, there will be other times when it will be necessary to record sound without the picture. The practice of recording "room tone" in each practical location for use during post-production sound design is an example of that. Therefore, it is foolish to think that you will need less audiotape than you do picture stock. If any audiotape is left over from production it can always be used in post-production or on your next project.

Finally, the walkie-talkies that are required to facilitate the production process are assigned to the Production Sound Department budget. Walkie-talkies may be rented or purchased, and are requirements on every project. The production manager determines the exact number of walkie-talkies needed by looking at the choreography on the production board. The minimum is usually four. On a lower budget project you may want to purchase the consumer type of walkie-talkie or headset intercom system. (First check carefully to see if it can handle the distance that you need for production. Don't forget this!) Communication will be greatly improved during production with the addition of walkie-talkies or some other wireless intercom device and will save you time in production. And saving time is saving money and adding creativity for the director.

TRANSPORTATION

Transportation Coordinator (IATSE Teamsters Local 399 *Los Angeles*, Local 385 or 390 *Florida*, Local 714 *Chicago*, Local 85 *San Francisco*, Local 817 *New York*)

The Transportation Department is the lifeline to the project. It is the department that must move the production, its personnel and its elements. They may move a single element during a production day or all the elements at the end of, or the beginning of a production day. Murphy's Law will certainly run amok if the Transportation Department is not on top of the company movement detailed in the production board. This department is directly responsible to the production manager, and the coordination and communication between the production manager and the transportation coordinator must be in sync at all times. This can be accomplished by having the production coordinator assist both the production manager and the transportation coordinator (see Figure #18). In that way the production coordinator becomes the pivot point for the successful movement of the production.

You should permit the transportation coordinator to have almost as much preparation time as the production manager. The transportation coordinator must read the script to determine if any picture vehicles are required and then meet with you, the director and/or the production designer concerning the type and color of picture vehicle desired. He or she then works with the Property Department to secure and transport the vehicle on the days it is needed for production. The transportation coordinator should start solving all the transport problems of the production as the needs of the various departments are known, locations are secured, personnel are in place and the production schedule is planned. The coordinator must arrange for the necessary vehicles and assure that drivers are scheduled. Transportation coordinators are like military strategists, since they are given the responsibility of moving large companies of people and equipment. They must visit each location and determine the position and establishment of "base camp" and the logistics of transit as it relates to time and production creativity. The Transportation Department must make sure that everything is set up before the production company reports to work and they are often the last department to leave a location at the end of a production day. On nonunion productions you often assign production assistants to work with the production manager and transportation coordinator to make sure the loose ends regarding production movement are tied up.

The Teamsters represent transportation on an IATSE signatory project. But since union transportation coordinators do not have the duty of driving vehicles, the salary is generally negotiable, though they may not be paid less than the lowest paid full-time driver employed on the production. This policy allows Teamster drivers to elevate themselves to the responsible position of transportation coordinators if they have the skills and knowledge required.

Teamsters primarily drive. Although the Teamsters local also includes animal wranglers and mechanics, it primarily covers the drivers of vehicles used on productions. Once the vehicle has reached its destination, the driver waits until it is time to again move the vehicle. If your project is an IATSE signatory make sure your production manager and your production accountant understand the details regarding the Teamster locals since they are complicated and vary from region to region.

If your project is not a signatory to IATSE—depending on the size and complexity of the project—a three-person Transportation Department will probably suffice. However, ideally one of the two crew people should be a certified and trained mechanic as it will aid in reducing the possibility of Murphy's Law adversely affecting the project.

Nevertheless it will be impossible for these three-people to drive all of the production company's vehicles from location to location. Therefore you should designate onset production assistants, grips or electricians as drivers and give them an additional weekly bonus or "crew bump" for this service. Your production manager and transportation coordinator must make sure that the assigned driver has the appropriate drivers license, knows how to drive the vehicle and does so safely. It is not a smart policy to have multiple

Acct. #	Account Name	Units	Rate	Amount	Sub Total	Total
3200	TRANSPORTATION DEPARTMENT					
01	Transportation Coordinator					
	Prepare					
	Shoot					
	Wrap					
02	Driver Coordinator (IATSE)					
	Prepare					
	Shoot					
	Wrap					
03	Drivers					
	Prepare					
	Shoot					
	Wrap					
04	Driver/Mechanic					
	Prepare					
	Shoot					
	Wrap					
05	Crew/Driver Bumps					
06	Labor Overtime					
07	Vehicle Rental (Detail attached)					
08	Dressing Room Rental					
09	Fuel					
10	Special Equipment Purchase	Allow				
11	Special Equipment Rental	Allow				
12	Transportation Taxes and Permits					
13	Mileage Allowance					
14	Repairs and Maintenance					
50	Other					
	Total 3200					

Figure 31

drivers for a specific vehicle; try to maintain the same driver for the vehicle throughout the production. This will keep you in the clear should there be any claims under your producers' package vehicle insurance policy.

Besides necessary production vehicles to transport people, other basic vehicles required for production are a grip/electric truck with a lift gate, a wardrobe vehicle, a camera vehicle and a prop vehicle. Of course, you may add to, or remove from, this caravan depending on the size and demands of the production.

The Transportation Department is also responsible for ensuring that mobile dressing rooms on location are clean and in place. Dressing rooms are also called star wagons or honeywagons and are contracted from independent rental companies. They are pulled by a truckcab and consist of a trailer with one or more small separate rooms, each with its own entrance. Latrines used by the production crew are found at the back end of the trailer. Usually the person from the contracting company brings the honeywagon to the location and stays with it for the entire day of production to assist with its maintenance. The Screen Actors Guild requires each actor to have a separate dressing room or place where they can get away from the confusion of the set. The same rooms on these wagons may be used for several actors during a shooting day, depending on when each are called for work and the time each finishes. The 2nd AD closely monitors this schedule from the production board and works out the dressing room assignments with transportation.

In some instances you may wish to provide motor homes as dressing rooms for your principle actors. This may be a requirement in the actors' contract or something you provide for the actors' comfort. This can be costly.

— • • • —

On The Clonus Horror *I contacted a senior organization in order to rent five motor homes from their members. (Senior citizens are the largest group of people in the United States to own and use motor homes.) My insurance package provided insurance for the vehicles, and I offered each owner $250 a week, guaranteeing that each motor home would be occupied by one of the main leads in the project. Appealing to their ego, I further invited them to visit the location, meet the actors and have lunch with the production company. I had no problem finding the motor homes. We had to provide drivers for the motor homes while we were using them, and transportation had the responsibility of maintaining them. The seniors were happy with the additional rental income and the actors were happy having their motor homes. And I was happy because it was a cost-effective transaction which translated to happy actors giving the director a creative performance.*

— • • • —

A transportation crew often solves problems before the producer and director are even made aware of them. When they are doing their job, they are thinking ahead. They must always consider Murphy's Law as their nemesis, since almost anything that happens during a production will impact transportation. *Therefore, you must make sure that the budget allows for any special equipment that might be needed.* On one project, I had a director decide to shoot an unscheduled scene using a grip as stunt driver for the sports utility vehicle we were using as a picture car. (The scene was originally scheduled on a day when the stunt coordinator was working.) The result was disastrous. The SUV got stuck in the mud and the more the grip tried to get it free, the deeper it went. The production manager and transportation coordinator called in a tow truck to pull it free. By the time the tow truck was hooked to the SUV, it was up to its floorboards in mud. The tow truck tried to raise the SUV, and the suction was so powerful that it pulled the tow truck into the mud. So the transportation coordinator brought in a second tow truck and together (with the first tow truck) they were able to raise the SUV from the mud. Murphy's Law! Be ready for it!

LOCATIONS

Location Manager (IATSE Teamsters Local 399 *Los Angeles*, Local 385 or 390 *Florida*, Local 714 *Chicago*, Local 85 *San Francisco*, Local 817 *New York*)

The Locations Department is another breeding ground for Murphy's Law. It is common to find appropriations in LOCATION EXPENSE to solve or prevent problems that might arise. The location manager must not only be creative, but also a master of organization and detail. A location manager first reads the project, then meets with the producer and director to discuss its locations. Creative location managers will also discuss production problems and parameters with the production manager. Once the producer has determined the geographical location of the project, the location manager, armed with the creative concepts and production parameters, begins the tedious search to find several options for each of the discussed locations. The location manager considers not only what may work creatively for the story, but also what may appear to work logistically for production. Creative location managers may make suggestions to the producer or director if they come across an interesting and cost effective location with picture value and that might work for the project. They research possible locations using information from their network of relationships, or from sources like film commissioners, real estate agents and Internet web sites. They get in a car and drive around with a cinematographer's eye for the image. Location managers generally scout around armed with a panorama view still camera, a digital still camera, and a Polaroid camera. Some even use a video camera. They must bring back the visual and practical information for the creative and logistical production teams to accurately and efficiently make choices to scout. Through this initial work of the location manager, the production team then scouts the possible locations.

The location manager also considers locations in relationships to the production board. When Costa-Gavras was preparing *Mad City*, his location manager scouted the television studio at UCLA. The location manager discovered that the location was ideal for Costa-Gavras because the studio could be seen from the control room. This was something the director specifically wanted since the studio was supposed to be a small television station studio where Dustin Hoffman was a news reporter. When the loca-

Acct. #	Account Name	Units	Rate	Amount	Sub Total	Total
3300	LOCATION EXPENSES					
01	Location Manager					
	Prep					
	Shoot					
	Wrap					
02	Below-the-line Production Travel					
03	Below-the-line Production Hotels/Motels					
04	Below-the-line Per diems					
05	Meals On Location					
06	Location Site Rentals (see attached)	Allow				
07	Local Location Connection					
08	Location Production Assistants					
09	Policemen, Firemen, Security					
10	Labor Overtime					
11	Location Scout Expenses					
12	Production Office Rent					
13	Office Equipment Rentals					
	Computer Rentals					
	Internet Hookups					
	Fax and Copier Machines					
	Other					
14	Amenity Payments	Allow				
15	Cellular Telephones					
16	Hard Line Phones on Location					
17	Shipping and Postal	Allow				
18	Film Shipment	Allow				
19	Location Permits	Allow				
20	Foreign Travel Permits	Allow				
21	Export Taxes	Allow				
22	Custom Fees, Duties	Allow				
23	Flight Insurance	Allow				
24	Government Censors	Allow				
25	Interpreters	Allow				
50	Other					
	Total 3300					

Figure 32

tion manager originally scouted the studio and took photographs, he found adjacent hallways and entranceways that could be used for other scenes in the movie. It also helped that the dressing rooms and equipment trucks could be parked near the building. When Costa-Gavras, the producer, the production manager, director of photography, gaffer, key grip and production designer visited the site, they artistically and logistically agreed with the location manager.

Once the locations have been selected, the location manager arranges all the clearances and details for their use with the appropriate owners and authorities, and arranges for the necessary security (if the production company or the location requires it). The complexity of these tasks requires the location manager to work with local and state government officials, the pro-

duction manager, the transportation coordinator, the production accountant, the producer, the assistant to the producer and a variety of other people
who might tangentially be involved. Therefore, you should have a location
manager who has the patience of Job and the diplomatic skills of Kissinger.
The location manager stays with the project throughout the production
process. In some instances, you may want to assign a production assistant to
work with the location manager, or employ a local location contact, as the
work often gets quite complicated and the poor or untimely results of the
location manager's work will have a direct impact on the production.

Travel, Hotels, Per Diems

The production philosophy will be reflected in the area of travel, hotels and
per diems for below-the-line crewmembers. If the project requires production in a geographical region different than your production base, you may
decide that you will arrange for all or a portion of your crew to travel to the
region. If you travel with only a portion of the crew you are deciding either
to use a smaller crew or pick up local people as crew. Your production board
will help you with this decision. Guidelines for travel, housing and per
diems are provided in all union and guild contracts. Common sense, personal respect and dignity should be the guideline for nonunion crews.
Coach air travel is perfectly acceptable, and airlines often have special lower
rates if you fulfill certain requirements (such as travelling at certain times,
advanced booking, or purchasing multiple tickets). These discounts are
good to have, but they can also be a problem since the tickets may not be
refundable or may have a penalty attached should they need to be changed.
The travel of crew personnel can be in a continual state of flux, so consider
all travel arrangements carefully.

Housing on location should also be a consideration. IATSE crew members
each must have their own rooms according to the IATSE agreement.
Although it is acceptable to put two people to a room on a nonunion project, you should remember that crew people may want to get away from one
another at the end of a long production day and may welcome having individual hotel or motel rooms. If you do decide to put two people to a room to
save a few dollars, make sure you ask the crew members if it is all right with
them and give them a chance to choose their own roommate from the crew.
However, regardless what you do with the rest of the crew, make sure that the
director, cinematographer and production manager have private rooms.

Per diem (translated from the Latin means *per day*), is the money you pay
each member of the crew for meals each day they are away from home due

to your project. A set amount would be decided for breakfast, one for lunch and one for dinner. If you feed a meal during the shooting day, deduct for that meal. As an example, if the per diem is $10 for breakfast, $20 for lunch and $30 for dinner, then the total daily per diem will be $60. For a week, it would be $420. But, you feed a lunch to the production six of the seven days of the week, then the weekly per diem would be $300.

Your production board will let you know the statistics relating to travel, hotel and per diems to help you calculate the precise amount needed.

Meals on Location

The meals you serve on location during production are very important to the morale of your production. The quality and creativity of each meal will have a direct affect on the results in a shooting day. Serving a meal is not a requirement in the industry, but it is a practice. Producers provide meals to the production crew only on location for one very good reason: to save valuable production time. When a meal is served near the set, the crew knows that it will be ready when they need it and the producer can relax knowing that no time will be wasted in getting a crew to and from a set location on time. Also, when the serving of the meal is coordinated with the production of the day, the production manager is able to manage the distribution of the meal to the needs of production. The meal that is served in the middle of the production day should be a "sit down" meal. That is to say, a meal at which people stop working and sit and eat. The Screen Actors Guild requires its members to have a sit down meal within six hours of their members' call time. This is a good policy to adhere to for crew members as well. The meal period begins when the last person has gone through the meal line, so to save time it is common for part of the crew (those not busy) to begin eating before the production has broken for the meal. SAG requires that a sit down second meal be fed to their members' six hours after the first meal ends. However, since many times the second meal comes close to the wrap time of a shooting day, the crew often opts for the second meal to be a "walking" meal. This is usually food that can be eaten while they are working. You only need to feed those people who work before and after the scheduled meal. Some people on your production may be called into work after the scheduled meal and some may complete their work before the company breaks for its meal. You may want to do the honorable thing and invite the people excused before this meal to eat with the company anyway. They worked, so they deserve to eat.

The meal served on location should be of excellent quality. Although there are many ways to cater a meal on location, a motion picture catering company knows the importance of the quality of the food expected by the crew and its success to the day's production. Motion picture catering experts also know the portion sizes for a hungry film crew. A normal menu would consist of at least two entrees, five salads, starches, two beverages, soup, several deserts and bread and butter. There should always be a vegetarian dish and the food should be prepared with an idea towards maintaining the energy of the company. Caterers will often do thematic meals, such as a luau or barbecue. They even provide decorated cakes to celebrate birthdays and other occasions.

The caterer eventually becomes part of the production family and learns and caters to the tastes of the various crew personalities. A meal will cost you anywhere from $7.50 to $15.50 a person, including the set up of tables and chairs. You will pay extra for the catering staff. If you choose to use restaurant caterers, make sure the restaurant provides *enough* food. Usually restaurant menus are fixed and they run out of food because it is not portioned out as in a restaurant. You may, however, find that this is suitable with smaller crews.

The production board will help determine the number of meals you need each day. It will also tell you if there is a probability of a second meal on any particular day. Rarely do you feed the company three meals in one day. You only need to provide a "walking breakfast" if an actor or a member of the company is called to work before 6:00 a.m. Although craft service usually has bagels, fruit, toast and coffee for anyone who may want it, this is not considered a breakfast. Whatever you decide about meals remember the quality of the meal is most important. Tainted or poorly prepared food can cause sickness in your company and affect your production, and bad tasting food serves only to make your crew cranky and edgy.

Location Site Rentals

You must make sure that you have enough resources for the rental of locations. Although you should try to make the best deals possible, the budget you prepare is a guide and should be prepared as if there were no deals. Even if you decide to make the project in another state or country (because of the dollar exchange or other benefits), you will still need to rent locations. So, although you don't have to spend it all, make sure that you have the resources budgeted for that purpose. Make sure that your location agreement has clauses in it in case you need to prepare the location in any way for the shoot. The rate you pay for preparation and wrap at the location should be less than the rate you pay for production. It is also important that you include a clause in the agreement that permits you to come back to the location at the same rate you paid when you first used it for production. If you do not have that agreement up front, the location owner may increase the rate if you need to come back for any reason. Everything must be in writing and structured as a binding contract. The location owner can always turn you away or give you problems but with a written agreement you have appropriate recourse in a court of law for any recoverable loss or expenses.

Be creative when looking for locations, since locations can be other than what they appear to be on film. As an example, it may be difficult to get a real courthouse lobby—but perhaps the lobby of a public library or an office building with federal architecture will work with the proper set dressing and atmosphere.

Not only do you have to consider the look of the location, but also how the location works within the schedule. Most projects will have one or two primary locations that are critical to the story. These are usually the locations in which a lot of the story takes place. The production will probably be scheduled to stay in those locations for several days, possibly for weeks. Other locations may only be seen a few times in the story. You should first find the primary locations and then look nearby for any secondary locations. This will help when you finalize the production board and schedule. You can always make the shoe fit the foot and rewrite the script to adjust for secondary locations that might be near the primary locations you secured. It doesn't make sense to move the production company for smaller sequences when it may be possible to adjust these locations for the production schedule. I was presented with this problem in *Hunter's Blood*. Although the picture starts out in Oklahoma and moves to Arkansas, I decided to shoot the picture in Los Angeles. The problem was finding locales that could stand in for both the Oklahoma countryside and woods of Arkansas. We searched all over the Los Angeles area trying to keep it within the fifty-mile studio zone radius so we would not have to travel or house people on a distant location. There were three important locations in the story and I knew I had to find those first. One was a campsite that would be the hunters' camp. Another was the poachers' cabin that needed to have a backwoods rural feeling. The third was the poachers' gully, which had to look like it was hidden deep in the woods. After weeks of searching in the obvious woodsy areas around Los Angeles, we called a backlot company near Valencia, California, and explained what we needed. This was just on the outskirts of the fifty mile radius. The location contact for the company took us out to an undeveloped part of the property to show us woods that closely matched the kind of woods we would find in Arkansas. The minute I saw this location I knew we could shoot our project in Los Angeles. While driving around that area the location contact pointed out a very large 200-year-old tree that was isolated and had an ominous look. This was to be our poachers' gully. About one hundred yards away, the location contact showed us a riverbed that he said would be a raging river with the right rain. I thought it would help sell the location if we were able to use the riverbed in some way and I knew that the director could easily find a suitable place near it that could be dressed as the hunters' camp. The third location was still a problem. I told the contact what was needed for the poachers' cabin. We drove to another part of the area and he showed me a rural cabin on stilts in what looked to be a dry weeded piece of land. He told me that they could flood the area and the cabin would then appear to be sitting on stilts in a wooded swamp. Perfect! The cabin was surrounded by woods. The projects' breakdown had many scenes in the woods. And since a tree is a tree is a tree (at least for the purpose of this production), I knew that nearby the cabin we had choices for many of our secondary and tertiary locations.

The production board also told me that we needed to find other important locations and though they were used only once they were more difficult to find. The trick was in finding them so the project could be shot in twenty-two days. Two secondary locations in particular presented a problem. One was a rural bar, both interior and exterior, the other was a rural gas station where the hunters stop for gas and where Sam Bottoms places a call to his girlfriend (played by Kim Delaney), asking that she meet him the next evening. Right behind the tree we were going to use for the poachers' gully, but hidden by woods, was an empty tin-roofed shed. I turned to the art director and asked what he could do with this structure. In no time flat, and with a minimum of rented set dressing, we had our rural bar. Near the same area we spotted a Western town circa 1880. With a little imagination, the rental of gas pumps and an agreement with the director that he not stage the scene in one particular direction, we had our rural gas station.

Finally the story called for the hunters to escape the area by water. We were hoping for rain so they could make their escape by the river. But (as Murphy's Law would have it) we did not have enough rain that season to completely fill the riverbed. However, railroad tracks and a freight train were nearby. This gave us the opportunity to change the escape to a train and devise an exciting stunt in which Lee DeBroux (as the lead bad guy) falls sixty feet to his death. Although we budgeted $25,000 for site rentals, everything—including the train and the labor to run it—cost $17,000. Not bad for a picture whose total budget was $750,000. They even bulldozed a road for us to get back into the woods.

In *The Clonus Horror* we had an escape that had to be devised for our clone hero. I didn't have any idea how we were going to do it or find all the locations to sell the escape. Robert Fiveson, the director, told me not to worry about it. As he scouted locations he had decided he would create the action: find the alleyways, open fields and drainage pipes that we needed to sell an exciting escape. I didn't have a notion how we were going to pull it off, but we had our collaborative creative vision of the story and I put my faith in his ability to make it work brilliantly. Although I saw the strips on the production board and saw the footage during our dailies, I couldn't fathom how it would cut together as an exciting chase sequence, but Robert did an astounding job. Inventive thinking in the use of locations will bring creativity to the project. Don't be afraid to be inventive.

Further Location Expenses

You may need a distant location production office or a local production office for the project. The office will require such equipment as fax and copier machines, and Internet access. The use of the Internet is becoming a standard situation in producing and you should plan for its use. It is used for e-mail communication, instant messaging, research, purchasing and sometimes the viewing of footage. The computer has replaced the typewriter and you will have to supply location and production planning staff with computers by either buying or renting them. Some of your staff will be better served with laptop computers since a lot of their work is away from the production or location office. This is the communication millennium so you will need to arrange for cellular phones as well. Make sure that the phone service reaches all the areas you need. Nothing is worse than a mobile phone that cuts out in the middle of a conversation.

During production you will find the need for amenity payments. Simply put, these are payoffs. Your director may be shooting on a street and one of the residents will decide to mow his lawn just as the camera is about to roll. Your production manager can use every power of persuasion with the resident but an amenity payment may be the final solution.

Other factors affecting location shoots are dependent on the structure of the production. If you are shooting the project a distance from the processing laboratory but editing at the location, you will need to make arrangements for shipping and transporting the film or video transfers to and from the lab. If you are shooting in a foreign country, you may have to work with a customs broker to purchase flight insurance, work with government censors or require an interpreter. The location cost center will reflect the producing structure of your project. Creative thinking in this area is critical.

STAGES AND STUDIOS

Chapter six discusses the possibility of set construction for your project. If that is the direction you are going with all or a portion of the project, then you will need a space in which to put the sets once they have been built. In major cities, where production is an industry, there are spaces all over. These may be film stages and studios, converted warehouses or lofts on the outskirts of town. They have sprung up all over because of music video, industrial and commercial industries. The advantage in using these spaces is that they provide a controlled environment for your film or video production. They have been sound-proofed and have the electrical power, air conditioning, heating, and the accoutrements of comfort that are necessary for a production. Their downside will be their cost, limited availability, and the need for separate crews to set up, rig lights, and strike the set when finished. In addition, you may be required to use their equipment or union people.

Sometimes it is necessary to use a space *like* a stage, where a bit of imagination can turn a high school gymnasium, auditorium stage, or even a circus tent into a production facility. Unless the need for a stage is obvious, sometimes the production board and the requirements of the story will direct you towards using a stage space. *Coming of Age*, a project that is currently in development, has thirty-two pages of the story taking place in a college dormitory room. As the director of the project I want to use practical locations for the picture. After many months of planning, the production

Acct. #	Account Name	Units	Rate	Amount	Sub Total	Total
3400	STAGE /STUDIO EXPENSES					
01	Local Stage or Studio Rental					
02	Distant Stage or Studio Rental					
03	Supplementary Stage or Studio Facilities					
04	Process Stage Production					
05	Required Studio Personnel					
06	Purchases					
07	Rentals					
50	Other					
	Total 3400					

Figure 33

designer and cinematographer have convinced me otherwise. The cinematographer said he could do a much more creative job of visually interpreting the story if the walls of the dorm room could be "wild." (Wild walls are not weight-bearing, but instead are walls that can be moved independently to suit the needs of production.) I got to thinking about it and realized that movable walls would also allow more flexibility in the staging. And because there are some fairly emotional scenes in the dorm room, the actors might also feel more comfortable working in a more controlled environment. So the project is being planned for seven or eight days of production on a stage. The design of the room will be specific to the staging and the final result will match the texture and details of a practical location.

Some projects may require the use of a blue- or greenscreen stage for photographic effects. Chapter 5 discussed effects that might be needed to create the story. Either a first unit production team or a second unit production team can do process photography. This would depend on the desired final result. If actors are to speak, develop their characters and their relationships in the structure of the sequence, then more than likely the first unit will do the process work. It is then handed off to a digital effects house, which has the task of marrying it to a background or foreground image for inclusion in the story. If it is just the process that needs to be photographed (without character development), a second unit may be used. In *Star Trek: The Next Generation*, a second unit team was employed to do the transporting effects with the actors, but the first unit would do any sequence when they move or speak after they have been beamed aboard.

In *The Girl, the Gold Watch and Everything*, which was produced before the development of digital technology, we scheduled work on a bluescreen process stage as first unit. In the story the real world stops at the beach, at a boat marina and in the interior of a yacht when the actors use the watch to move into the world of stopped time. I decided we would do the effects by marrying film negative with tape transferred to film negative using an experimental video format (at the time), of 655 lines at 24 frames a second. The director was not familiar with video, bluescreen or film matting processes. I had the sequences storyboarded so everyone on the creative production team knew what shot was to be film and what shot was to be tape transferred to film. I brought Emory Cohen and Leon Silverman (now of Lazer Pacific Media Corporation), and Bob Ringer of Ringer Tape Transfer together with the technicians from the film laboratory to figure out how to make it work. Together we came up with the following plan: The director would shoot on film the storyboarded shots and the background plates for the bluescreen stage. When we transferred the film background plates to tape in preparation for the bluescreen stage, we removed the electronic focus on the image.[1] Then in preparation for the bluescreen process the cinematographer (Jacques Haitkin) recalculated the television camera lens to match the film camera lens of the background plate. A video truck was brought in to the bluescreen stage with the machines that would record in 655/24. When we played back the out-of-focus background plates now on tape, and matted in action with the actors against a bluescreen, we recorded the action in 655/24 removing the electronic focus once again. Then we brought Bob Ringer the married image of the background plate and the foreground bluescreen action and had it transferred back to film adding the electronic focus to the married image. It worked, and at 1/6th the cost and time of doing it all on film. Digital technology would go on to change the way it would be done today, of course. However, no matter how it is done, the bottom line is always the story. It is and must be your motivating factor. Technology doesn't change the story, just the way we tell it.

SECOND UNIT PRODUCTION

Second unit has been mentioned several times. A second unit team is a mini production unit that has specific tasks to accomplish towards the creative storytelling of the project. It may include some or all of the departments indicated in Figure #34. This would depend on what is required of second unit. Sometimes this crew works simultaneously with first unit—especially when the second unit is being used to alleviate a backup in the production schedule of the first unit. In those instances you should make sure that there is close communication between the cinematographers and directors of both units to ensure the creative continuity needed for the project.

Sometimes a second unit is needed after the first unit has completed production. In those instances, the second unit is working specifically on sequences that will be worked into the project. They may be action like the aerial sequences in *Top Gun* or they may be establishing sequences like the wide angle shots of the *Thelma & Louise* car as it travels cross-country. Your project may require shooting certain sequences in a miniature set for digital inclusion with main action, or a stand alone sequence, like the destruction of Los Angeles in *Volcano*. Whatever the reasons, a second production unit

---

[1] The very fine focus in video is through the electronics of video to enhance the focus of the optics of a camera lens.

Acct. #	Account Name	Units	Rate	Amount	Sub Total	Total
3500	SECOND UNIT, & MINIATURES					
01	Production Staff					
02	Cast					
03	Extras					
04	Set Construction					
05	Set Striking					
06	Set Dressing					
07	Properties					
08	Camera					
09	Sound					
10	Set Operations					
11	Electrical					
12	Wardrobe *Mens* *Womens*					
13	Makeup and Hair					
14	Locations					
15	Transportation					
16	Special Effects					
17	Purchases	Allow				
18	Rentals	Allow				
50	Other					
	Total 3500					

Figure 34

creatively is guided by the your vision and the vision of the director. The creative process is always a collaborative one.

PRODUCTION FILM—TAPE LABORATORY
Production Link to Post-production Decisions
Your project will either be shot in film, videotape or digitally, and technology may yet find new ways of recording your project. You must determine the post-production process of your project in the planning stage and it must be reflected in your budget when detailing the process flow. There are several paths that you can take, all of which follow different procedures but end up with the same results (see Figure #35). Each path has its own fiscal upsides and creative downsides that will be discussed in the next chapter.

Figure #35 shows the various paths starting with the origination of the material. Figure #36 allows for the planning for any of these paths.

Originate on Film Shoot **1**	Develop Negative	Print Dailies	Edit dailies on Film	**Conform Original Negative – Answer Print**		
Originate on Film Shoot **2**	Develop Negative	Transfer Negative to Video through Telecine Process	Digital Nonlinear Editing	**Conform Original Negative from non linear edit – Answer Print**		
Originate on Film Shoot **3**	Develop Negative	Print Dailies	Transfer Dailies (positive) to Video through Telecine Process	Digital Nonlinear Editing	Conform Dailies to digital non-linear edit	**Conform Original Negative – Answer Print**
Originate on Film Shoot **4**	Develop Negative	Transfer Negative to Video through Telecine Process	Digital Non- Linear Editing	Print and conform only Dailies that conform to final digital edit	**Conform Original Negative – Answer Print**	
Originate in Video Shoot **5**	Digital Nonlinear Editing	Original Video conformed to final digital edit. **Final Product in Video**	Or **Transfer final video to film – Answer Print**			

Figure 35

Acct. #	Account Name	Footage	Rate	Amount	Sub Total	Total
3600	**Production Film & Laboratory**					
01	Picture Negative					
	Tape Stock for Digital Video					
02	Process – Develop Film Neg					
	Forced Develop Film Neg					
	1 Light Dailies - Film					
	Timed Dailies - Film					
	Telecine Film Negative					
	Telecine Film Positive					
	Sales Tax *(everything in 01 and 02 is taxable)*					
03	Special Lab Work					
04	Stills- Neg & Lab					
05	Sound Trans. Dailies					
	Labor					
	Mag Stripe					
06	Tape Stock for Video Transfer					
50	Other Charges					
	Total 3600 Detail					

Figure 36

Picture Negative

The volume of picture or film negative you purchase (and use) for the project will have a major impact on the budget. This is determined by the shooting ratio. Shooting ratio is the quantity of film that needs to be shot to realize one foot of film finally used in the project. As an example, if you are shooting a 35mm film that will be approximately ninety minutes in length and the shooting ratio is 10 to 1, you will be purchasing slightly less than

82,000 feet of negative film stock. (1000 ft of 35mm = approximately 11 minutes.)

If you are shooting 16mm film with the same shooting ratio you will be purchasing approximately 35,000 feet of negative film stock. (400 ft of 16mm = approximately 11 minutes.) *The shooting ratio should be your barometer for maintaining your directors' fiscal responsibility towards the project.* The more film stock used, the more time it takes to use it, and the more it will cost to process. There are camera techniques like dolly shots, Steadicam and multiple camera sequences that use up a lot of film. Your director's style and creative approach to the project will have a direct impact on your time and budget. So be sure to discuss the shooting ratio very carefully with the director and cinematographer and plan accordingly. If you have a completion bond on the project, the bonding company may require that you strictly adhere to the stated ratio. This is one of the reasons why the production report on each day of shooting indicates the amount of footage shot both that day and up to that day; the information is used as a budgetary yardstick.

Kodak, Ilford and Fuji are the major manufacturers of motion picture film (Ilford is used extensively in Europe, especially for black and white film). Your cinematographer should be familiar with the technical differences between the brands. You can purchase the stock from the company for its retail list price, or there are companies that offer discount rates on film stock. You can also arrange a comfortable discount rate from the manufacturer but it may not be as favorable as the rate you can get from other discounters. Many discount companies buy back unopened leftover stock and resell it at a discounted rate. However, the stock may be short ends or from different manufacturing batch numbers. Short ends consist of the leftover film stock from full camera rolls that have been used. The unused portion is removed from the camera and repacked for sale or use at a later time. Short ends limit your director if he or she was planning on using long camera takes. Different batch numbers also pose a slight risk of affecting the color timing of the final product. Also, although the stock may be unopened, you are never quite sure how the stock was stored before it was sold to the discount company. Many producers generally have a positive experience with these discount companies, but you should take this into account. Purchasing stock from a discount house can also have an impact on the faulty stock insurance you may purchase for the project. However you wind up purchasing the film stock, you should budget using the list rate from the manufacturer. If you get a discount on its purchase, you can apply the savings elsewhere in the budget.

Developing The Film

Generally you should budget the same amount of film negative to develop as you do to purchase. If you decide to make a positive of the selected printed dailies, then the amount of footage budgeted will vary with the millimeter film stock you use. A *one light daily* is a positive print of what is shot each day of the production. If you are shooting 35mm film, 75 percent of the total footage you purchase should be budgeted for a one light daily process. When processing 35mm, motion picture laboratories, although developing all of the film, only print the circled takes indicated on the camera report. Circled takes are the takes of each shot that the director has determined to be the best performances of both the actor and the camera. If you are shooting 16mm film, budget 100 percent of the total footage you purchased for a one light daily process, because motion picture laboratories develop and print all of the film in the 16mm daily process.

Typical dailies are named "one light" because the laboratory picks one timing light in the process and uses that as a basis for making the positive daily print. Do not worry if it doesn't look as you expected. The important thing is the density (thickness) of the negative and its ability to be properly color timed at the end of the process. If there are any questions about the color timing capacity of a sequence, you can always order a timed daily (which of course costs more). The question of color timing is considered during the production phase so you are able to re-shoot a sequence if it eventually cannot be color timed appropriately. If you find this information out after the production period, it will cost you more money to resolve the problem than timing the daily during production. Of course the notion of budgeting either 75 percent or 100 percent of the film footage is applicable only if you use post-production paths #1 and #3 indicated in Figure #35. If you choose path #4, then you only have to budget for positive daily film footage that corresponds to your final length of the film project plus an additional percentage (anywhere from 50 percent to 300 percent). This is because the entire take needs to be printed even if only a small piece of it is used in the final edit.

Your director, cinematographer, editor and you must all see the daily footage every day of production either it be on film or tape. You must not wait until the project has completed shooting before processing dailies or transferring to video to see the dailies. If you want to save money, you can choose to print the dailies on film only for the first few days or weeks of the production—to assure that the director and cinematographer are on track with their creative vision—and then see the remainder of the dailies in video. If you make that decision, make sure your cinematographer talks to the technician at the processing lab each day to ensure the quality of the developed negative.

Telecine Transfer

If you choose path #2, #3 or #4 in Figure #35 you will have to transfer your film to video through a telecine process. The video will then be digitized into a nonlinear editing system. Make sure you check the rates with the laboratory for the telecine process. They are competitive and will depend on what you require for the transfer. For example, if you want to transfer sound with the picture, it will cost more than if they only transfer the picture. This decision must be thought through carefully, because, if you transfer only the picture, the assistant editor will have to spend time during the edit process synching up the sound. This may delay the edit process. You will be faced with these decisions of time to money and its impact on creativity throughout your producing career. Time versus money becomes even more critical during the post-production process (and will be discussed further in the next chapter).

Sound Transfer

If you decide to follow path #1 in Figure #35, then you will need to transfer your production sound to magnetic stripe film. The amount of magnetic stripe film you budget should be about the same as the amount of printed film. The labor and transfer process for the production sound should be part of the bid by your post-production sound company.

Determining the film, tape and laboratory issues of your project affects the post-production and vice versa. Look to the End Result Use of the final project to help guide you.

TESTS—MAKING SURE YOU ARE READY TO SHOOT

It may be necessary to do tests of one sort or another before you start shooting the project. At the very least, you should test the camera equipment by shooting 50 to 100 feet of film and having the lab process it. In addition, you should test any visuals you might be unsure of before you start production. This may include testing out a visual design process, screen testing the actors to assure if they are right for the role, or may include testing film stock to

Acct. #	Account Name	Units	Rate	Amount	Sub Total	Total
3700	TESTS					
01	Stage Rental					
02	Equipment Rental					
03	Crew					
04	Lab Processing					
05	Projection					
06	Purchases					
50	Other					
	Total 3700					

Figure 37

determine which is best suited for the project. It is better to test and be sure than to discover problems later.

BELOW-THE-LINE FRINGE—PRODUCTION PERIOD
Creative Budget Protection #4

The below-the-line fringe of the production period reflects the structure of the below-the-line labor of production. If you are planning the project as a Directors Guild signatory, you will have to budget 12.5 percent of the below-the-line DGA gross payroll for pension, health and welfare (5.5 percent for the pension plan and 7 percent for the welfare plan). If the End Result Use of the project is for theatrical release, there is a salary ceiling of $200,000 for the pension plan and $250,000 for the welfare plan. You will also need to budget for vacation and holiday at 7.719 percent of gross wages for DGA personnel. (Four percent for vacation and 3.719 percent for holiday). This is required only for the below-the-line DGA personnel.

If the project is a signatory to IATSE, you must budget 4 percent for vacation and 3.719 percent for holiday, for a total of 7.719 percent as a payment based upon all gross below-the-line IATSE salaries. However the IATSE percentage to the pension, health and welfare plans vary depending on the craft local, and are not as easily calculated as it is for guilds. Many craft unions are based on a certain amount per hour with a twelve hour day per employee maximum, plus certain daily charges. You will have to consult the rate book of the IATSE for the precise amounts. For budgeting purposes you should be relatively safe if you budget 16 percent for a project shot in Los Angeles, 19 percent for one shot in New York and 12 percent for Florida. If you are using a nonunion crew, the pension, health and welfare and vacation and holiday payments do not apply. But, as in the case of above-the-line wages, you will be liable for the employers' share of payroll taxes for all below-the-

Acct. #	Account Name	Amount	Computed Rate	Sub Total	Total
3800	**FRINGE BENEFITS Below-the-Line Production Period**				
01	D.G.A. Pension Health Welfare		12.5%		
02	D.G.A. Vacation and Holiday		7.719%		
03	IATSE Pension Health Welfare		16%		
04	IATSE Vacation and Holiday		7.719%		
04	Payroll Taxes		17%		
	Computed on $				
	Total 3800				

Figure 38

line production wages. This was discussed in Chapter 5 under "Employers Tax Obligations."

Here again you are creating *a fourth method of providing fiscal security to protect against possible budget overages.* As in the case of above-the-line, the employer's share for below-the-line payroll taxes can go into an interest-bearing account before making the payments to the appropriate government agencies. Once the payments are made, the interest remains in the account. The same holds true for payments for pension, health and welfare, vacation and holiday. These payments do not have to be made until the end of the work assignment. Therefore, as payroll is met weekly on the project, you may want to transfer the additional funds into the same interest-bearing account until it is time to make the payments. This will generate additional resources through the earned interest, which can then be applied elsewhere, should the need arise.

———— • • • ————

Recently I cut a picture for a producer who had to deal with an executive (the wife of the head of the studio) who was at considerable odds with the director. The producer's task was to honor the executive's opinions (which, though cinematically naive, were not without insight), while at the same time protecting the director's vision for the picture. He also had to beat off "friendly" interference from the composer, the writer, the director of photography, his co-producers—and of course from me—all without stifling appropriate contribution and creating dangerous battlegrounds. From my Avid-side perspective, the creative producer is the film's enabler—and its ultimate friend and protector.

—Robert Gordon, Editor, *Toy Story, The Blue Lagoon, Return of the Living Dead, Girl in a Swing*

———— • • • ————

CHAPTER 8   THE EDITING PERIOD

The editing period should begin even before the first day of principle photography. The interplay between the post-production process and the production process begins during production through the marked script notes, the continuity log and continual communication between the editor, the director and the producer.

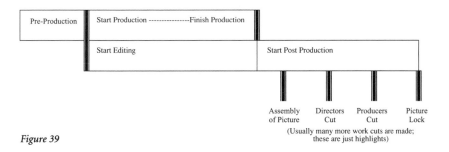

Figure 39

PICTURE EDIT—PART I

During production, the editorial staff monitors the path of the original material through the laboratory and, if need be, synchs the sound with the picture for screening of dailies. *Dailies must be seen each day during production either on film or video. Do not wait until the end of production to see the footage. It will be too late to make any corrections or repair any problems.* The picture editor should be present at the screening of dailies, along with the director and producer, so montage assembly ideas are exchanged and considered. While the director continues with production the editor should assemble the footage into a linear story. The assembled scenes, which contain all dialogue and action, are usually screened by the director to see how they conform to his or her vision. This way, any missing shots the director may have overlooked can be picked up without affecting the budget. Shortly after the completion of production the editor should have an assembly of the project ready for you and the director to see. You should then give the director time to work with the editor to deliver the director's cut. If your project is a DGA signatory, the director is entitled to a "director's cut" which you view with temporary sound effects and music to provide you with the full intention of the director's creative interpretation of the vision. After viewing the director's cut, you may want to make further changes before locking or finalizing the picture edit of the project. Once the picture has been locked it is then (and only then) that the major creative sound work begins. Up until that time, you, the editor and the director may be thinking about the elements of sound or you may have asked your sound designer to provide temporary effects and your composer temporary music, but the actual work cannot be started until the picture is locked. By locking picture you are determining the specific lengths of the scenes and the feel of the story. This will make up the map for the creative use of sound.

The post-production process has a creative magic unto itself. But it is only as effective as the material provided from production. What is not shot, you cannot use.

Again, "*What you don't do (or plan for) in pre-production will affect you in production and what you don't do in production will affect you in post-production.*" The old expression "we can fix it in the mix" comes from not adhering to that truth or from not thinking through the end result when planning out the project. And once again, fixing a problem is always going to be more expensive (and less creative) than preventing one.

POST-PRODUCTION PROCESS DECISIONS

In the last chapter Figure #35 indicated four separate paths in the post-production editing period, all of which lead to the same result. Each of the paths has its own specific pros and cons in terms of budget planning. The End Result Use of the project will have a direct effect on the path post-production should take. For example, if the project you are making on film is intended for television, then there is no reason to conform (or print), the negative to a film answer print. For television the final product is delivered on video (normally digital video). If you use path #2 in the diagram, you will transfer the negative through a telecine process, edit the project with a non-linear digital process and transfer in high resolution to video or digital video. You will not need to conform the original picture negative to an answer print. You have completed the project for its intended marketplace. Be sure you know what the End Result Use will be before you plan out the project.

If you are doing a film project for a theatrical release you must take into consideration other factors besides economics when deciding what post-production path to take. Do you have a film festival or distribution deadline? What creativity do you compromise using the various paths? Is the compromise worth it?

1.

Originate on Film Shoot **1**	Develop Negative	Print Dailies	Edit dailies on Film	**Conform Original Negative – Answer Print**

Figure 40

The first path works entirely with the physical film negative. It involves editing film using the linear film editing technology that has been in existence almost thirty years. The process is slower than working in the (digital) nonlinear environment but every step of the way, you are working with film, touching it, sensing it and viewing it in its intended format. Since this editing method involves the cutting apart and putting together pieces of celluloid, and then projecting them on a screen, creative decisions take longer to make. Film projects that have shot thousands (if not hundreds of thousands) of feet of film have a massive organizational and handling process associated with this path. It is, however, a tried and true path and every step of the way you are seeing the project in its intended format.

2.

Originate on Film Shoot **2**	Develop Negative	Transfer Negative to Video through Telecine Process	Digital Nonlinear Editing	**Conform Original Negative from non linear edit – Answer Print**

Figure 41

The second path shoots on film, develops the film, then transfers the developed negative to a positive video image which is then input digitally into a nonlinear editing system. A nonlinear editing system allows the editor to immediately edit and transpose images digitally, quickly slipping them in and out of a sequence without adjusting other shots within the sequence. The most common of these systems is the Avid, although Apple has developed a software program called Final Cut Pro that is quickly taking over certain segments of the marketplace. It is less expensive than the Avid and is easier to understand and use. The Avid, however, still remains the professional system of choice. The fundamental principle of digital nonlinear editing systems use a syntax developed from traditional film editing, linear videotape editing and computer language.

There are editing advantages to using a nonlinear method other than speed. For example, digital nonlinear editing permits the editor to store an edited sequence while trying other versions of the same sequence. This allows for a creative side by side comparison of two or more cuts of the same scene. This would be impossible in path #1 without an additional expense. When the picture is locked (that is, finished editing) the digital nonlinear system produces an edit decision list (also called an EDL or a film cut list), with code numbers that match numbers on the original negative. A negative cutter then assembles the original picture negative. Although this is the least expensive of the film paths, it includes an important creative compromise. If the project is intended for theatrical distribution, you will not see the picture in intended form until the end of the process, because the entire time you are viewing the edited image you are either watching it on a computer screen or through video projection. You will not have the opportunity to view it in its intended format until you view the final answer print.

3.

Originate on Film Shoot 3	Develop Negative	Print Dailies	Transfer Dailies (positive) to Video through Telecine Process	Digital Nonlinear Editing	Conform Dailies to nonlinear edit	Conform Original Negative – Answer Print

Figure 42

The third path shoots on film, develops the film and then prints the dailies which are then transferred to video for digitizing into a nonlinear system. After the picture is edited, the dailies are conformed to the picture edit. This is called a workprint. This workprint is then projected to see if the project works in its intended format. Sometimes it is projected with a temp sound track to assist in creative decisions. Changes can be made either first through the nonlinear system or directly with the workprint which can then be projected again for its creative impact. This path provides for the greatest amount of creative flexibility and decision making in the shortest amount of time. But it is the most costly of all the paths.

PRODUCERS VOCABULARY

Black Track Print—Silent answer print (with picture only, no sound).

Final Cut—1. The finished version of the work print from which the negative is conformed. 2. An important negotiating point for a director's or producer's contract when determining who has the last word on the form and content of the film that will be released.

Workprint—An untimed print assembled from dailies with tape splices. When the workprint reaches the final cut stage, the negative is conformed to it. Also called a picture workprint or cutting copy. In addition to the picture workprint, there may also be a sound workprint (also called a magnetic film worktrack) used in the synchronized editing of sound.

4.

Originate on Film Shoot **4**	Develop Negative	Transfer Negative to Video through Telecine Process	Digital Nonlinear Editing	Print and conform only Dailies that conform to final digital edit	**Conform Original Negative– Answer Print**

Figure 43

The fourth path shoots on film, develops the film, telecine transfers the film negative to video for digitizing into a nonlinear editing system. After the picture has been edited, *only* the dailies of those shots that have been digitally edited in the picture are printed and a workprint is edited to conform to the nonlinear digital picture edit. The workprint is then projected in its intended form. It is sometimes projected with a temp sound mix. If changes need to be made, they could be first made in the nonlinear format for viewing and approval. Then the changes may be printed and conformed into the workprint for projection and picture lock. This path allows for creative flexibility and decision making in a short period of time. It is a cost-effective manner to edit the project quickly and see it creatively in its intended form.

Regardless of the path you choose there are always limitations. For example, in paths #2 and #4, once you develop the negative of your film original and transfer it to video you may choose to digitize only the "printed takes," indicated in the continuity notes. Since digitizing takes time and the information you digitize requires data storage, selective digitized sequences will save you both time and storage. But not having the nondigitized sequences at your disposal may have an impact upon your creative results.

There are also moments that may cost you additional time. For example, if you select path #4 and make changes in the picture cut, you will have to wait for the lab to print the dailies needed for the change and further lab expenses will be charged to your account.

5.

Originate in Video Shoot **5**	Digital Nonlinear Editing	Original Video conformed to final digital edit. **Final Product in Video**	Or **Transfer final video to film – Answer Print**

Figure 44

If you originate your material in a video format as indicated in path #5 such as digital high definition video, you can digitize directly into a nonlinear editing system and then output the final product in high resolution video using your original material and an EDL. This process is a video process called online and is the final process for picture when working in either linear or nonlinear video. If you wish to transfer the final result to film, make sure you find out ahead of time what it will cost and what the creative technical requirements might be for both camera movement and lighting to achieve the desired end result. Unless you have considered and planned ahead, the transfer may not meet with your expectations, requiring very expensive changes.

Technology is continually offering the producer choices in the post-production process. As digital techniques makes creativity easier and quicker, you must consider the expense of the entire process and weigh its cost effectiveness very cautiously against the end result. When you choose the path your project will take, you must be willing to carefully examine the creative pros and cons and accept any limitations as a result of your decision.

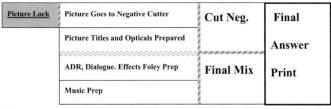

Figure 45

SOUND EDIT—PART 2

When the picture is locked, it is turned over to the negative cutter who conforms the negative to include the locked picture (See Figure #45). Title and optical negatives are prepared and given to the negative cutter as well. Simultaneously the creative preparation of sound begins in post-production. Although the picture editor has worked with the production sound as a reference, sound design and editorial sound specialists now take over. The creative preparation of sound should be thought of in three components. The first component involves cleaning up production tracks, automatic dialogue replacement (ADR), foley and sound effects. The second component is music. The third component is the mixing of the sound.

Although music and sound effects are different from one another, they have similarities of tone and rhythm. You have only to walk down a busy street and listen to the sounds of everyday life to understand this concept. The creative people involved with the first two components of sound preparation work independently of one another. They rarely know what the other is doing until they meet during the mix process. This may present some problems—the composer may have a tempo or rhythmic idea for underscoring a scene, while the sound designer creating the sound effects may have a very different notion of tempo or rhythm for the same scene. It is too late to solve these problems if you wait until you are mixing the project. It will cost you more money to shut down the mixing phase and make the corrections. You find yourself faced with choosing between the effects or the music. You can avoid this potential problem by using either a creative post-production supervisor, or by you, your director or your editor monitoring the creative work that both components are doing independently before the scheduled mix dates. By the time you are in the post-production sound process you will be totally immersed in your project and your creative sense of what you are hearing will be finely tuned to the resonance and texture of the story. Do not leave anything to chance; you and your director want no surprises during the mix phase. You must be free to make the creative sound choices based upon sound mix levels, not its creative content.

Post-production sound can go out for bid to post-production sound companies during the planning stages of the project. The bid should be included in the budget, which will lock post-production in place even before you start production. This practice will maintain fiscal regulation during post-production and limit volatility to the production phase only. This will also assure that you have the resources in place for post-production since the contingency will primarily support the vagaries of production.

Some companies have the capacity to do it all: the creative preparation work of the ADR, foley and effects, as well as the final mixing of the sound. Some companies do one or the other. Your choice of the right company should not be solely a fiscal decision. You must consider the creative ability of the company. To quote my friend David Lewis Yewdall, M.P.S.E. — one of the finest sound designers in the business and the author of *Practical Art of Motion Picture Sound* (Focal Press, 1999), "The best sound design is done with a sable brush, not with a ten pound sledgehammer. The sound designer has failed if the sound design distracts the audience from the story. If the sound design succeeds it is in concert with and elevates the action of the picture to a new level."

The same is true for the post-production sound mixer. There are creative subtleties that make mixers different from one another. Although you and your director will be supervising the mix and making the final decisions, I have found that mixers still use their own subjective creative subtleties to shade the project. If you find the right creative mixer, you have found a person who has an emotional link to your project. They are motivated by ego and will do an exceptional job. I am a big advocate for bringing post-production sound into the planning stages. The bid process will do this for you. Have the creative sound people read the script and discuss potential contributions; listen to their opinions and their feedback. Their egos will then encourage their participation and help the bid. The amount of the bid will not only be based on creative and ego incentives, but also on supply and demand. If the company is busy with other clients when you are scheduling the project, the bid may be higher. They will base the bid on the complexity of the work and the date of delivery.

You will need to let the sound mixing company know what kind of stereo mix you want. Will it be four track, two track, or surround sound? What stereo system do you want to use? This information affects the cost as you will not only be paying for the creativity of the sound mixers, but also for the amount of time to do the mix.

Before you accept the bid, visit the facility to see how they work and check out the finished projects the company has worked on. Ask for a client list and check their client relationships. See what technology is being used for the mix, as it may effect the creative decisions that will be made. A mix to video projection of a theatrical feature will not have the same creative feeling as mixing to film projection. Video technology may be cheaper, but is it cost effective creatively? Always keep in mind the End Result Use of the project when making decisions that maximize creativity.

Picture Editor (IATSE Local 700)
Picture editors are storytellers right along with the director and cinematographer. Your selection of the picture editor is as important as your selection of the director. Picture editors will get emotionally (and proprietarily) attached to the project, so make sure you find a picture editor who shares a creative vision with you and the director.

Picture editors are only as good as the footage they receive from the director, since they only see the story from the standpoint of footage. Because they offer this different viewpoint, have your editor create a linear assembly of the footage after the end of production. This will also give your director time away from the memory of production details before working with your editor. Your director will then see the project from a new angle and will probably see in the editor's assembly some storytelling points that may not have been thought about during production. Some directors may also want to edit the project. If your director is also the editor, insist they take a vacation to clear their head and change perspective before beginning to edit. Their artistic contribution during editing will be more effective.

Acct. #	Account Name	Units	Rate	Amount	Sub Total	Total
4000	**Editing**					
01	Picture Editor					
	Assistant Editor					
	2nd Assistant Editor					
	Additional Editing Assistants					
02	Digital Post-production Effects Supervisor	ALLOW				
03	Digital Post-production Effects Bid	ALLOW				
04	Post-production Sound Designer					
	ADR Editor					
	Sound Effects and Foley Editor					
	Music Editor					
	Company Inclusive Bid					
05	Non Linear Editing Suite Rental					
	Flatbed Rental					
	Editing Room Rental					
	Additional Equipment Rental					
06	Film Coding	ALLOW				
07	Projection (Production and Editing)	ALLOW				
08	Projection on Location	ALLOW				
09	Purchases	ALLOW				
10	Film Messenger	ALLOW				
11	Video Transfers	ALLOW				
50	Other Charges					
	Total 4000					

Figure 46

The picture editor's primary job ends once the picture is locked. However, you will often employ the picture editor as your post-production supervisor to see the project through to its answer print. This will require the picture editor's involvement in other areas of creative post-production supervision. Your editor may be someone who is so critically important to you creatively that they earn the title of associate producer or co-producer and you involve them in more than just the editing of the picture. This affinity generally evolves from long-standing relationships based on creative trust and understanding. Although the editor will work with a director, the editor is working for the producer, so this relationship must be treated with a great deal of respect. The editor's creative contribution is extensive, as your editor may see usable story and character moments in footage you or the director may have overlooked. It may be the tilt of an actor's head, the movement of the camera or the image of the actor after the director has said cut and before the camera stops. Editors understand the editorial juggling that can enhance a moment or shorten the spatial connection in a scene. Their contribution to the storytelling will be invaluable to you, and often their perspective on an artistic moment will be just as valid as the director's. I firmly believe that producers need to spend time with editors. You began with the vision and put together the collaborative team to make that vision a reality so don't let go of it after production has been completed. On *The Girl, the Gold Watch and Everything,* my executive producer (the late Arthur Fellows), believed that the director and producer shouldn't be involved with the editing process. Arthur was a legend in the profession having worked his way up in production on important pictures like *Gone With the Wind,* to the President of Production for Paramount Pictures. He knew all about making movies and believed that the editor should be left alone to edit the picture without any input except his own; Arthur relished the creative process of working with the editor. The director was fine with Arthur's edict. I was not. I would often show up at the editing room and make suggestions when he and the editor were working. Arthur was annoyed by this and wanted me to wait until after the cut was finished to make my suggestions. He knew that by then it would be too late to lock the picture, because the delivery date of the project was upon us. Knowing that the flatbed was on the wall behind the door into the room, he drew a line in the doorway and told me I could make all the suggestions I wanted—from the other side of the line. I thought about it and then had the studio prop shop construct a periscope that would allow me to see around the corner and over the shoulder of the editor. I made my suggestions from behind the line, just as Arthur requested. When he saw my initiative, he laughed, invited me in and left me alone to work with the editor to meet our deadline date.

Most medium and higher budget projects employ the editor through the completion of the sound mix and answer printing process. Lower budgeted projects will often release them after the picture is locked. If you hire your editor only for picture editing, then the employ for that period of time should be on an exclusive basis. If you want to have a direct association with the post-production sound process and do not want to work with a post-production supervisor, then employ the picture editor on a non-exclusive basis from picture lock through the final mix. This will allow the picture editor to take another job, and at that same time do the necessary follow

PRODUCERS VOCABULARY

ACE—An abbreviation for American Cinema Editors, an honorary professional society of film editors in the United States that promotes the advancement of the art and craft of editing; it also bestows annual editing awards. Membership is by invitation only. Founded in 1950 and based in West Hollywood.

AFM—An abbreviation for American Federation of Musicians, the union of professional musicians.

ASC—Honorary organization, comprised of directors of photography and others related to cinematography, that works to advance the art and craft of motion picture and television camera work. Membership is by invitation only. Founded in 1919 and based in Hollywood. The British counterpart is the British Society of Cinematographers (B.S.C.); Canadian counterpart is the Canadian Society of Cinematographers (C.S.C.). When giving screen credit it is customary to include the appropriate organization initials after the name.

through on post-production tasks for your project. These may include working with the title company or the optical company preparing any dissolves, fades or wipes, or interfacing with the negative editor.

By the time picture has been locked, your picture editor, impelled by ego, will have an emotional attachment to the project. Music editing is one of the last bastions of emotional editing. The ego of your picture editor might compel them to edit the music and creatively fine tune the music cues, getting the project ready for sound mixing. This eliminates the need for a music editor who, of course, does not creatively have anything at stake on the project.

Editing Issues

The path you decide to take will affect what you budget in Figure #46. As an example film *coding* is needed only if you are going to print and edit with the dailies. Although your laboratory development deal will include screening your dailies, you may be in situations or locations where it becomes difficult to view dailies. You might need to rent a local movie theater, or have the dailies transferred to VHS and sent to the location for viewing in a hotel room. Digital technology has brought the post-production editing phase closer to production. You and the director are now able to see edited sequences of the story while it is being shot. Technology will let your editor send dailies or an assembly of a scene to you and the director over the Internet instead of waiting days for the material to be shipped and finding an available local projection facility. Or you can rent (or purchase) a suitcase-sized nonlinear editing system and bring your editor to the shooting location to work with the director. The creative association between you, the editor and the director is significant so it is important that you plan out this stage of the process and have it in place before you begin the project.

DIGITAL POST-PRODUCTION EFFECTS

The editor must, in some situations, work closely with a digital post-production supervisor to realize the image for the storytelling. Using digital technologies to solve production problems is not always cost effective, so various other methods of telling the story should be carefully thought out. Narrative visual storytelling is an illusionary art and the audience only knows that which they see and hear—not how it got there. The digital work can be done separate from live action or it may incorporate live action. Much of it is done in post-production and as it is completed, a positive image of the final picture negative is given to the editor for editing into the project. The work is usually supervised by a digital post-production supervisor who reports to the visual effects supervisor. Like visual effects companies, digital post-production companies will bid on a project.

SOUND EDITING

Post-production creative sound designers should view the locked picture with you, the director and the picture editor to gain an overview of the soundtrack. They will hear different things than you will when they view the picture. They hear variations of sounds and subtleties of texture that will heighten the feel and concept of the project. Their creativity is the foundation for the sound, and finding a good designer with the sensitivity, commitment, love and passion for the art of sound will be difficult. Your designer must be told the intended End Result Use of the project as it will affect the creative contribution. The soundtrack for a television project is different than a soundtrack for a theatrical project. It is smaller in scope and doesn't require hundreds of post-production sound specialists. A good soundtrack should be done by an artist who is inventive and experienced, and who is passionate about the work.

After you have completed editing the picture, you, the director, the picture editor and a sound designer will sit down with a copy of the project (usually on video) and go through it, foot by foot. This is called a "spotting session" because you will be spotting where all sound (excluding music) will eventually go in the final mix. Discussions about ADR also occur during spotting sessions so it is common to have your ADR editor there as well. Make sure that the video you are spotting with is prepared to the proper specifications of your sound house.

Automatic Dialogue Replacement (ADR)

Automatic dialogue replacement, often called "looping," is done for many reasons. You may have shot on a noisy location. Perhaps the actor mumbled the lines or maybe a performance is just not good enough. Whatever the reason, although it is not preferred, ADR is unavoidable. Through ADR the intonation and performance of the dialogue is altered. The words are the same as originally recorded, but the subtext of the performance can be changed. You may be able to change the occasional word, if the movement of the mouth matches the new word. (This is common especially when changing foul language for public broadcast of the project.) If actors are doing ADR during the production phase you, your associate producer, your editor or your post-production supervisor will usually direct the recording sessions. If you wait until production is completed, your director may be available to supervise the actors' performance. Actors who do ADR after production receive payment for ADR based on their original contract, with the exception of day players who received a SAG-mandated minimum of $5000. In their case, the producer is entitled to one free day of ADR.

The bid you receive for ADR post-production sound work is only for the creative work of the ADR editor, who functions as a supervisor at an ADR session. As a supervisor they must communicate with the actors, some of whom may be intimidated by or inexperienced with the ADR process.

Most ADR studios record with video playback. It is cheaper, and quicker than film. The ADR editor prepares the cue sheets and the playback of the sequences and functions as ADR supervisor. You may be surprised at the amount of dialogue that a supervisor is having re-recorded at some ADR sessions. You may think that the original production tracks sound fine, but the supervisor should quickly articulate to you why certain cues are being (or should be) recorded and how this will improve your project's soundtrack. The ADR supervisor will be extra picky about the quality of the dialogue since their selection is based on their ego and their desire to do a thorough job on the project.

The ADR editor is only as good as the recording made for him or her. So the ADR mixer, who does the recording, is key to quality ADR. The mixer must not only be experienced in the use and placement of microphones but must also know how to listen to the production track to seamlessly match the colorization and timbre of the ADR recording with it. Since the egos of actors are involved, the mixer must also be diplomatic when communicating with whomever is directing the ADR, or feelings get bruised. However, the last word on the performance should be with whomever is directing the ADR session. *The ADR mixer must not make creative decisions as it relates to performance.*

Foley

The sounds that people make onscreen other than dialogue (footsteps, putting guns down on tables, taking off their coats, etc.) are referred to as foley. It is created separately since the sounds people make onscreen when recorded with dialogue are not a specific focus of a production track. Recorded sound during production is specifically for dialogue.

Foley had its origins when the creative people at Universal Pictures realized that after the premiere of the talkie, *The Jazz Singer*, their silent production of *Showboat* was outmoded. As often happens with technology,

Universal found a way to add sound to *Showboat*. On a soundstage, an orchestra performed the music and it was recorded live to the picture. At the same time a group of people watched the projected image and also recorded various sound effects and crowd vocals creating the technique called "direct-to-picture" recording. The head of this team was Jack Foley. As sound developed so did sound effect libraries, and editors began cutting in the sounds of footsteps from the sound libraries. But it became hard to find the exact footstep to match the image. Jack Foley re-entered the scene and began to record footsteps and other sounds "direct-to-picture." The stage he used at Universal to do this work was called the "Foley Stage" and the activity that was done on that stage was always referred to as foley. It is now part of the language of the industry.

Foley artistry is a major component for creating reality. Good foley artists, also known as "walkers," will act the part and get into the spirit of the characters. They will create sounds that are motivated by the image. The sounds should be subliminal to the dialogue. Foley artists study the way people move in order to create a real-life auditory experience for the audience. They use a variety of props, wear a variety of clothes and walk or run on a variety of surfaces in a variety of ways, to do their creative work. The work is done in specially designed recording studios equipped with various "pits" and surfaces on which to move. Finding the right foley facility is important. Your sound designer or sound house will be able to refer you to appropriate facilities since they work with these facilities all the time. The post-production bid you receive for creative sound work may not include the cost of either the foley artist or the foley stage. So go over the bid carefully as you may have to budget this separately. The mix facility bid may include foley and ADR stages and, if the bid makes sense, this might be the best solution. The more sound recording you are able to keep with one vendor, the fewer technical problems you will have at your final sound mix. The fewer technical problems you have at the sound mix sessions, the greater the creativity and fiscal savings.

Sound Effects

Effects from other sounds provide the layers and recognition of reality that an audience expects. Good sound effects can lead, entice, forewarn or shock an audience. They give the sensibilities of audio reality that take a flat image and give it dimension. They can bring the audience into the action rather than have them watch it at a safe distance. They are an essential part of storytelling. Sound effects can be originally recorded, created digitally through nonlinear systems or a combination of both, in which a realistically record-ed sound is enhanced or altered digitally. Many sound effects editors have their own unique individual specialties. One may be creative with mechanical sounds, another may be creative with explosions. All sound effects editors know how to sync up the sound and edit cues into scenes, but the more experienced know how to elevate the cue and make it a creative spark. Sound effects editors will also take the room tone recorded for a scene and add that to the effects track to balance out the dialogue and provide a presence for the sound. The post-production sound design house whose bid you accept will probably use several sound effects editors.

THE M&E TRACK

Sound effects and foley should be created for the entire project even in areas where the original production tracks contain enough sound. They will provide a full presence soundtrack, even when the dialogue is removed, and one of your delivery items for distribution is a separate "music and effects track" (also known as an M&E). An M&E track contains all of the sound except the dialogue and ADR. This track is required for distribution sales to the foreign market as it is used by foreign exhibitors as a basis for dubbing the project into their native language. If the M&E track is void of foley or other effects, the foreign soundtrack will not be a full soundtrack once dubbed. And without the ability to make a quality foreign soundtrack the value of your project in the foreign market will be reduced. *End Result Use!*

———— • • • ————

Sometimes I hear a producer describe him or herself as "very hands on." Frankly, this usually scares me. A good, creative producer is a supportive producer, who respects the director's vision and works to keep that focused. Sometimes this means "hands off." There is an element of trust, not only in the director but also in the other key creative people—the cinematographer, the editor, the production designer, the composer. The producer creates the environment where everyone can do their best work.

—Nancy Richardson, A.C.E. *Stand and Deliver,*
Roadside Prophets, Mi Familia, White Man's Burden,
Selena, Down in the Delta, Why Do Fools Fall in Love

———— • • • ————

MUSIC

Music propels the action and increases the audience's emotional involvement in a project. It is a powerful and manipulative art form that never needs translation into a foreign language. It can stretch the soul of a story, tell us when danger is near or let us know the emotional passion of the characters. It reflects the entire spectrum of emotions, moves us to think and feel a certain way, and can take us into realms we have never experienced. In some instances it sells the project and millions of records as well. The creation of the music comes near the end of the post-production process and often if the project is over budget and funds are in short supply it is the first place that producers go to trim costs. This is a major mistake! Music is so critical to the creative nature of the project that you must protect its planned budget at any cost.

Music is used three ways. The first is as background composition that underscores the dramatic action (called the "score"). This is the most common and is motivated by the image, plot or the characters. Score music causes us to tear up at the right time, or warns us that danger is lurking. It can make our hearts beat faster as the killer shark is swimming towards shore in *Jaws*. It can excite us when we are taken on a space adventure in each of the *Star Wars* movies. It makes us scream when the knife rips the shower curtain in *Psycho*. Or it makes us feel the power of the military when "Ride of the Valkyrie" is played over the loudspeaker as the helicopters land on the beach in *Apocalypse Now*. Background music will tell us when we

Acct. #	Account Name	Units	Rate	Amount	Sub Total	Total
4100	**MUSIC**					
01	Composer/Conductor					
02	*Musicians*					
03	*Arrangers*					
04	*Lyricists*					
05	*Singers*					
06	*Instrument Rental*	ALLOW				
07	*Instrument Moving Labor*	ALLOW				
08	*Studio Rental*					
09	Composer Underscoring Fee (*all inclusive*)					
10	Music Contractor					
11	Composer Original Songs					
12	Music Rights					
	Synchronization	ALLOW				
	Re-Use	ALLOW				
	Performance	ALLOW				
	Songwriters, Composers, Publishers	ALLOW				
	Record Producers	ALLOW				
	Record Companies	ALLOW				
	Artist Performance in Film	ALLOW				
	Artist Performance Use on Soundtrack Album	ALLOW				
13	Music Clearance Fee	ALLOW				
50	Other					
	Total 4100					

Figure 47

should laugh or cry at a situation; it can be dramatic, melodramatic or over-ly dramatic. It can be heard alone or with special effects, dialogue or foley. It can be subtly influential to the mood or intrinsic to the storyline. Background musical compositions can make a weak project stronger or weaken a strong project. It can comment on the characters and heighten the dramatic intention of the film. And it can make a project stay in our emo-tional system for days after we have seen it.

The second use of music is as "source" material or as part of the story. It might appear to come from a radio or CD stereo or be motivated by live musicians. Think about the opening scene in Coppola's *The Godfather*, which takes place at a wedding reception party; or the end of the Copacabana Nightclub scene in Scorcese's *Goodfellas*.

The third treatment of music in a project involves the use of songs as either source material, background score or underscoring of titles. The pro-ducers of *Sleepless in Seattle* used various styles and types of songs through-out the project to underscore the characters' emotional feelings. *Good Morning, Vietnam!* took advantage of the radio DJ aspect of the story to motivate the use of songs as an underscore to the dramatic action. Can we ever forget hearing Louis Armstrong's version of "Wonderful Day," while seeing the images of killing and destruction in Vietnam? Songs are often used over titles and in some instances incorporated into the main action of the story. In the opening title sequence of Mike Nichols' *The Birdcage*, we hear the song "We are Family" while we see a night shot travelling over water to a digitally created shoreline full of people. The image then quickly dis-solves to a matching live action shot as the image comes down to ground level, moves across a busy street full of summer tourists, through the doors of the Birdcage Nightclub and right up to the performers on stage who are singing the song.

Songs are also used to motivate the characters or the action in a story. In *Hudson Hawk*, Bruce Willis and Danny Aiello use the Sinatra tune "Swinging on a Star" for the timing they need to do their cat burglar act, while *Risky Business* has the iconic scene of Tom Cruise sliding onto screen in a dress shirt, briefs and socks while belting out the words to "Old Time Rock and Roll." Bette Midler, Diane Keaton and Goldie Hawn triumphant-ly sing "You Don't Own Me" at the end of *The First Wives Club*.

Music is an art form that is creative and motivated by the project. Even though you will not pay a lot of attention to its need or its use until post-production, it must be incorporated into the vision of the project from the development and preplanning stages. Although there are music libraries and

Internet companies from which you can purchase pre-recorded music cues, most background scores are written specifically for a project. Background music licensed from these stock music companies ("stock music" or "needle drop") is not inspired by your project and, since it is premixed, will not allow you to be very creative. You will also not own any of the music publishing. Consider these three issues carefully before making the decision to use "canned licensed" music. You might, however, want to re-record existing music or use music that has already been recorded for another medium. In those situations you must first acquire the rights to the music.

MUSIC RIGHTS
Publishing Rights

You will have to purchase publishing rights to any existing music that talent performs onscreen or you re-record for the score. These rights are purchased from the publisher, lyricist, and composer of the musical composition. In some instances the composers and publishers are the same entity. This is also true if you use existing music from a pre-recorded disc. The only exception to this would be music that is in public domain (such as most classical music). The fees vary and are based upon the final use of the project. You can easily find the publishers of existing music by calling BMI or ASCAP, the two registers for music published in the United States.

Synchronization Rights

There are other rights you will have to purchase if you wish to use music from pre-recorded discs. The first of these are called synchronization rights. This is the right to use the music in timed synchronization with visual images, and include pre-recorded songs if the song is synchronized with the action on the screen. Synchronization rights are required no matter how the project is being used. Although these rights are not as yet determined for Internet use, it may very well be necessary to include this medium in the future.

Performance Rights

Performance rights are the rights to use the performance of the artist (or artists) performing an already recorded musical composition. These fees may vary depending on how the project will be distributed throughout the world. Synchronization, publishing and performance rights are the major rights you must acquire for previously recorded musical compositions.

Reuse Fees

In some instances you may have to pay re-use fees. This might be required if the recording was made for one medium and is being used in another medium. The musicians union, the American Federation of Musicians (AFM), assesses this fee in the United States. It is also called a "new use fee." The logic behind this fee is that the use of the existing recording will prevent musicians from being hired if you were to re-record the composition. Theoretically, you are putting union members out of work, so the fee is assessed. The amount of re-use fees payable for a particular recording is in direct proportion to the number of musicians on the track. Therefore, a three-piece band can be inexpensive but the L.A. Philharmonic will not be. Re-use fees occur chiefly when your project produces a soundtrack album. If the score is recorded under union auspices then a new use payment is made to players on release of the soundtrack album. In addition, there is a "special payment fund commitment" through the union, which is based upon the success of the project and gives the musicians a tiny percentage of your profits when the project is sold into markets such as cable television, DVD or videocassette.

Record Producers and Record Companies

Other fees you may be responsible for when using pre-recorded music are to the producers of the composition or to the record company in order to use the original recording masters or put the composition on your project's soundtrack album. Also, if you want to use the performance of the artist on a soundtrack album you must clear it with the artists' record company before negotiating the deal. The negotiations will include a royalty to the artist and the record company. It may also include any recoupment of dollars to the record company, recording rights to the film company, and music video responsibilities.

If the artist is performing onscreen, then the artist is paid a fee that falls within the guidelines of the Screen Actors Guild. This is only in cases when there are no soundtrack recordings involved with the project. However, if the project is planned to eventually go to the home video or DVD market, then the artist's recording on the project is treated as a home video device and may require the artist's record company's consent. Under most music deals home video and DVDs are treated as records or CDs. This is a very complex issue and must be approached carefully through music attorneys or a music clearing company in consultation with your attorney. Just make sure you do the clearances before you use the music in the project.

Music Composer

The fee you pay a composer may vary. "A-list" composers earn between $750,000 and $1,000,000 for a project. This does not include the costs for orchestrating, copying and conducting if the composer doesn't conduct. The music budget may easily be in the millions of dollars. Excellent musicians for composers to use are found in Los Angeles, Czechoslovakia and London. Many Los Angeles musicians are members of the American Federation of Musicians, or AFM, while London and Czechoslovakia musicians are not, so their fees may be lower than those in Los Angeles. Many large orchestral scores are recorded in London to avoid the re-use and other fees that the AFM requires for its musicians.

A composer can write a score that can be recorded either by a full orchestra or by a handful of musicians. Many excellent but not yet well-known composers have the ability to record the score in their own home recording studios using synthesizers and other keyboards that electronically create a musical or symphonic sound. They write, score, compose and record the background music, bringing in musicians to supplement the sound if needed. Usually motivated by ego, they call upon their relationships within the music community to assist them. In this instance the composer should provide you with a "flat bid deal" to do the music for your project. It should be inclusive to the delivery of the music ready to edit into the project in preparation for the final sound mix.

When employing a composer on a flat deal the composer will be an employee for hire who renders certain services that will include furnishing a complete and original musical score. The deal should include the writing, composing, orchestrating, performing and recording—with the composer bearing the full cost of any musicians, studio or equipment rental, guild or union fees. You want to make sure that you have the non-exclusive right to use the composer's name in perpetuity in connection with the project. You should also provide suitable credit or billing for the composer. It is customary to give credit on a separate title card in the main titles of the project. You may also wish to provide the same credit on advertisements that are under your control. (Credit in advertisements can be a powerful negotiating tool.)

Because it is your project that provides the creative motivation for composing the songs or a background score, and since the project had its creative impetus with you, make sure that all the material written, composed or prepared for your project will be the sole property of your production company. This will require you to establish a company for the publishing and copyright of the music. Background music is often published by the project's publishing company. On the other hand, songs created for a project may share joint publishing with the composer, depending on the name and status of the composer. Music publishing companies receive royalties from distributors and exhibitors for projects that are sold not only in the foreign theatrical and television markets but also the ancillary domestic markets, such as video, DVD and cable television. This revenue is in addition to the revenue the project earns for its distribution and is split by the composer and the parties that share the ownership of the publishing.

WORKING WITH THE COMPOSER

Although your composer began thinking creatively during the pre-production stage of the project, you, your editor and your director should view the picture lock with the composer, selecting moments that feel like they need music as underscoring. This is called "*spotting for music.*" The spotting session, much like your sound spotting session, is used to discuss the particular underlying intent for specific music cues and to talk through the moments that you hope will be enhanced with music. Hopefully you will avoid having to tell your composer, "Maybe music will help this scene!" Except on low budget projects it is normal to hire a music editor, who will also attend the spotting session and take thorough notes. This music editor will work as the composer's aide in making sure that all of the music that he or she writes will work perfectly with the cues in the project. To that end, the music editor—under the direction of the composer—will prepare music timing notes, make sure proper videotapes are made for the composer and for the music recording, assist in all preparations of the recording, attend and assist in recording sessions, and finally, edit the recorded music cues for the final mix. The music editor will also normally be present at the mix to correct or improve on any technical music issues that arise there.

After spotting for music, the composer begins the task of writing the score, usually working with a videotaped copy of the project as a picture reference. When the score is completed, the composer should deliver it to you with the lead sheets of the musical compositions and cue sheets noting where each cue is to begin and end. The cue sheets will be used by the music editor (or picture editor if no music editor is used) in preparation for the final sound mix of the project. Some composers like to have the final creative control over how their music is mixed so they do a music mix of the tracks before delivering it to the producer. You should ask for the music cues to be delivered on no fewer than four tracks. One track should have either SMPTE or Video Time Code, while rhythm, melody and percussion sounds should be separated out on the other three tracks. If the music tracks are delivered separated, you have more control over the creative intent of the sound during the final mix. If the music is pre-mixed for any scene, you will be stuck with predetermined levels of musical tones, which may fight other sounds that are being mixed into the scene.

Also, new or inexperienced composers do not always have a sense of how a scene will play with their music score, so they have a tendency to deliver tempos that are a little slow. The music is intended to play against the picture and slow tempos make a picture feel slower. You can avoid too-slow tempos by visiting the composer from time to time during the preparation process and asking to see the cue played against the picture.

Do not be surprised if the composer asks to have the levels of the music raised during the final mix. Composers are sensitive to their music and their egos want to make sure the audience hears every single nuance intended in the score. Try to handle these requests with care, as egos can be fragile and you are building relationships for future projects.

Original Songs

Music for your project should be thought of as being a separate but vital component of the project. The business of music has its own structure, different from any other business. Publishing and performance royalties are necessary for music played on the radio, sold in record stores, played on videocassette and DVD. Songs or musical themes that are written and recorded specifically for your project may be used to promote the project or a soundtrack album. The song "Two Hearts in Perfect Time" was played over the title sequence in *The Girl, the Gold Watch and Everything,* and the characters in the movie were thematically motivated by the lyrics. The song was written by the film's composer and sung by Ritchie Havens, who recorded for Elektra Records at the time. I contacted the president of Elektra records and offered to supply him with the musical tracks of this new Ritchie Havens song if he would press 300 discs of the recording. I also guaranteed him radio play of the song in every major market in the United States. He agreed. When the discs arrived, I gave them to the project's publicist and instructed her to put one recording in every press kit sent to the television stations that had licensed the movie. I knew that each television station had a sister radio station which would play the song to promote the movie the week it aired in their city. As happened, the movie aired during sweeps week and was the top-rated show in the Los Angeles and New York markets—due in part to radio disc jockeys saying, "Two Hearts in Perfect Time," sung by

Richie Havens from *The Girl, the Gold Watch and Everything* on channel XYZ this Saturday night!" Ritchie was paid a SAG wage for singing the song and Paramount Studios' in-house publishing company owned the publishing. The entire cost of the song was under $2000, and it helped deliver the number one movie for television during the spring sweeps.

You don't necessarily need to commission a song to be written in order to use original songs. Many new musical artists and bands are represented by music agents and managers who look for opportunities to put one of their clients' songs in film or video projects. They will gladly provide you with the tracks and free synchronization and publishing rights. You will not, however, be entitled to any ownership of the song. If you are creative and find an artist or group who is on the way up the musical ladder, you may be able to increase the longevity and promotion of your project by making arrangements with groups like these.

——— • • • ———

While scoring a trailer of a feature film for Gramercy Pictures, I went through numerous revisions of the music for a one minute spot and finally got the approval of the Marketing Department. Upon the recording of the trailer, I specifically asked the client (producer) if they wanted to be present for the music mix to the picture. They said, "No, it's fine—we trust you." When the project was delivered, I got a call from the client—they loved the spot, but they wanted the snare drum a little louder throughout the mix. (The same mix that they had chosen not to be present for.) This caused me to have to re-book the room in one evening, re-hire the musicians, find subs for those who were unavailable and find a new engineer. All for a snare drum! The spot turned out great, but it cost the client double what it should have.

—Steve Kaminski, Composer

——— • • • ———

———— • • • ————

I was talked into designing the sound for this low budget independent "helicopter action/adventure" film. The project had a small fleet of very sexy helicopters (Long Ranger, Hughes 500, Dauphine, etc.) - just my type of sound sandbox to play in. The producers assured me that they had custom recorded each helicopter for its exact sound effect so not having to re-record the sound, I felt that the low-budget price tag was at least doable. I carefully filtered through the sound reports and listened to each and every roll of production tape. Each so-called wild track of a helicopter was filled with people talking and the noises of a production crew getting ready for another shot. Every "sync" shot was filled with assistant director radio squawk that rendered the actual recorded sound useless. This threw me into a position of having to "sound design" helicopter series for each machine. As we were given no budget for custom recording and at $500 an hour helicopter rental (not including recording equipment, materials and crew) there was no way I was going to personally absorb that cost, so I used effects I already had of UH-1s. On the re-recording stage my sound effect mixer found my redesigned UH-1s which had been sped up 60 percent and re-EQ-ed extremely fitting. However, one of the executive producers at the mix stood up and snapped at me, "We had all this stuff recorded on the set, why didn't you use the real thing!?" At this point, I had had enough of executive producers who were totally ignorant of the filmmaking process, and the art of the soundtrack. Especially one who never secured and/or consulted a supervising sound editor prior to starting such a difficult and challenging audio project. I decided to give him a valuable piece of custom sound recording advice. "I would have used your *!@!$& helicopter recordings if your crew had kept their *!@#*&# mouths shut while your *!@#*&# helicopters were performing. But your *!@#*&# crew didn't know how to keep *!@#*&# quiet so your *!@#*&# recordings are *!@#*&# useless!! Have I made my *!@#*&# point?!" With that I turned back to the mixing crew to continue work. He immediately left the stage and went to the line producer to have me fired. When the line producer heard the story, he told the executive producer that I was absolutely right and that he should be grateful that I had not dumped the show weeks before when I discovered the shabbily recorded helicopter tracks. I went on to do six more pictures with that line producer.

—David Lewis Yewdall, M.P.S.E.,
Post-production Sound Designer, *Reindeer Games,
Jackie Brown, Starship Troopers, The Fifth Element*

———— • • • ————

CHAPTER 9   THE COMPLETION PERIOD

POST-PRODUCTION SOUND LAB
Sound Mixing

Sound mixing, or re-recording, is a process in which separate audio elements are mixed together into a combined format. The more seamless this mixing is, the better for the final project. It is a creative process that combines the separate sound and music processes and is motivated by the story, its characters and its concept. The readying of ADR, foley, music and effects in preparation for a sound mix is analogous to what wardrobe, art direction and properties provide for shooting the picture. Just as you gear up all the creative elements for the moment of production, you gear up all the creative sound elements for the moment of sound re-recording.

At a mix session there is a team that usually consists of the head mixer, the effects mixer and the music mixer. The head mixer is responsible for the dialogue. During a final mix the head mixer usually instructs the effects and music mixer to raise or lower their elements during any particular creative moment, since the head mixer has the final word on the balance and dynamics of the sound. The effects mixer generally works in tandem with the head mixer because effects, background and foley are critically tied to dialogue. When an M&E track is made, it is the effects mixer who must tie in the background and foley to the effects track. The music mixer generally comes to the mix during the final mix phase. In some instances the head mixer also mixes the music after pre-mixing the dialogue.

Much of what happens during the pre-dubbing mix phase is in preparation for the final mix so it is not necessary for you or the director to be present. Pre-dubbing is required in order to distill the sound into a workable order while still allowing for aesthetic options during the final mix. It is at the final mix that the creative egos of everyone involved kick in. Therefore

Acct. #	Account Name	Units	Rate	Amount	Sub Total	Total
4200	**Post-production Sound Laboratory**					
01	ADR Facilities (including recordist)					
02	Foley Facilities					
03	Foley Walkers (Artists)					
04	Voice Over Facilities					
05	Sound Transfer					
06	Temporary Dubs (Mix)					
07	Sound Dubbing (Mix)					
	Dialogue and ADR Mix					
	Foley and Effects Mix					
	Music Mix					
	Pre Mix					
	Final Mix					
08	Stereo Royalty Fee					
09	Magnetic Stock	ALLOW				
10	Digital Tape Stock	ALLOW				
11	Equipment Rentals	ALLOW				
12	Optical Track Negative Stock and Transfer (2)	ALLOW				
13	Music and Effects Track (M&E)	ALLOW				
50	Other					
	Total 4200					

Figure 48

don't be surprised if there is a change in the mixer configuration and that the head mixer mixes music during your final mix, since music contributes emotionally and aesthetically to the final result. Although the supervising sound designer comes to the final mix with a specific sound design and the composer arrives with music ideas, the decision on the final vision and texture of the sound should be yours or the director's. Since your focus is on the End Result Use of the project, your voice—as to the details of sound and picture—must be the final word. Once, during the final mix of a television project that I was producing, I complained about one of the scenes we were mixing. As we listened, it felt like the actors were not really in the scene. The head mixer explained that the scene was an ADR scene and the scene was missing actor presence because there was no foley created for it. When I questioned the sound editor about the missing foley, he told me that it was not done because it was "only television." I immediately cancelled the mix and told the sound designer to do what he should have done already and foley every scene in the project. Two days later we continued the final mix with the foley intact. What the sound editor did not know is that the project was to be released theatrically in the foreign market and required an M&E track. He also poorly judged the integrity of the people behind the project.

The process during the final mix involves carefully listening and massaging the various sound cues reel by reel. Since you will probably be mixing in stereo, the creative decisions made will involve perspective, presence and in some cases, speaker selection. You and your head mixer should evaluate how much of the project can be mixed during any mix session. At some point your ears will no longer be attuned to the project and this will affect your creative decisions. The final mix is very much like listening to an orchestral composition; the subtleties in the shift of one sound or another will affect the aesthetics of the project. Therefore, you should not only play each reel after you have completed it but also the entire project at the completion of the mix. A lot can be heard by watching a complete playback, and for a variety of reasons it is common to change specific cues. However, if you are indecisive in your creative decisions and cause the mixes to be changed continually, thus using more time than was originally agreed upon, you will have to pay more money than what was agreed in the bid. So make sure you have clarity in your vision. You will hear a lot of opinions during the final mix, and you need to be able to trust your own creative instincts.

The End Result Use and creative integrity of your project should be the basis for your decision concerning a stereo or mono mix. Narrative projects targeted for a worldwide theatrical release must mix in stereo because it affects the return on the investment. You will have to pay a royalty for the use of the stereo system you choose. This royalty is based upon the type of stereo (i.e., 2 track, 4 track, SurroundSound tracks etc). Before completing the final mix, you, through the post-production sound house, must arrange for either Dolby or Ultra*Stereo to have a representative on hand to supervise the print mastering of the final mix. Post-production Sound Designer David Lewis Yewdall, M.P.S.E., recommends that your project always have an analog stereo mix on the print, although many theaters are able to play digital stereo soundtracks such as Dolby SR-D, SDDS or DTS. In his book, *The Practical Art of Motion Picture Sound*, he indicates that on "many occasions a theater that offers a digital sound presentation has a technical malfunction with the digital equipment for some reason. Sensors in the projection equipment detect a malfunction and automatically switch over to the analog 2-track matrixed track."

Temporary Dubs

Temporary dubs are becoming very common. They may be required if you have to screen your project early for potential distributors, or if you want to get an idea as to how something may sound against the images. Producers and directors are notorious for asking for temporary dubs before the sound has been fully prepared. This can be a dangerous practice to employ. Temp dubs always use sound effects or other elements that are truly "temp" effects and not intended for the final mix. Constantly hearing the temp mix will close down the creative process for everyone involved; if there is a constant flow of temp dubs, by the time you reach the final mix, the creative freshness, inspiration and spontaneity will be missing. Even more importantly, you are constantly paying for temp dubs, which may eat into your final mix budget. Therefore consider the need carefully, and use temporary dubs judiciously.

Music and Effects Track

In the last chapter we have referred to the creative and fiscal impact the M&E track has on the project. Some producers think that as long as they have the sound elements they are able to produce an M&E track when and if it is necessary. This thinking will require going back to a sound house, paying a fee and re-monitoring the elements in synchronization with the picture. The time to create the M&E track is at the time of the final mix. If the mixers are not only thinking about the project's completed mix, but also the M&E track, then when the final mix is completed it will be easy to produce a quality M&E. The same care that is taken in the final mix will be taken in the M&E. There is a saying which I have been hearing for years: "If you can get by Munich then your M&E is A-okay." The German foreign market is one of the most inflexible markets regarding quality control and censorship so this saying implies that your picture image and M&E track must be of the highest quality. If the M&E track is faulty in any way it will not be used and thus will affect your financial return. If you have the original elements it will have to be recreated by your foreign distribution representative who will charge it back to you. Therefore, it is best to produce the M&E at the time when quality is a priority.

POST-PRODUCTION FILM LAB

If the End Result Use of the project is to be in a film format, then the final phase of work on the project involves film laboratory specifics. This is comprised of such items as titles, opticals, the answer print and specifics for multiple prints of your project. Most of the particulars relating to post-production film laboratory may be accomplished through the contract bid system, while the expense of other items is dependant on the length of your project.

Black and White Reversal Dirty Dupes

A black and white high contrast positive image processed on reversal film stock is commonly referred to as a "dirty dupe." They used to be created for sound editors as the image to which they created sound effects and foley.

Acct. #	Account Name	Footage	Rate	Amount	Sub Total	Total
4300	**Post-production Film Laboratory**					
01	Reprints (1-light)					
02	Black and White Reversal Dirty Dupes					
03	Optical Effects					
	Fades					
	Dissolves					
	Others					
04	Main Titles	ALLOW				
05	End Titles	ALLOW				
06	Titles and Opticals Laboratory Processing	ALLOW				
07	Process Plates	ALLOW				
08	Stock Footage	ALLOW				
09	Negative Cutting (per reel or per cut)					
10	Develop Sound Track Negative					
11	Online Video Assembly					
12	Answer Print					
13	Foreign Textless Rendition					
14	35mm Blowup					
15	Tape to Film Transfer					
16	Protective Master Posit - Internegative (IPIN)					
17	Color Reversal Internegative - CRI					
18	16mm Release Print					
19	Lo-con Print	ALLOW				
20	Videotape Master	ALLOW				
21	Videotape Cassette	ALLOW				
22	Shipping and Cartage Charges	ALLOW				
23	Sales Tax					
50	Other					
	Total 4300					

Figure 49

Although this process has been replaced with videotape, it may still be necessary to manufacture a dirty dupe from time to time. If you can find a laboratory that will make one, they are relatively inexpensive. It is possible to negotiate for dirty dupes when you set your processing deal with the film lab. Thinking through the entire process of post-production will help you determine if there is a need for dirty dupes. You should base any decision concerning dirty dupes after speaking to your sound designers to determine what picture format they prefer to use.

Laboratory Optical Effects

Optical effects that are considered laboratory optical effects and are created by an optical company (often called an optical house), are usually fades, dissolves, wipes and other such photographic effects. If you are working in 16mm, however, these effects are executed using the original negative shot during the answer print process. They are created by the picture editor and prepared by the negative editor for the A and B roll developing process that laboratories render in 16mm. In all other film formats optical effects are created by an optical house, through an internegative process. Once the internegative of the effect is finalized, it becomes one of the final elements used by the negative cutter (see the section below on "negative cutting") in preparing for the answer print.

Optical effects should be supervised by your editor, unless they involve effects such as traveling mattes, blue- or greenscreen, or digital manipulation in combination with laboratory manipulation. Your visual effects supervisor (or picture editor) will be shepherding those effects. Both your visual effects supervisor (if you use one) and your picture editor will be involved in the creative look of the project from the pre-production phase. Therefore, by the time you are in the post-production laboratory phase, their creative egos will be the driving force in assuring that the effects look and work well with the story.

An optical house should provide you with a detailed bid for the services they will perform. However, you will have to furnish them with specific information, such as the number of fades (fade up and fade out) and dissolves, as the cost is based on the number and type of effects. You should attempt to provide as realistic an estimate as possible early in the pre-production phase. But, allowing for Murphy's Law, it is probably better to overestimate than underestimate. Since the optical process is an internegative process, the optical house will require a signed document giving them laboratory access to your project's negative. Nevertheless, their bid is a creative bid and will not include any of their lab expenses. These will be charged to your laboratory account. This is one of those "hidden" expenses that can shock a producer as it usually comes late in the post-production process after you think your laboratory bill is paid. Not tracking outstanding laboratory processing bills can be the nemesis of the independent producer and is often the fault of optical and title houses. These entities never consider the expense being attributed to the producers' account when they order the work to be executed; they take it for granted and the fees mount quickly. Plan for these expenses so that there are no surprises. You may want to negotiate certain specific limitations with the optical or title houses to try to keep this expense in line.

MAIN AND END TITLES

These same hidden laboratory expenses can also crop up when using a title house contracted for your project. Title houses will provide you with a bid for their creative work both for the end and main titles. Main titles should not be an afterthought, but should be integral to a project's concept as they encourage the egos of the people involved. Not all projects use a main title sequence. Some projects are conceived with credits given at the end rather than the beginning. This is entirely a creative decision. It should be made in concert with your director as it affects how the project will be directed.

There are three basic types of main title sequences each having a different creative and fiscal impact on the project. The first is the least expensive—white letters on a black screen. This is the most simple to create and the laboratory work is kept to a minimum. Creatively, you are asking the audience to focus only on the titles and nothing else. Your viewers may be hearing music, sound effects or a creative production track to help them get into the mood, but generally when using white letters over a black image, you are saying, "These are the people involved, lets get this over with, and then on to the story!" (Woody Allen uses white letters over black in most of his films.)

The second type of main title is the most common sequence—letters superimposed over picture. This involves generating an internegative from the original picture negative and putting the titles over the image. This type of main title is more expensive than the first because it involves access to your original negative and more laboratory work (that you pay for). Creatively it allows for the visual action, mood or character of the story to begin right away and says to the audience, "By the way, while your settling into the story these are the people who are involved with the project!" Today's audience is used to this type of main title sequence, which allows them to assimilate the credits and get into the story pretty easily. If these are the type of main titles you wish to use, plan for it when the script is written. Images that have superimposed titles have to be photographed with the title sequence in mind. When you see superimposed main titles that go on too long, you know that the main title was an afterthought.

The third sequence is the most expensive. This is a title sequence that stands alone creatively in the project. It is a visual representation of a tone or theme that the producer wants to get across. Movies produced from 1940 into the mid '60s always began with a separate title sequence before starting the main action of the movie. The classic examples are the ones created by Saul Bass for such films as *Man with a Golden Arm, Dial M for Murder,*

PRODUCERS VOCABULARY

Billing—The placement of names, titles, etc., in the credits. In addition to salary and profit participation in a film, billing is a major issue when negotiating a deal for talent. Other considerations for billing include: size of credit (in relation to the main title and to other performers or crewmembers); placement on the screen; how many other names are on the same screen, etc. If billing is not found to be satisfactory, it can be considered a "deal breaker."

Postproduction—One of the four stages of work of a film, television program, commercial or video production (the other three stages are development, pre-production and production). Post-production includes the steps necessary to complete a project for distribution; it occurs after principal and any second-unit filming has concluded. Examples of post-production work include picture editing, sound editing, dialogue improvement or replacement (ADR), music scoring, the inclusion of optical or computer-generated visual effects, etc.

Exodus and *West Side Story* (although these titles came at the end). The *Pink Panther* movies had their own title identity, and the title sequence for *Around the World in 80 Days* kept you interested until the very last frame. These sequences generally gave credits to everyone making the movie and did not usually separate talent between the main and end credits as we now do. Today we can see these opening sequences used in a couple of ways. They happen starting with the first frame of film as in *The Devil's Advocate*, or in the case of a James Bond movie, right after an opening action sequence as in the film *Tomorrow Never Dies*. They can be accompanied with a song or a main title theme that motivates the image. They say to the audience, "While you get a taste of the tone and feel of what you are about to see, these are the people who made this project!" These sequences must be planned as part of the creative style of the project. They involve graphic artists working through concepts with you, your director or your visual effects supervisor. These sequences often involve digital image manipulation.

It is your responsibility to give a list of the correct title credits and their sequence to the title house. These are either customary or contractual. The strongest position for an onscreen credit lies in the last credit before the start of the principle action of the project. This position is customarily given to the director. It is also contractually given to the director if the project is a DGA signatory project. It is considered the strongest because in a main title sequence audiences usually remember the last credit they read. It also allows for the latecomer to the theater who might miss the earlier credits but make it in time to see the last credit of the main titles. The next strongest sequence position is the second to the last position for the same two reasons. This position in theatrical features is awarded to the producer, while in television it is given to the writer. This is both customary and by contract with the WGA. In the theatrical market, the writer would receive the third to the last credit of the main titles. In the event that you decide that your credits will be at the end of the project and not at the beginning, a similar sequence (but reversed) is used: the first credit at the end is the director, then the producer, then the writer. The sequencing of other credits in both the main and end titles is at the discretion of the producer and is usually one of the areas for negotiations. The size, type and positioning of a credit onscreen affects the egos of the talent. Credits are determined during contract negotiations and can be used to garner a lower fee for the creative services of the talent. You have to provide the talent with an onscreen credit anyway, so make it work to your advantage. Main title credits will include key actors, composer, editor, cinematographer, production designer, producers, executive producers, writers and director. It can include other creative talent such as associate producers, line producers, casting directors, costume designers and visual effects supervisors. These decisions, and others, are yours and should be based on the desired length of the main title sequence in relationship to the project. The "A Film By" possessory credit and the position of a credit over the title of the project are the most valuable of all in contract negotiations. If you use them, do so wisely, especially when you have high-powered talent and egos to contend with. You can always elevate your credit and use "A John Doe Production" of "A Film By," or any combination to appease the creative soul.

When executing contracts for actor credits in the main title you will be faced with issues of whose title is first, second, third, etc., and whether the credits are shared card credits or solo credits. These are all problems of producing and must contractually be in place by the time you turn the information over to the title house. Credits are important since they provide acknowledgement of work well done, which we all need to massage our own egos and raise our self-esteem.

Your end titles should also be created with that statement in mind. The end credits should list everyone who worked on the project both in front of and behind the camera, from the pre-production through the post-production periods. It should not only acknowledge the people and organizations that helped on the project but also the contractual elements of product and service logos. Music credits are necessary if you use any original or recorded songs as well as disclaimers when and if you use animals in the project. If your project is fiction a disclaimer is also essential. Finally, for legal protection, the project should include copyright information. Keep the end credits simple since in most instances people will be leaving the theater way before the last credit has rolled onto screen. On occasion you may want to go for a novelty or unique end credit sequence that keeps people in their seats a bit longer, but it will also cost you more. Many audiences are appreciative of these, however, so if you previously planned for it, why not go ahead?

Stock Footage

Stock footage is film or tape footage of images that are catalogued in an archival format and available for licensing and purchase. They usually consist of newsreel or generic images that can be used to support almost any story. It is essential to use stock footage when either the director has been unable to get the appropriate footage or production issues move you in that direction. Once, a movie I directed in Lake Tahoe called for a hang-gliding sequence with two of the principal actors. We shot the landing sequence before the actual flying, which was scheduled a week later using stunt doubles. By the time we got to the flying sequences the weather had changed drastically and there was now snow on the ground. This was not going to match the already shot landing sequence so we kept pushing the flying sequences further and further into the schedule, hoping the weather would change. But as Murphy would have it, the winter came early that year in Lake Tahoe and we never shot the sequence. It was also too late to rewrite the story to work for the weather change so we had no choice but to search for stock flying footage over matching mountainous terrain. After we exhausted (what felt like) every stock library in existence, I called a friend at ABC Wide World of Sports to see if they had produced a show on hang-gliding. They did and we made a rights deal to use some of the footage in the movie.

If you plan to incorporate stock footage when you break the project down, you should try to locate and see it before you begin production. Knowing what the image looks like and how it works in context of the story will help the creative linkage for your director and cinematographer. The director, with the stock footage in mind, will be more creative when directing the sequences before and after where the stock footage is intended to be used. This technique was employed brilliantly in *Forrest Gump* and *JFK,* both of which used carefully edited stock footage to great advantage.

Stock footage is purchased and licensed by the foot, not the minute, and you will often need to purchase and license more footage than you use since there is always some degree of waste when editing the footage into the project. You are also responsible for the laboratory work for the internegative, and any telecine, which might be needed. Many producers think that stock footage is inexpensive. It is not! The licensing payment is based upon the end use of the project and the wider the distribution the greater the expense. Never try to "steal" footage for your project. You must always maintain a legal right of ownership for everything in connection with the project. Without it, you jeopardize your ability to get the project in the marketplace.

Negative Cutting

Once the picture edit has been locked it is given to the negative editor or cutter, along with a numbered list of where the cuts are to be made. If the negative is cut from the final picture edit created using a nonlinear system during the editing process the computer will print out a "film cut list." If the locked picture is available in the film format, the negative editor will make use of the cut workprint and use the edge numbers on the film. Negative editing is a business of math and accuracy and the cost varies depending on the size of the negative film stock. 16mm negative cutters assess by the cut, while 35mm negative cutters usually charge by each 1000' reel of film; if it is a short film, they will charge by the cut. It is a competitive situation, because every negative editor is an independent contractor, so make sure you receive an appropriate bid for the services. 16mm editors have the greatest variable in price, while 35mm editors will charge anywhere from $750 to $1000 a reel for the services. Do not look for shortcuts when seeking a negative editor. The bottom line is that once you turn the original negative over to the negative cutter, you are putting your investor's money in someone else's hands. You want no mistakes. Check out the negative editor; ask for references and a list of projects they have cut. If you have a completion bond, discuss the choice of a negative editor with the bonding company. They have something at risk with this decision as well. Consider carefully the location of the editor. There are negative editors who are based at film labs, and others whose operations are based elsewhere. Negative editors based out of a laboratory (assuming it's the laboratory you used) make a simple request to the film vault when working on your negative, while transportation has to be arranged for the negative to leave and return to the laboratory if the negative editor is based elsewhere. Do you want your negative to leave the laboratory? Is there any possibility that your negative can be misplaced or lost in the transport? Who will be doing the transport? What will the transport cost and who pays for it? These and other questions should be considered before you make your final decision for a negative cutter. Once you have made your decision and it works out, you will probably use that editor for all your projects.

If the project completes on video using a nonlinear system during the editing process the computer will print out a series of numbers where each edit is made. This is called an "edit decision list" (EDL). The video assembler uses the EDL to match the edits to the address track time code numbers from the video of the original material that was digitized for editing. This is done at an online session using the original video material and results in a final video edit.

Answer Print

The best possible positive image of your project will be made from the original cut picture negative. This is called the answer print and once the final mixed sound has been processed and married to the print, it becomes a composite answer print. Some producers use the non-composite answer print to mix their sound. This is not recommended, since you pay the lab for each answer print that is struck from the original picture negative and it is a costly lab expense.

The color timing of the answer print is the last area when creativity can be applied to your project. Color timing of the negative involves color correcting the print from the negative scene by scene for tone, mood, texture and dramatic feelings. This process must be done with you, the cinematographer, the director and the color timer assigned by the laboratory. The cinematographer discusses the timing in technical terms, and you should discuss the timing in terms of descriptive emotion. The color timer is able to translate words of emotion to what has to be done technically to achieve the apt effect. Color timing is subtle and affects an audience subliminally. When timing *Hunter's Blood*, we decided to start the picture with a warm feeling and gradually made it cooler as the terror of the story unfolded.

If your project is in video and you intend to transfer it to film, you follow the same process of timing the final result. However, there is a color timing process in video (suitably called the "daVinci process") that allows for shot by shot color timing, thereby providing a wider range of timing capabilities. Color timing in film is chemical, while color timing in video is electronic. The daVinci process is costly and time consuming, while color timing of an answer print is part of the normal cost of the print.

Projects are now being created with color timing done in the digital medium before transferring to film negative, thereby heightening the final result of the color.

Foreign Textless Rendition

The FTR or foreign textless rendition (often just called "textless") is a distribution delivery item. It refers to a version of the project in which the reels that normally would contain any titles have the footage without the titles. As an example, if your project has titles superimposed over picture, a FTR would be a print that only has the picture without the superimposed titles. The foreign textless rendition is given to foreign non-English speaking territories when the project is sold for distribution. The individual distributors in each of the foreign countries use this version to make their own internegative, inserting the titles in their own respective language. This is simple to provide since the background images are one of the elements used in making the titles. Your optical house should be able to create these textless elements immediately after they've finished your normal (or "texted") titles.

35mm Blowup

If your project is produced in 16mm or super 16mm and you intend to distribute theatrically (domestic or foreign) you will have to blow up the project to 35mm as very few public theaters in the world are able to project 16mm. The 35mm blowup will be a second generation negative. From that 35mm blowup, another negative (third generation) will be generated from which multiple prints will be struck for theatrical release. First-time filmmakers often believe that shooting in 16mm is less expensive than shooting in 35mm. The stock and the processing may be less expensive, but the printing ratio and the consideration of a 35mm blowup may negate any savings. As an independent producer, you must always consider how the project will be distributed and focus on the needs of the End Result Use. In order to be eligible for Academy Award® consideration, narrative films must be screened in either 35mm or 70mm for three days before a paying audience in New York and Los Angeles before the end of any year.

Protective Master Positive, Internegative (IP/IN)
Color Reversal Internegative (CRI)

The composite answer print is the final result of your efforts on the project. Additional negatives are needed for distribution. Since you must preserve your only physical asset (your original picture negative), you need to avoid using it for multiple prints. The IP/IN and CRI processes are two alternate processes that can be used to create additional negatives from which release prints are made. This expense can be negotiated with your distributor. The distributor may pick up the cost of an IP/IN or CRI as their expense, or require you to foot the expense of the IP/IN or CRI. In the event of the latter, a distributor will often advance the funds and either share in the expense or charge the expense back to you. When an answer print is manufactured from an IP/IN or CRI it is a good idea to once again meet with the color timer to ensure that your creative and emotional intent is carried through to these release prints.

Videotape Versions

In order to make a videotape version of your project you must telecine from a 35mm film element (16mm if it is originally shot in 16mm). There are several choices for the film source. With 35mm, some directors of photography like to create their video master from the cut 35mm negative. Others prefer to use an interpositive instead. Still others prefer to use a specially struck low contrast print (called a "lo-con"). There are pros and cons to each of these methods. Using the original negative may create the best video image, but will always take the longest to telecine because each shot will need to be video color timed. Since the interpositive is already color timed, the telecine will take less time and, therefore, cost appreciatively less. However, some cinematographers feel that the quality of a telecine from a lo-con is superior to an interpositive, though the expensive lo-con print has no other use, other than the telecine.

The cheapest way to telecine is from the 35mm (or 16mm) answer print, since no additional lab prints need to be made, as opposed to the lo-con method. However, the quality of the video image is generally inferior to any of the methods mentioned above. Still, you should choose the method that best suits your needs.

The video master should be in a high end format (preferably digital) from which you can make videocassettes for viewing. This video master can be used for any domestic video distribution duplication. Eventually, once your project is distributed, you will need to have a video master in the PAL or SECAM formats with music, effects and dialogue on separate tracks for foreign television distribution.

Fringe Benefits—Editing Period

Most of the labor during the editing period can be contracted through bids from individual companies. The exception is your editorial staff who begin their work at the start of principle photography. So the fringe expenses for the editing period should not be as large as during the pre-production and production periods. You may want to include any Screen Actor Guild fringes that might apply for post-production ADR work, but again, you can contract that work out to companies formed by experienced actors.

Acct. #	Account Name	Amount	Computed Rate	Sub Total	Total
4400	**FRINGE BENEFITS Editing Period**				
01	IATSE Pension Health Welfare		16%		
02	IATSE Vacation and Holiday		7.719%		
04	Payroll Taxes		17%		
	Computed on $				
	Total 4400				

Figure 50

CHAPTER **10** ADMINISTRATION

A good creative producer, like Jeff Katzenberg, is always looking for clarity. Jeff pushes me beyond where I would probably go . . . always working towards the very best, the clearest, most entertaining and dramatic way of telling the story. I think it is important that a director (of animation) embraces his producer as a partner, never as a client. Good animated films are the result of a well-structured collaboration based on mutual trust and respect. A creative producer's job is to maintain that trust and respect, and nurture it.

—Kelly A. Asbury, Feature Animation Director;
Director, *Spirit: Stallion of the Cimarron* (2002);
Story Artist, *Chicken Run, Prince of Egypt, Toy Story,
Beauty and the Beast, The Little Mermaid*

Every project will have certain administrative expenses associated with the needs of the independent producer. They include those areas that involve the creative and the organizational and position the project toward its intended end use.

PUBLICITY

The motion picture and television industry is an industry of middlemen. Although you make a project for an audience, you first must generate interest from a group of middle people who in turn get it to another group of middle people who get it to the audience. These middle people have names like distributors, exhibitors, network executives, festival programmers and studio executives. It's a crazy system but it exists. Your tool to generate interest to these people is publicity. This is a very different kind of publicity than

Acct. #	Account Name	Unit	Rate	Amount	Sub Total	Total
5000	**Publicity**					
01	Public Relations Fee					
02	Photo Suppliers and Expenses					
50	Other					
	Total 5000					

Figure 51

the electronic press kits, Internet exposure, newspaper articles, press releases and other such plans that are generated to sell the project to an audience. The Publicity Departments of the middlemen handle those once they have acquired your project. The publicity you need during the producing of the project is what will expose it to the middlemen. This kind of specific publicity often includes the preparation of biographies and photographs of the major creative people involved with the project. It may also include appropriate photographs of the cast, to be used later for distribution. This is usually handled by publicity people who have the relationships to do the job. They are familiar with the trade press, *Daily Variety* and the *Hollywood Reporter,* and know what festivals are important to your project. Publicists are usually paid a flat fee (plus expenses) for their services.

Although a publicity person is not mandatory on a project, it is helpful to have one. Your attention as a creative producer must be in the management of the project and not in trying to promote it at the same time. Ideally, you want distributors to come to you, rather than you going to them, as it will put you in a stronger position for negotiating the distribution deal. If this can be done before you complete the project, all the better! Once the project is completed, the distributor can find many reasons why they should not distribute the project. However, if the project is yet to be completed, their imagination and a certain degree of public relations hype will drive their ego towards wanting the project. A wise producer will take advantage of that leverage.

INSURANCE

Insurance is mandatory when producing a project as it reduces the fiscal risk. Your funding entity will require that the project have the appropriate insurance; you can obtain this from insurance brokers who are experts in film and video production.

The first step in assessing the risk will be the insurance company's review of the script and budget. From this assessment they gather preliminary information with respect to stunts, pyrotechnic effects, computer generated effects, specialized equipment, processes and production problems. This will allow the broker to identify risks and recommend coverage that will be best suited to the needs of your project. You need not take all the coverage that is recommended, but you will need the basic "producers package" coverage. This includes general liability, property damage, props, sets and wardrobe, faulty stock and processing, miscellaneous equipment, and auto liability and physical damage insurance.

Cast Insurance

Cast insurance provides coverage for the additional expenses to complete principle photography, or the aborted costs should the project be abandoned. It will also cover you if an insured actor, animal or other declared person cannot begin, continue or complete their duties in a production as a result of death, injury or sickness. Under the terms of this policy you declare the people (or animals) without which the project cannot be made. (There is a limit as to the number you can name without paying an additional premium.) Those listed will be required to take a physical exam by the insurance company's appointed doctor who will exclude from the coverage any pre-existing condition. (You must bear the expense of these medical exams.)

If you file a claim under this coverage, the insurance company audits your production budget and schedule to determine the amount of the claim. On one project I was involved with, my lead actor had a grand mal seizure the second day of production, which hospitalized him for a week. We had to adjust our schedule, and although we still finished on time after he returned to work, it cost us an additional $50,000 in overages. He was insured under

Acct. #	Account Name	Quote	Rate	Amount	Sub Total	Total
5100	**Insurance**					
01	Cast Insurance					
02	Props Sets and Wardrobe					
03	Extra Expense					
04	Miscellaneous Equipment					
05	Property Damage Liability					
06	Negative Film and Videotape					
07	Faulty Stock and Processing					
08	Errors and Omissions					
09	Guild/Union Travel Accident					
10	General Liability					
11	Foreign Liability					
12	Excess Umbrella Liability					
13	Railroad Protective Liability					
14	Auto Liability/Physical Damage					
15	Workers Compensation (United States)					
16	Foreign Workers Compensation					
17	Aircraft and Marine					
18	Animal					
19	Contingency					
20	Medical Exams for Cast Insurance					
50	Other					
	Total 5100					

Figure 52

our cast insurance policy and after the audit, the insurance company paid us the $50,000.

Props, Set and Wardrobe Insurance
This provides coverage for owned property and the property of others while used in connection with the production on an all-risk basis. Certain prop houses or wardrobe companies from which you rent or borrow will require this insurance, as will some tradeoff (promo) houses.

Extra Expense Insurance
Extra expense insurance provides coverage for any additional costs necessary to complete principle photography due to the loss, damage or destruction of property used in connection with the project. This also covers any loss due to generator failure or the mechanical breakdown of cameras (providing your Camera Department performs the appropriate camera tests before accepting the camera from the camera rental company).

Miscellaneous Equipment Insurance
This coverage is for owned equipment and the equipment of others, such as cameras, lighting, grip and sound equipment. This coverage also includes physical damage for all rented production vehicles.

Property Damage Liability Insurance
This is absolutely mandatory as it covers loss, damage or destruction of property belonging to others. It is required for any location that you secure for the production and includes any loss of use of that property while it is in your keeping, custody or control.

Negative Film and Videotape Insurance
This covers all risks of physical loss, damage or destruction of the film negative, of computer generated images or of sound, videotape or soundtrack. It provides coverage for the extra expenses incurred by re-shooting or re-recording the lost or damaged material.

Faulty Stock and Processing Insurance
Faulty stock and processing insurance provides coverage for the extra expense incurred in re-shooting or re-recording lost or damaged material when the loss is a result of faulty materials, equipment, developing, processing or editing. This coverage applies only if you employ appropriate professional companies with qualified personnel.

Guild and Union Travel Accident Insurance
If your project is a signatory to any union or guild, this is required for their members when traveling to distant locations.

General Liability Insurance
This insurance covers any claims of bodily injury and/or property damage arising out of production. This is mandatory and is required prior to filming on federal, city and state roads or property, or on any location sites that require permits or certificates. General liability certificates are usually needed quickly during production, so being with an insurance broker who provides you with immediate service is critical. You should be able to make a phone call and have a certificate of insurance in your hands within minutes.

Foreign Liability Insurance
Foreign liability insurance is required when a project is to be scouted or produced outside of the United States or Canada. This does not include auto liability in a foreign country, which you should get in the country where the vehicles are rented as insurance criteria vary from country to country.

Railroad Liability Insurance
Railroad companies require specific insurance that provides coverage protecting any railroad company against third party claims or claims arising in connection with the use of their property. The property can be a terminal, or the actual trains they own.

Auto Liability and Physical Damage Insurance
This covers owned, rented and non-owned autos associated with the production company. This also provides coverage if you are sued as a result of damage caused by an employee during the course and scope of the business of the production. Physical damage insurance can be tied to this coverage as well.

Excess Umbrella Liability Insurance
This is often required when liability coverage needs to be over the limits provided in the general liability, auto liability, employers' liability (workers compensation), and third party property damage policies. It will apply in certain locations which your location manager will know about.

Workers Compensation and Employers Liability Insurance
State laws require workers compensation insurance. If one of your employees is injured during the course of their work, the coverage pays for hospi-

talization, medical bills, and disability or death benefits. Although workers compensation insurance can be purchased from an insurance company, some states have state-run workers comp programs. The premium for workers comp is based upon a stated payroll. At the end of the production an auditor from the insurance company will audit your payroll to determine if the payroll matched your original statement. If you underestimate your payroll, you will have to pay an additional premium. If you overestimate, your payroll you will receive a refund. To err on the side of the refund might be preferred, as it will provide you with a *fifth method of providing fiscal security to protect against possible budget overages.* The majority of your payroll will be during the production period, so the refund can offer you unexpected resources for use during post-production. The Screen Actors Guild requires that their members work only on projects that are covered by a Workers Compensation Policy.

Foreign Workers Compensation and Employers Liability Insurance
This may be required for your personnel when a project is scouted or produced outside of the United States or Canada. It will depend on the structure of the labor and the country in which you will be working.

Aircraft and Marine Insurance
This is available when a plane, helicopter or watercraft is rented, leased or borrowed for the use of scouting locations, production on water, or aerial photography. You are also able to insure the hull of a boat against damage or destruction due to the production.

Animal Insurance
This provides for loss or damage to animals used in connection with the project.

Contingency Insurance
There is also insurance that affords for any loss sustained by reason of any insured person on the project being necessarily prevented from beginning, continuing, or completing their responsibilities, caused by the hazards that have been insured against.

Errors and Omissions Insurance
The E&O insurance provides against libel, slander or other forms of defamation, as well as invasion of the right of privacy and publicity. It also

affords protection against infringement of copyright and coverage against purported claims of unauthorized use of names, trade names, service marks, titles, formats, ideas, characters, character names, characterizations, plots, musical compositions, performances, slogans, program material or any similar material. The E&O policy also covers any breach of contracts or circumstances surrounding any facts with respect to the alleged submission of any literary, dramatic, musical or other similar material, or a breach of any trust and confidence that surrounds the submissions. An Errors and Omissions policy is not necessary for the project to move forward. However, *it is necessary for the project after it has been completed.* You must make sure that you have all the written clearances, contracts, authorships, copyrights and releases upon the completion of the project. If the project is unable to acquire an E&O policy, you will be unable to get the project in the marketplace, or to screen it in a public forum. Providing you have the documentation, the Errors and Omissions policy may be considered a distribution expense and be included in negotiations with your distributor since it must be valid for every year the project is in distribution.

These policies are fundamentally for the production period and will contain exclusions and terms and conditions that you and your attorney should read very carefully. Your production manager, location manager, accountant and bonding company will all be concerned with the type of insurance you purchase for your project, while the cast and crew rarely think about insurance. But it must be in the back of your mind at all times. Any claims against

...one of the smartest things a creative independent producer can do at the onset of a production of any size, is to work closely with their insurance broker, who is experienced in insuring motion pictures or television projects. By reading the script and going over the budget in detail, the broker is often in a position to point out potential insurance problems that might have gone unnoticed—like auto and pyrotechnic stunts being excluded from the coverage. Your broker, thinking creatively and working with the producer, can frequently work out ways to allow for the scripted stunts with a minimum of additional cost.

—Truman Van Dyke, Insurance Broker,
*The Wedding Planner, The English Patient;
Reservoir Dogs; sex, lies and videotape*

these policies will be on a per incident basis and you will be responsible for the declared deductible. So there are a couple of points to keep in mind.

First, make sure you rent equipment from qualified vendors. You may come across a situation where an individual who owns a special piece of equipment rents to your production at a reduced rate. The equipment may appear functional but there may be some minor damage to it not caused by your production and, when it is returned, the owner may declare the equipment was damaged during use by your production—thus forcing you to file an insurance claim.

Second, make sure that your location manager takes photographs of all locations before you use them, noting any pre-existing damage. Location owners are notorious for declaring damages knowing that insurance will provide a new paint job or new wallpaper. A little precaution and some sensible production practices will save you money in the long run. Insurance provides protection against the effects of Murphy's Law. The best protection, however, is your own common sense, creativity and decision-making capabilities.

MISCELLANEOUS

Many production budgets forget obvious items that should be applied to the negative cost of the project, assuming they will be absorbed "somewhere." But any actual expenses should be assigned to the project in the budget. These include particulars such as office rentals, telephone, office equipment, copying and those occasional meals that you must pick up when you and your staff discuss the creative elements over a breakfast or lunch.

MPAA Rating Fee

The Motion Picture Association of America (MPAA) provides ratings on all theatrical motion pictures. The ratings are G, PG, PG13, R, NC-17 and X. You pay a fee each time your project needs to be rated and each time the ratings board views your project. The fees are not less than $2500, and are charged on a sliding scale, depending on the size of the submitting company. If you want to wait until you have a distributor, the fee may be lower, but the distributor will still charge it back to you as a negative expense.

It is a well-kept secret as to who the specific people are who view the project and recommend the rating. Although the only game in town, the rating system is currently under scrutiny. Jack Valenti has been the vocal representative of the MPAA for many decades and was originally responsible for setting the rating system standard. Almost two thirds of today's motion pic-

Acct. #	Account Name	Unit	Rate	Amount	Sub Total	Total
5200	**Miscellaneous**					
01	Office Rentals					
02	Telephone					
03	Office Equipment Rental					
04	Printing and Duplicating					
05	Business Sundry Expense					
06	Office Supplies					
07	MPAA Rating Fee					
08	Dialogue Continuities					
09	Production Wrap Expense					
10	Premiere Screening Expense					
11	Production Service Organization Administration					
12	Fringe Benefits - Administration					
50	Other					
	Total 5200					

Figure 53

tures receive an R rating for one reason or another. Currently, there is a movement afoot for a new Adults Only rating that would help parents distinguish different types of explicit material, since the modern cultural scene is changing. At the moment the adult ratings are NC-17 and X (*Midnight Cowboy* was originally released with the X rating). But X is generally reserved for pornographic projects. X and NC-17 rated projects are barred from advertising in many forms of media. This is one reason that distributors often make a certain rating a specific requirement for their acceptance of the project, and this may force you to creatively re-edit the project.

Currently the rating system is under attack, not only by conservative legislators, but also independent film producers, who feel their artistic freedom is being battered. Studios are suggesting expanding the rating systems to indicate isolated ratings for sex, objectionable language or violence. Some studios are asking for a universal rating system for all entertainment, including television. You can already see a difference between original programming for subscribed cable television and free television. The content in such shows as *The Sopranos, Sex and the City, Oz, Queer as Folk,* or *Real Sex* would never be seen in network television. Also, such shows as *Will and Grace, Law and Order* and *The Practice* use subject content that would not have been accepted on network even five years ago. The content of projects is also an issue in the foreign market, especially in territories that practice various degrees of censorship. If you recognize the content differences between these markets, then you should attempt to have your director shoot dialogue and sequences for both. When shooting an R rated project intended for the theatrical market it is not unusual to also shoot the R sequences as a PG or PG-13 for network television (this is called "television coverage").

Dialogue Continuities

Your project may change from the time the script was originally written to when the project is finally completed. Along the way, dialogue may have been changed, deleted or added. A text of the completed script, including the final dialogue, is required for foreign distribution as it is used as a reference for dubbing into foreign languages. This is referred to as a dialogue continuity. The distributor can create it once you have secured a distribution deal. They hire someone to watch the project several times, write every line of dialogue, and then charge that expense back to you. This expense can be avoided by making sure that your production keeps an accurate and up-to-date running record of all dialogue changes during the production and post-production processes.

Production Wrap and Premiere Screening Expenses

It makes no difference what the project is, you will always want either a party at the completion of the production period, a party to premiere the project, or both. These occasions are almost always an afterthought and independent producers generally scramble for supporting resources. The production wrap party is usually limited to only the production people and is generally very casual, while the premiere screening party may be more formal and may extend to many more people. Both events are morale and ego boosters and establish the deep-rooted relationships that will be important to you in the future. At both events you must state your appreciation for as many people as possible, knowing that each of them has provided their own creative expertise on the project. Attempt to be one of the team, since the people you meet going up the ladder may well be the same people you meet going down. Begin those relationships with warmth, dignity and respect. It will take you far!

PRODUCERS VOCABULARY

Domestic Version—The cut of a project that is released in the United States and Canada (domestic market) which may have been edited to achieve a particular rating by the MPAA. This will be different from an Overseas Version or Television Version, which will be appropriate for those markets.

MPAA—The Motion Picture Association of America represents the interests of the major distributors in financial, legal, ethical, and domestic and foreign trade as well as monitors the pirating of motion picture projects throughout the world. Organization in the United States comprised of major producers and distributors. Among its various activities, it issues ratings (which are trademarked) for theatrical films and direct-to-video movies; promotes foreign distribution of U.S. films; operates a film title registration service; and provides a voice for the U.S. film industry in news media interviews and government hearings on such matters as film and video piracy, censorship standards, the impact of new and future technologies on moviemaking and industry financial trends. The Motion Picture Export Association (MPEA) is the foreign arm of the MPAA. Founded in 1922 and based in Washington, D.C. and Encino, California.

MPAA Code Seal—An on screen endorsement that a project or advertising has been conformed to the regulations and standards of the MPAA.

FEES

Any project you do will usually have fees attached. It can be a broker or investment fee paid to entities who help structure the deal, or fees for legal and accounting services. These fees are included in Figure #54.

Finder Agreement

Many independent producers offer a fee to the "finder" of the funds for the production. This is called a finders fee; it is included *only* on the top sheet of the budget (Figure #11) as Other Fees. The finders agreement should indicate that you have the right to produce the project and own or control it and that the finder is engaged in finding financing for investment projects such as yours. The finder may be an agent who arranges foreign or domestic distribution as a source of the financing structure. In your agreement the finder should be encouraged to introduce you to other parties who may be interested in lending, investing, distributing or financing all or any portion of your project. After you have defined the finder's fee clearly within the structure of the agreement you should include a clause that gives the finder exclusivity for a finite period of time. However, the fee should not be paid until all the financing is in place. Many finders ask for a credit as an executive producer. (This is fair if they are responsible for at least 90 percent of the financing.)

To determine the legitimacy of a finder, try to determine if they have had prior substantial experience in raising funds. They should also provide you with proof they are not insolvent or in any danger of bankruptcy. This will give you aid in the event of any problems that may result involving the investors the finder may bring to the project. All agreements should always be in writing and always be prepared by your attorney.

Legal

Your attorney is your cohort, confidante, friend, partner and colleague and should be an expert in all legal aspects related to independent financing, producing and distribution. Your attorney is involved with you and your project from the moment of development through the completion of distribution and beyond, and can be a link to many relationships that are essential in between. The legal advice your attorney renders should always be considered and analyzed very carefully since you are the one ultimately responsible for all creative and business decisions. Do not be afraid to discuss every business situation with your attorney, as having the legal perspective will make your producing easier. Attorneys usually receive an

Acct. #	Account Name		Rate	Amount	Sub Total	Total
5300	Fees					
01	Company Accounting Fee					
02	Company Legal					
03	Miscellaenous Fees					
50	Other					
		Total 5300				

Figure 54

hourly fee for their services, although some may be willing to take equity participation as their fee. You should openly discuss this with your legal counsel so there is no possibility of a misunderstanding. Regardless of the arrangement, you need to budget resources for legal fees as attorneys send out some of the specialty work to other attorneys and fees will be involved.

Accountant

Your accountant or CPA firm is *also* your cohort, confidante, friend, partner and colleague advising you on fiscal matters in relationship to your project. Different than the production accountant, the accountant for your project should be responsible for the larger fiscal issues of the investment, partnership, recoupment, tax liabilities and profit acquisition. Accountants or CPA firms usually receive a fee for these services, but often receive equity participation in lieu of a fee. When your attorney and accountant are on board and immersed in the project, you will have the security of knowing that both the legal and the fiscal attributes are secure and your energies can be focused on the creative producing decisions.

——— • • • ———

DISTRIBUTION DELIVERY ITEMS
Once the project is complete and you have arranged for its distribution, there are several delivery items that you are responsible for. These items have been discussed in detail throughout the previous chapters:
1. Still Photographs—Page 142
2. Rights and Clearances for Errors and Omissions Insurance—Page 232
3. Lo-con and Video master—Page 214
4. Dialogue Continuities—Page 236
5. Color Reversal Internegative (CRI) or Interpositive (IP/IN) - Page 225
6. Music and Effects Track—Page 216
7. Foreign Textless Rendition of Main and End Titles—Page 224
8. Biographies of the Creative Team—Page 227

——— • • • ———

CHAPTER 11 PUTTING IT ALL TOGETHER

There are no set views on how to produce. You just go and do it. Producing involves the developing, creative and logistical processes of the project and may include the details of its funding. Sometimes the economic structure is through co-financing, or partial financing and partial contribution through goods and service relationships. In other instances the structure may utilize deferrals, which are payments made in the future for services that are provided during the producing of the project. This structure is preferred by independent producers when they are either desperate or have no other choice. It is an arrangement that can work for you or work against you.

DEFERMENTS

Deferments can be looked at as a structure that "allows for something now and allows you to worry about its payment later." This can be dangerous. Although deferrals are necessary in certain instances, it is imperative that you structure a deferral that protects the assets of the project. The low budget agreements of the Directors Guild of America, for example, allows for directors to receive a deferred payment after the project has returned 200 percent of the investment. In this case, the deferred terms of payment are favorable to the producer and to the investment and therefore make sense.

Is the deferral payment put in first position before investment return? If there is more than one deferred entity are all deferrals paid at the same time when resources become available? If they are, how do you pay them equitably? Deferral participants may ask for equity participation in exchange for either a lower fee or an entire deferral. How will this arrangement work? These and other questions should be carefully worked through with your attorney, and clearly defined and agreed to by your investors before arranging any deferrals.

Deferred elements may insist upon a security interest in the picture negative or some other collateral until they have been paid their fees. Although the Screen Actors Guild requires a security interest in the negative to assure their actors will receive any and all residual payments, it is usually quickly relieved once you have a distribution agreement. Independent producers often try to work deferrals with labs and post-production sound companies in case they run out of funds during production. Because they usually get payment for their services late in the production schedule, labs and post-production sound companies are wise to this practice, and will usually insist upon their fees up front. Some may, however, agree to deferrals, keeping a security interest in the negative. This is not a practice you should agree to, since it puts legal bindings on your only asset (the negative), and can affect the investment and cause all kinds of legal problems by tying up your project and preventing it from getting distribution. If you must use deferrals as a method of producing your project, use them wisely, always protecting the End Result Use of the project at all costs. Deferrals should be included in the negative cost of the project!

PSYCHOLOGY OF PRODUCTION LAYOUT

Many of the hair-trigger creative decisions you will make will be during the highly volatile production period. These decisions will set the course for the philosophy of your producing. Your knowledge of the details of your budget combined with the details of production choreography as reflected in your production board will give you the wisdom you need to keep the project on the creative track.

It is almost never cost effective to shoot projects in story or script sequence. The burden of maintaining consistent creative performances is the responsibility of the director who must be attuned not only to the demands of production, but also to its effect on the talent in front of the camera. Your skill as a creative producer lightens this burden. Your total objective is to be creative and to permit, encourage and nourish the director and cinematographer to be as creative as possible. This must be your primary focus and one that your production board will help you achieve.

Another priority is, through your production team, to creatively make sure they complete each day's work within the prescribed and planned hours. To do this you must consider several factors. One concerns the first day of the project. There are three basic doctrines for scheduling the first day. The first is to schedule work that is very easy to complete so that the director and production company will feel satisfied about getting the project off to a good start. The second theory is to schedule difficult work on the first day, pushing the director and the production to finish what is planned.

The logic behind this blueprint is that if the work is completed and the project is still on schedule, everyone on the production crew will know that they can complete any other day in the schedule. The third theory is to schedule a day that is neither too easy nor too hard but comfortable, with the idea of completing the days work. This planned logic opines that if the first day is completed, when the schedule becomes tougher the director and the production crew will be able to handle it easily.

These three choices should be discussed amongst you, your director, cinematographer, first assistant director and production manager. The final decision, however, will be most important as the outcome of the first day of the production schedule sets the tone for the rest of the schedule. If you end the day behind schedule, the psychological factor for the production company will be one of trying to "catch up" and the director will be under pressure to make up for being behind. This may affect the creative decisions made on the set. At the same time, if the day is too easy, the production crew may adopt a lazy attitude on the project and expect that the rest of the schedule will be equally problem-free. This too may affect the creative decisions made on the set. The first day of the production is a day when everyone is getting to know everyone else. Grips and electricians are trying to find where equipment is stored, the assistant directors are getting a feeling of how the director and cinematographer work, the Camera Department is trying to get its working relationship in place, wardrobe and props are learning the particulars of the characters in the story and many actors are meeting one another for the first time. Although some of the people may have worked together during planning or with one another on other productions, they are not as yet into the rhythm of the project. It takes time for

---

PRODUCERS VOCABULARY

Calltime—The time and location for the next day or night shooting.

Call Sheet—A list typically posted or distributed at the close of each shooting day. Prepared by the second assistant director under the supervision of the first assistant director and approved by the production manager, the call sheet displays the call time for each cast and crew member (e.g., the time when one must report to the set or to the area for pre-arranged transportation to the location); informs the cast and crew which scenes are to be shot; the order of the scenes to be shot; which sets or locations will be utilized; what the cover sets are; and any unusual equipment needed (crane, Steadicam, etc.).

Closed Set—A studio set or location set that is closed to anyone not immediately connected with the production. (Sometimes, when an intimate scene is to be shot, only the most necessary crew members are allowed on the set; henceforth, the set will be "closed" to remaining crew members.)

Cover Set—An alternate film location and timetable to be used in the event that shooting cannot proceed as planned, e.g., if exterior shooting is thwarted by weather, it is imperative to have a backup schedule of interior locations which can be substituted.

individual crewmembers to know the idiosyncrasies of one another and reach a comfort level for working in a harmonious environment. This is called the "ease factor." Your hope is that the ease factor sets in as quickly as possible, because it is one of the building blocks of a successful production.

There are some production issues you should stay away from on the first day, because they rely heavily on the ease factor already being present.

First—delay the stunts. Stunts often involve a lot of rehearsal and onsite planning and execution. When they involve actors rather than stunt people, the stunts may take even longer to stage. Stunts can be complex and are better planned later in the schedule.

Second—avoid shooting love scenes early in the schedule unless the love scene is motivated by the characters meeting one another for the first time. Love scenes are tough to do well and you want the actors to be as comfortable as possible with one another before asking them to be intimate.

Third—stay away from sequences that involve dialogue in moving vehicles. The production techniques for these scenes are different and complex and take a lot of time. They are better suited for later in the schedule when the ease factor has been established.

Fourth—stay away from special effects. Special effects are time consuming and may result in Murphy's Law when scheduled for the first day of production.

Fifth—keep away from crowd scenes. Working with large numbers of extras is difficult enough; doing it on the first day of the schedule only reduces the odds of completing the first day's work.

And you *must* complete the first day's work. It should be a constructive day and a day in which people learn about one another. It should be a creative day and one that goes well. At the end of that day, your cast and production people have to feel good. They must know the train that they are on has left the station and it's going to be a congenial ride.

The rest of the schedule will depend on a variety of factors, the most important of which is which sequences your director most wants to spend time with in telling the story. These are usually (but not always) the scenes where the director needs to focus on the actors' performances rather than the production elements surrounding the actor. They are sequences that are emotional or passionate and demand the director's uninterrupted attention and concentration. The schedule should be planned out with those sequences in mind regardless of the script page count. Producers on theatrical projects try to complete two to three script pages each production day. Producers on television productions plan on four to five pages each production day (and sometimes seven or eight). Many independent producers plan on completing anywhere from two to five pages a day depending on the elements of each boarded sequence. Budget restrictions and creativity will always be the driving force in terms of the daily page count.

Shooting on location versus in a studio is another scheduling factor. Studio production is controlled, which allows you to move the production elements quicker. But you will also have the problems of set construction, rigging and striking to contend with. Locations may give you more realistic picture value, but they have their own related problems, making this a major factor affecting the production schedule. A location is selected primarily for creative reasons but you should consider the logistics of the location as well. What is its accessibility? What are the restrictions of its use, its cost, and its production limitations? Productions shot on location all share one great truth; *it is impossible to move a production company more than once in any day and still complete the production day.* Even one "company move" becomes problematic, because when you move a production company in the middle of a shoot day you are inviting Murphy's Law in the front door and offering milk and cookies. As a result, most location projects attempt to board out by location groupings first, both interior and exterior, and then by day and night sequences in a location. This could play havoc with actors' schedule and the SAG budget, so you need to monitor the day out of days as the board shifts due to locations. Most projects have primary and secondary locations that are needed to tell the story. The primary locations are ones that you will focus on either finding or constructing. If you can find secondary locations within the immediate vicinity of the primary location, you will save yourself a production move and therefore valuable production time. You should consider this option even if it means making the shoe fit the foot by selecting an alternative location other than the one written in the script.

Interior day sequences always take longer to set up than exterior day sequences, and interior night sequences take longer to set up than interior day sequences. (Note: Interior night does not have to be shot at night.) Exterior night sequences always take the longest to set up because of night weather conditions and the additional crew and equipment that are often needed. Exterior night sequences are also more difficult for the production crew to get accustomed to because their internal clocks are thrown off. But since it is a creative necessity, it must be prepared for very conscientiously within the structure of the production schedule. Care should be taken to make sure that the crew and cast are given the pertinent number of hours between workdays (or nights) to avoid potential burnout. Too little time off can result in forced work calls, an increase in cast and crew payroll, and a diminished crew performance that will affect the creative contribution. To allow for this, if exterior night work is mixed with either interior or exterior day work during a week, the production board might schedule out the exterior night work towards the end of the workweek, rather than the beginning of the workweek. Or it might make more production sense to start the week with an early call time and each successive day make the call time a little later so that by the third day you are scheduling some of the exterior night work and increasing it during the remainder of the workweek.

The time of year you shoot will have an impact on the schedule. If the project boards out with more exterior day sequences than exterior night, it might make sense to shoot the project in the spring or summer when there are more hours of daylight in the Western Hemisphere. Or, you may want to shoot in another part of the world, where the weather conditions will correspond to these needs. If your cinematographer and director want to shoot an exterior sequence at "magic hour" your production day will be boarded around that requirement. Magic "hour" is a misnomer because it actually lasts about twenty minutes and occurs just as the sun is rising or setting. It offers a wonderful lighting quality that only Mother Nature can create. The scene needs to be set up and rehearsed for camera before magic hour hits and at the right time (when the quality of the light is ideal) the director calls action. (Remember the wonderful magic hour shot in *City of Angels* when all the angels are standing on the beach at sunset? Perfect!)

Adverse weather conditions can have a huge negative impact on your schedule and budget. Annual regional weather conditions have a greater degree of predictability in some months of the year than in others. Probable weather problems may dictate that the exterior sequences, for example, should be shot as soon as possible, while holding the interiors for later in the schedule. Or it might require the interiors be used as cover sets throughout the production schedule in case of bad weather. (A cover set is an interior location that is on standby in case scheduled exteriors cannot be met.)

PRODUCERS VOCABULARY

Day for Night—The use of under exposure, filtration and placement of the sun in relationship to a shot to create the illusion of night exterior, though photographed during the day. The consideration of shooting a scene day for night is based upon the production schedule, location, the length of the scene and the sequence that comes before it and after it in the project. The technique was devised in Hollywood, and therefore is called, in French, "La Nuite Americaine." François Truffaut's film *Day for Night* (1973) is an excellent example of this practice in filmmaking.

Night for Night—Night sequences that are actually shot at night. This usually pertains to night exteriors or night interiors where the cinematographer wants to see night usually through windows.

Story elements can also affect how a production is scheduled. For example, if the story calls for characters to watch something on television, then the television sequence has to be shot first before you shoot the scene.

An actor's personal requirements can also have an impact on the production schedule. Your project may have children in the cast, and child labor laws permit minors to work only a certain number of hours per day. Therefore, you will have to schedule to accommodate those issues. If an actor is unavailable until a certain date, you may have to schedule around the availability or hire a different actor. Or your schedule may have to be arranged for the actors' workweek. *Hunter's Blood* had a six-day week production schedule. Because it was a local project, the actors' workweek was five days. We scheduled only Sam Bottoms on the sixth day of the week. Sam worked on a weekly agreement so the sixth day was an overtime day. It proved to be cost effective to shoot a six-day week and pay the overtime for one actor.

Production techniques will also affect the production board layout. Your production board schedule is affected if your director plans on using special technical equipment—such as camera cranes, Steadicams, camera cars, helicoptercams or helicopters. Special technical equipment is provided by independent companies with which you will have to schedule the equipment's availability. The equipment takes time to set up, rehearse with and use, so the schedule will need to reflect its use on any specific day. These days should be talked through before they are scheduled, keeping in mind the director's need to creatively tell the story.

Scheduling the sequence of scenes to be shot on any specific day is part of the production layout. This is best determined by the director and first assistant director. For creative reasons your director may want to schedule specific scenes earlier or later in the day. Certain production and cast elements may only be available at certain times. There are many reasons for laying out a daily shooting sequence. But there are two basic truths about daily sequence scheduling that should be foremost in your thinking.

The first truth is that the time the first shot of the day takes place will determine the pacing for the entire day. The director must set a time marker each day when he or she wants to do the first shot of the day. That time is a gauge for the first assistant director for the day's work and the 1st AD pushes the crew and plans accordingly. If that time is met, the day has a chance of getting completed.

The second truth is that more work gets done before lunch than after lunch. The production crew is fresher at the start of the day. The meal period is the break that takes them to and through the halfway mark. Because they have more energy at the start of the day, they work harder and look forward to the meal break. The meal allows them to relax a bit and enjoy the wonderful catered food you provide. They may feel a bit lazier on a full stomach (as many of us do) so usually things slow down after the meal. A smart producer will plan on doing the more complicated scenes before the meal when the production crew is freshest and most alert, knowing that their creative focus is most attentive to the needs of the project then.

Also, if you have a lot of extras or cast members working in one or two scenes you may want to schedule those scenes before or after the meal. If they are excused before or come to work after the meal, you save on the catering for that day.

Four Scheduled Days

Separate each production day with a black strip once you have arranged the board (see Figure #55). The production board constantly changes. You begin with an ideal proposed schedule and, as elements come together (or don't), you shift things around on the board. The changes that this causes in most instances are minor, as they relate to logistics and availability. Change has its greatest impact on your cast budget, as the day out of days will shift each time there is a change. For that reason it is wise to hire actors with an "on or about" date. Any time there is a shift in the schedule, your production accountant should analyze the cast budget and update its projected expense.

Since there will always be days when the director does not complete what is planned, try to design days in your schedule that can be used to pick up any scenes your director may not have shot when they were scheduled. This affords the production a safety net. If you use the shoe fit the foot theory you do not necessarily have to return to a location to get the scene. Your creativity will find a solution. Tom Denove and I were shooting a project several years ago that I was directing but not producing. Poor producing on the project caused us continual problems during the production. I was unable to shoot two 1/8 page scenes that were important to the story. One was an exterior low angle window shot of Mitzi Kapture, as she looks and reacts to a fight taking place on the street below. The other was a sequence with Miles O'Keefe. He needed to go into a closet and open a chest full of war memen-

FOUR SCHEDULED DAYS

Breakdown Page		1	4	D	5	8	D	10	D	6	3	D
Day or Night		N	N	A	D	N	A	D	A	D	N	A
Location or Studio		L	L	Y	L	L	Y	L	Y	S	S	Y
Sequence		INT	INT		EXT	EXT		EXT		INT	INT	
No. of Pages		5/8	2		1 1/8	1/8		1 1/8		3 1/8	2	
Blue: Ext. Night, Green: Int. Night White: Ext. Day, Yellow: Int. Day Red: Traveling sequences				#1			#2		#3			#4
Title: Love in a Handbasket		Eyan's Bedroom	Eyan's Bedroom		Beach	Beach Pier		Eyan's Apartment		Euclid County Jail	Trish's Livingroom	
Director: J. Moore												
Producer: C. Bradley												
Asst. Dir.: R. Robles												
Script Dated: 2/4/01												
Character **Artist**		1	3B		4	7		9		5	3A	
Eyan Hayes	1	1	1		1			1				
Trish Malone	2	2	2		2			2		2		
Suny Malone	3				3	3		3		3	3	
Angela Hayes	4				4	4		4		4	4	
Tommy Joe	5											
Delphine	6											
Meredith	7											
June	8					8						
Bob	9											
Don	10					10						
Eyan's Stunt Double	11				11							
Trish's Stunt Double	12				12							
Delia Varni	13											
Charlotte Silver	14											
Cop #1 15 Mary	19	15			15							
Cop #2 16 Monica	20				20							
Fire #1 17 Leslie	21	17			21			17				
Tyler 18 Gower	22				18	22						
Waiter A Nun D	23	C/D						A/B				
Waitress B Teacher E	24											
Rabbi C Librarian F	25											
	26											
	27											
	28											
Atmosphere	29				3 ✕ 2			6 ✕ 4				
10 beach marines	30				30							
	31											
	32											
	33											
	34	Trish/Eyan make love			Trish/Eyan almost drown	The heist is planned (pos. magic hour)		Eyan's Apt. on Fire		Angela Bails Suny out	Suny/Angela Argue	
	35											
	36		Trish on phone									
	37											

Figure 55

tos from his past. He rustles around and finally finds a semi-automatic assault rifle he used in Vietnam. Both scenes were scheduled early, at specific locations. The strips in the board representing these two scenes kept getting moved to days when we would be at locations that could be adapted for the scenes. But we never seemed to have the time to shoot them. Finally, we were on the last day of our shooting schedule and it was a night exterior in an alley. Both Mitzi and Miles were scheduled to work that evening. We had not as yet shot those two scenes, both of which were needed to tell the story. Thinking on our feet, Tom and I had the property master rustle up a wall flat and a window flat from a college theater department. We arranged the flats on the scissors lift we were using as a light stand to illuminate the alley. We put Mitzi in the appropriate wardrobe behind the window flat on the scissors lift and raised the lift about fifteen feet off the ground. On "action" Mitzi stepped out from behind the wall flat and appeared in the window flat looking toward the camera below her. It worked in the picture. (How? Because the audience only sees what's on the screen, not how it got there!) The second scene was more difficult. Tom took the same two flats and positioned them in the alley at right angles to one another to look like the corner of a closet. We then put the camera on top of a ladder and focused it straight down the flats. We found an old piece of carpet in an alley dumpster and put it in the shot between the flats on the asphalt surface of the alley. Tom hung a practical light bulb in the camera frame to make it appear to be a light bulb hanging from a ceiling in a closet. We put the chest of momentos in the camera frame and I staged Miles to enter the frame and rustle through the chest until he found the parts of the rifle. He took the parts out of the chest, snapped them together and quickly turned off the light. Once again, the audience saw just what we wanted them to see!

Many more issues will arise during the production and you will usually be able to find their solutions using the production board. Working with the production board is like working with a giant puzzle. Once the production is underway, for one reason or another, the shapes of the puzzle pieces change. Since your vision is what the finished puzzle is to look like, you must find a way to complete the puzzle. If you complete the puzzle, you complete the picture.

THE LOX AND BAGELS MEETINGS

You will have many meetings during the planning stages of the project. Each meeting, usually on a specific topic, helps build the puzzle. But there are two meetings that you must have. These meetings are called "lox and bagels meetings" because you put out a spread of food that people can help themselves to during the meeting. These meetings can be as long as five or six hours for feature projects (so don't skimp on the food). If the meeting begins in the morning and goes throughout the day, have such items like bagels, lox, cream cheese, fruits, vegetables, juices, coffee, breads, cold cuts, etc. These meetings are critical to the success of the production as they put everyone on the same creative and logistic pages and you need people to pay attention to the meeting—not their hungry stomachs.

The first of these meetings should be held sometime during the first or second week of pre-production. You must require everyone hired to be present and invite those whom you intend to hire. By the second week, the people on your payroll should be the creative team, the department heads, your casting agent, production coordinator, location manager, transportation coordinator and production manager. All of these people should have read the project by the time you hold this meeting. Some of them may have had some discussion with the director and all of them will come to the meeting with creative ideas ready to flow forth. This meeting is held by your director and should be a detailed creative discussion of the story starting with the first scene and ending with the last page of the screenplay. The director offers the creative vision and shares ideas of the creative content and tone of the story, its theme and its characters. At this meeting, the director discusses the look of locations, wardrobe, set dressing, and props scene by scene and gets into the particulars of action, special effects, visual effects, and other areas that impact the aesthetic nature of the project. You should passively be participating, armed with your creativity and your knowledge of the budget limitations. You must never mention those limitations; but your participation must challenge the egos and creative abilities of everyone involved since one of the certainties of production is that creativity flourishes within limitations.

The second lox and bagels meeting is yours. This meeting must be scheduled no earlier than three to five days before the start of principle photography. It must be mandatory for everyone on the payroll to be present (except the actors) as well as those whom you intend to hire or are scheduled to begin work on the first day of production. Eighty percent of your production staff will be on your payroll by this meeting. The remaining 20 percent will be members of your production crew who begin work on the first day of principle photography. Although not being paid to attend the meeting, they will probably be there since their own creative egos will motivate them to be on the same page as everyone else when they begin work. It will serve you well to welcome them and appreciate their attendance. You and your production manager head up this meeting using the production board and script as the basis of discussion. Each of the production areas should have completed their preparation and bring their knowledge, skills,

---

PRODUCERS VOCABULARY

P&A—Prints and advertising, which is the expense for a project once it proceeds to distribution.

Production Report—Daily report itemizing all elements used for that particular day of shooting; filled out by the key second assistant director and submitted to the production manager for approval. The completed report is sent to the producer, director, production auditor, studio executive (if applicable), bonding company and any other party concerned with the daily costs of the production. The report includes such items as: the scenes shot, the number of pages completed, amount of footage exposed, any abnormalities to explain overage or underuse of material covered, any penalties incurred and their reasons, which crew members and actors were used, etc.

research and creativity to this discussion. During the meeting you discuss each production day and its creative and logistic problems. Your director and cinematographer detail how they want to tell the story in each scene. The Special Effects Department talks through its contribution scene by scene and estimates the amount of setup time required. The stunt coordinator discusses stunts and stunt safety in detail, and each of the other production areas has a similar opportunity to talk through the schedule. This lets everyone see if they have any logistical problems in relation to what is planned creatively. You will hear any potential problems that may erupt during the production and should be able to plan how to protect the choreographic creative moments that are critical to the story. This might require a change in the directorial approach to a sequence, a change in a location, a rework of the production board or a possible rewrite of the script. This meeting allows you to talk through each day as if you were already shooting the project.

These two meetings are very important to the production success of the project. The first prepares people to creatively think in a collaborative direction; the second reveals the results of their preparation and how it fits in the whole of the project. Creativity has a flow. These two meetings let you nurture that flow.

CHAPTER **12**   PRODUCING

THE PRODUCER AS COACH

The producer is the coach of the project; its guiding force. You hire the team, make up the plays, and with the quarterback (your director), you decide what plays are called and when. Sometimes your quarterback runs with the ball and sometimes passes it to someone else. When in doubt, your quarterback confers with you concerning what to do to succeed. And you and your quarterback lead the victory celebration when you win. When you don't, the two of you chatter enthusiastically about the plans for the next game. There's an old story about a meeting between a creative producer and a director just before principle photography begins on a picture. The producer takes a revolver out of his coat pocket and, with a knowing smile, points it at the director. When production begins, the producer gives the revolver to the director who points it at the producer and cocks it. This story has been told for many decades and illustrates the struggle for creative control between producer and the director. In *The Bad and the Beautiful,* a movie about movies, Kirk Douglas plays a very hands-on producer who keeps telling the director of his movie how to direct. The director finally says to Douglas, "You take over," and walks off the project. Douglas does and the project becomes a great fiasco.

The moral: producers must produce and directors must direct. It is impossible to have one without the other. They both must be clear on the vision and goal of the project. A good producer is not always a good director, and a good director does not always make a good producer. But a good director needs to know about producing and a good producer needs to know about directing so that both may understand, respect and creatively collaborate with one another.

Integrity and fairness are two words that you must keep in the forefront of your mind when you produce. Never approach a producing situation with the notion that you are always right or that you think the risk is yours and yours alone. Everyone shares in the risk in his or her own way. It may be their ego, their reputation, or their job. But they share in the risk. You should always be interested in *what* is right rather than *who* is right. Keep your eye on the project, not on the personal. This approach must be foremost in your mind whether it involves negotiations, production decisions or creative story choices. Always speak your mind. Since you are the producer always say what you think, because other people around you may be afraid to speak. But if you say it in the form of a question you are encouraging others to contribute creatively while nurturing their ego. If you are wrong about something, or something happens on the project that is your fault, never be afraid to admit it. This only shows you have failings and are willing to take the consequences for them. This humility gains you respect, reinforces your creative position and, believe it or not, moves things along on the project.

Your skill as a creative artist with an instinct for storytelling and your expertise as an organizer are both very important. Your gifts for spotting and assembling talent and then delegating authority to directors, writers, composers, editors, art directors, set designers, cinematographers and other above- and below-the-line professionals are honed as you refine your craft. Your passion and professionalism are signs of a truthful belief in the ability of others to support your dreams. During pre-production on a studio project, I was having some early budget control disputes with the studio production manager assigned to the picture. We did not see eye-to-eye on the sequence of pre-production spending in relation to the creative aspects of the project. He wanted to spend money right away on a coordinator, and I wanted to wait until we were further along in pre-production. He noted this to the studio brass and I was soon ordered to report to the head of the studio. One of my executive producers heard about the incident and asked me if I was sure I could bring the picture in for what I had estimated. I absolutely confirmed to him that I could and would, but I had to do it my independent way. That afternoon, putting all his faith in my response, we met with the studio brass. By the end of the meeting, we not only had the studio supporting our tenets of independent producing, but also agreeing that I would determine when and how the budget was spent on the picture. It was their money and they knew we were out to protect it for the project. (Ultimately, the picture came in $70,000 *under* budget.)

On the same project, a writer was assigned to write a screenplay based on a well-known novel. The screenplay that came in six weeks later bore very little resemblance to the novel. At the first story conference I patiently asked the writer if he had gotten it out of his system. He looked at me strangely and then a smile curled up his mouth and sheepishly nodded his head. I handed him back the script and told him to write it again—this time using the novel as his basis for the story.

You are the coach. People depend on you for advice, guidance, wisdom and knowledge of what must be done to complete the project (and win the game). Some coaches work from the sidelines, some from the air boxes. Some rely on their defensive or offensive coaches to call certain plays, while others do it themselves. Like coaches, producers work in different ways. Some producers delegate a lot of the creative above-the-line responsibility to a director, while others play a more active role. Some employ a line producer for logistical below-the-line decisions affecting creative production decisions, while others want to take that responsibility. Some producers share the producing chores in collaboration with other producers, and some give all the producing responsibilities to others but contractually take the onscreen credit as a producer.

Producing for television is very different than producing a theatrical project. Producers in television must learn how to "pitch" (verbally sell a story or idea) and work with a variety of writers. In television many writers are also the producers who work with network executives to refine the show's creative elements. They must know how to work with temperamental actors who make more demands as their popularity increases and how to reduce costs to conform to specific budgets while producing shows in volume with increasing creativity. And the shows must be entertaining, informative and thought provoking to stay on the air.

Producing has no age boundaries and its demands are different from project to project. These demands are challenged by the producer's creativity, knowledge of the process of production, the End Result Use of the project, and the producer's willingness to be the last word for the project. When any of these responsibilities are delegated or assigned to someone else, it may essentially be because the producer does not have the sureness to tackle the producing or does not understand the creative relationship of the story to the process and the budget. You must have courage and tenacity to produce. Knowing about some of the tools that are available to do the job will also be helpful.

PRODUCING TOOLS AND RESOURCES

Besides your passion, common sense, relationships, creativity, the budget and the production board, there are several other tools that a producer calls upon to assist in the role of producing. First are reference books that have digests of the various contracts and agreements of unions and guilds in the United States and throughout the world. You can buy these on Internet websites, at industry tradeshows or at various bookstores that specialize in books on the entertainment industry. Second are reference books that contain the names of companies involved in the process of film and video production. They are books like *The Hollywood Creative Directory*, *The Producers Motion Picture Directory*, *Kemps International Directory* and *LA411*. Again, you will be able to buy them and other books at bookstores, trade shows and on the Internet.

Third, there are subscription trade papers that provide daily and weekly information about the industry. The two largest are *Daily Variety* and the *Hollywood Reporter*. Although the trade press is often a tool for publicists to create hype around people, projects and events, if you are skilled at "reading between the lines" you will get an idea of what creative talent and businesses are doing and cull knowledge concerning the use of the latest technologies.

Along the same lines there are various subscription magazines that offer information regarding independent filmmaking, video production, Internet activity and technological innovations. *On Location* magazine focuses on issues involving shooting productions on location and publishes contact numbers for film commissions throughout the world.

Fourth, as an informed independent producer, you should visit the trade show conventions that take place several times a year. At Showbiz Expo (held in Los Angeles and New York), vendors demonstrate the latest technological equipment used in video and film production as well as the latest in digital and new media technology. NAPTE (National Association of Programming and Television Executives) is a buying and selling marketplace for television product throughout the world. A visit to this trade show helps you understand the marketplace for the end use of your product. It also lets you meet various buyers of product and sets future relationships. The NAB (National Association of Broadcasters) is one of the largest conventions in the world. A visit to this convention allows you to see the latest in sound and picture production and post-production technology. It focuses on video and the explosion taking place in the digital environment, its impact as a replacement for film and the possibilities of its end use.

Every state in the United States, as well as countries throughout the world, realizes the value of motion picture and video production to their economies. Therefore film commissions have been established by countries, states, counties and cities—each with the mandate of encouraging production in their locale. Most of them are members of an organization called Association of Film Commissioners International (AFCI) (afci.org). Several times a year they hold a Locations Global Expo to show producers, directors, location managers and other interested parties what they have to offer. Since they compete with one another for your business they offer inducements to the producer. Among them might be sales tax incentives, personal location services or housing and transportation assists. Some areas do not have unions or guilds; some offer financial discounts due to the exchange rate of the U.S. dollar. All commissions provide published manuals and guides that detail area vendors and local talent both behind and in front of the camera. A visit to a Locations Global Expo will open any producer's eyes to the creative possibilities that await their production.

Once you have decided on a geographic location for your project, make sure you contact the appropriate film commissioner during pre-production for whatever assistance they may be able to offer. The size of the project makes no difference. Several years ago I was producing a pilot for a reality television series. The segment we were doing focused on Roy Rogers, the famed television cowboy. The segment took my two-man crew and me to Portsmouth, Ohio. I contacted Eve LaPolla the Ohio Film Commissioner at the time, requesting whatever assistance she could provide. We had quite a surprise when we landed in Columbus, Ohio—as we disembarked from the plane, we heard the Ohio State University fight song and then saw a high

———— • • • ————

It's Sunday at 7:00 a.m. and I am just stirring in bed when the telephone rings. It is the voice of a Locations Manager who tells me to hang on as he turns the phone over to the Production Manager who says, "Del, I am in trouble—one of the talent for the film being shot is detained at the Miami airport. American Airlines will not allow him to board as he is of Colombian citizenship and does not have a visa to enter Jamaica. You must help me as the project cannot be delayed!" "It's Sunday," I tell him. "You have to do something," he says, "call somebody!" Jamaica being the island it is, I rushed to my office, made a few calls, faxed off a letter to American Airlines in Miami—and the Columbian actor was on the plane. In a few hours he was in Jamaica. Such is the power of the Film Commission.

—Del Crooks, Film Commissioner of Jamaica

———— • • • ————

school marching band in the middle of the airport. Standing in the midst of the musicians were Eve and her staff holding signs welcoming us to Ohio. We were escorted to a waiting limousine that drove us to Portsmouth. As we pulled up to our hotel, a sign on the marquee welcomed us to the "wonderful state of Ohio." The next two days of shooting went very smoothly thanks to the organization and enthusiasm of the Ohio Film Commission.

The computer is a major tool for the producer. If the producer is the writer the computer lets the writer/producer deliver changes on the spot. Software programs that are specific to budget and scheduling (like Movie Magic or Turbo Budget A/D), are a common part of the producer's tool bag. Be aware that this software only allows for the input and manipulation of information, not the tenets or philosophy of producing.

Finally, the Internet is a powerful tool for producers. It is full of sites containing easily accessible information about available services. Not only can you find information on vendors, locations and talent but the Internet also has many sites detailing festivals, cast and crew listings, and synopses of projects. Sites such as *www.laiff.com* (L.A. Independent Film Festival) and *www.e.bell.ca/filmfest* (Toronto International Film Festival) are fine examples. *IFCTV.com* links to production companies, film festivals, resources, information on channel programming and schedules and a chat room on film. *IFILM.com* links to 30,000 plus film sites and is also a netcaster for independent short films. *www.IFP.org* is the Independent Feature Project's home page and *www.IndieWire.com* has a lot of information about independent productions, reviews, deals and their structure and film and video festival news. *www.Indie.IMDB.com* is the Independent Film Internet Movie Database and spotlights independent films. It is a popular site since it contains 230,000 entries (that may or may not be entirely accurate—sometimes you get what you pay for when you use free data) on films produced from 1892 to those in pre-production. And *www.pbs.org* is an independent site geared towards nonfiction, archives and documentary projects.

The Internet offers product sites, music sites, legal sites, and other sites that you will want to bookmark permanently on your computer. The sites grow and change every month and it is worth a search to see which may be best for your needs.

PRODUCING FINANCE PARTNERS

There are many companies that actively finance projects (either as co-productions, or sole financing) or provide completion bonds for independent productions. Each will require certain documents or specific terms in order to consider a relationship with a producer. They may require creative involvement or approval and finance control. They may also increase your budget with a finance fee adding to your negative cost. Companies of this sort are international and are familiar with independent funds, tax shelters and private investment capital. There are Internet sites that offer these scenarios as well. Some websites, like *www.surfview.com* offer a complete list of projects looking for investors and investors looking for projects. Other websites, such as *www.investrum.com,* have set up extensive proprietary data collection mechanisms whereby qualifying producers may enter their project details and funding needs online and investors are matched with their projects. The match is always based upon certain parameters set by the finance partners. You must examine the reliability and integrity of these Internet sites and visit them cautiously. Your communication is through a computer and not face to face with a representative. You are never quite sure who you are negotiating with so caution should always be your byword. This can have an affect on a producer's financial risk, so legal advice is necessary before entering into any financial relationship.

FINANCE

Financing entities have affiliation with financial groups like KC Medien, CineArtists Entertainment, Imperial Bank; Entertainment Finance Group of Melbourne, Australia; Independent Film Financing of Toronto, Media Entertainment Funding; GmbH of Munich, Germany; General Motors Acceptance Corporation, Southern Pacific Bank and US Bancorp. They work through various financial structures including equity, tax sheltered investments, structured finance, private placements, full or partial collateralized loans, distribution presales or gap financing, and they may look for solid distribution situations to secure the funding. Usually these companies, before considering involvement, want solid and experienced producers, completion bonds and details of the project that may include a story synopsis, chain of title showing ownership and copyright, detailed budget of the negative cost, a possible project cash flow, details of the collateral for any loan and a minimum estimate of the value of the unsold film rights. Many of them have individual parameters and like to get involved with the project

---

PRODUCERS VOCABULARY

Cash Flow Statement—Weekly estimate of the flow of monies to be spent on the project. Usually required by a banking institution or completion bond company.

Pre-sales—Territorial sales of a project to distributors worldwide before the project is completed.

as early as possible. Their focus is on content and the package and they look towards projects that have good stories, ideas and characters.

Some companies will have a limit on the investment while others arrange financing for as little as $1 million to as much as $100 million dollars. A few of these companies are listed below.

Cinema Financial Services
112 Madison Ave. 12th Floor
New York, New York 10016
E mail: Support@cinemaFinancial.com

Natexis Banque
660 South Figueroa St. Suite 400
Los Angeles, California 90017
E-mail: bpozil@natexisny.com

Lewis Horwitz Organization
1840 Century Park East Suite 1000
Los Angeles, California 90067

Newmarket Capital Group
202 North Canon Drive
Beverly Hills, California 90210

Imperial Entertainment Group
9777 Wilshire Blvd. 4th Floor
Beverly Hills, California 90212

John Sloss
Sloss Law Office
170 5th Avenue
New York, NY 10010

Kramer and Kaslow
2029 Century Park East Suite 1700
Los Angeles, California 90067

Union Bank of California
1901 Avenue of the Stars, Suite 120
Los Angeles, California 90067

Law Offices of Mark Litwak
and Associates
9595 Wilshire Blvd Suite 711
Beverly Hills, California 90212
E-mail: litwak@attglobal.net

US Bank
1888 Century Park East Suite 915
Los Angeles, California 90067

CO-FINANCING

Co-financed projects are becoming commonplace. Co-financing makes sense for the larger studios as it shares the risk of higher budget projects—as in the case of *Titanic* (Paramount Pictures and 20th Century Fox) or *Meet the Parents* (DreamWorks and Universal). Studios are trying to make more projects while minimizing their financial outlay. Although co-financing reduces financial exposure, studios might look to how the projects are produced for the solution to higher budget projects. Today the independent film world is larger than it has ever been and projects take different routes to get into the marketplace. It is not enough any longer for the independent producer to have an independent voice, as there is a huge amount of product (good and bad) available.

The independent market demands more from the producer than just making the project. It requires the producer to maneuver through the film festival circuit or to find a distributor and make sure the distributor handles the project properly. The producer must look towards project marketability and audience demographics. This used to be the domain of just the distributor but since independent projects are now made for niche audiences (focusing on race, religion or sexual preference, etc.); the producer must have a stronger handle on these demographics. This market specialization is transpiring more and more in the cable market and with smaller pictures for theatrical distribution.

There are many independent companies who seek projects that fall within these guidelines and through their relationships can help to finance, produce and distribute independent projects. Each company has different methods and requirements for financing. In all cases they want creative input or control, a percentage of equity participation in the project, or complete ownership. They will be your creative partner, so make sure that the relationship is right for you. These companies look for projects within specific genres or budget ranges and may ask for packaged projects with high level names attached; they may look for projects geared for a specific market. What they all ask for, however, are strong narrative scripts with good characters or interesting non-narrative projects with unique approaches. You find these companies selling product and looking for projects and relationships at film marketplaces like the American Film Market (AFM), the Milan International Film Festival (MIFED), or the Cannes Film Festival. You also find listings of these companies two or three times a year in the trade papers or in periodical journals. Word of mouth can also lead you to the right doors.

COMPLETION BONDS

No matter how you finance your independent project, financing looks to the completion bond as security. Several completion bond companies aggressively seek independent projects and have experienced production people on staff; but they still will look at the expertise of the producer and director before considering participation. Many of them consider bonding lower budget projects while some consider only projects in the higher ranges (up to $100 million dollars). There are bonding companies that bond foreign projects and do business in foreign countries. Others only focus on projects that are produced in the United States and Canada. Completion bond companies establish production and location contacts through the course of doing business and are an excellent resource for you. Some of these companies are:

Cinema Completion International Inc.
4040 Vineland Avenue, Suite 204
Studio City, California 91604
e-mail: Filmbond@aol.com

Film Finances
9000 Sunset Blvd. Suite 1400
Los Angeles, California 90069
website: www.ffi.com

International Film Guarantors
Los Angeles, California

Motion Picture Bond Company
1801 Avenue of the Stars
Los Angeles, California 90067
e-mail: jhobel@mpbc.com

Worldwide Film Completion
2901 28th Street Suite 290
Santa Monica, California 90405

Producing today is fast paced. Years ago a producer could work at a slower pace, but not anymore! The computer, cell phone, palm pilot and other portable communication devices are all essential for the active producer. The decisions that producers make every day must be made quickly and confidently. Information is essential.

FILM FESTIVALS

The film or video festival circuit is becoming more important in getting your project distributed. It seems, however, that there are more festivals throughout the world than there are feature projects and more are springing up all the time. They are becoming one of the more popular marketplaces for independent productions. The oldest is the Cannes Film Festival, which premiered in 1946 and each spring becomes the center of world glamour as studios and producers send their stars and directors to France to help the promotion of their film projects. The granddaddy and most progressive of the current independent festival circuit is the Sundance Film Festival, the gold ring independent producers reach for in the festival circuit. Originally, it offered only feature projects, but has since expanded into documentary, short, animation and experimental forms.

Short narratives are becoming more important as the marketplace for shorts have opened up worldwide. The Nortel Palm Springs International Film Festival, founded by Sonny Bono, has two festivals—one for features and one for shorts. The Santa Barbara Film Festival is planned on the heels of the American Film Market held in Los Angeles and occurs just before the final Oscar® ballot deadline. The Berlin International Film Festival focuses on independent features, shorts, documentaries and animation. The festival of festivals is the Toronto International Film Festival which compiles the cream of the crop of films from festivals throughout the world and likes to screen specialty and art films that might have a difficult time getting started. Toronto has become an important festival; in 1999 *American Beauty* premiered there, in 2000 it was *Billy Elliot*. The Television Academy of Arts and Sciences has a video festival competition every year, and more and more digital festivals are appearing throughout the world.

But getting into a festival is one thing. Having the support from the festival is another, which is why you must examine the festival circuit very cautiously. Researching the right festival for your project can make all the difference. Some people think that with short projects, the more festivals you are in, the better, while others believe that you need to find a festival that will premier and back your feature project. The festival circuit can create a buzz and help you find a domestic or international distributor. It can help you get the ultimate prize, an Academy Award®, or it can help you raise your goals to a new level.

The Internet is a good source for film festivals throughout the world. Several good web directory sites with links are *www.ifilm.com*, *www.filmthreat.com* (independent movies), *www.moviebytes.com*, *www.marklitwak.com* and *www.insidefilm.com*.

——— • • • ———

In the multicamera format a creative producer is invaluable. The technical considerations while directing a multicamera shoot can be overwhelming and distracting. A well-trained, talented creative producer can offer an objective eye and provide insights toward realizing the potential of the work. A strong collaborative relationship between the director and the creative producer is an unquestionable asset for any production.

—Herb Stein, Director, *Days of Our Lives*

——— • • • ———

EPILOGUE

NOW WHAT?

Now what? The digital revolution is here. It is in our life, in our daily work. It is very much a part of producing. It cannot be ignored. Not only is it part of the pre-production and production process, but it is opening up new sources of revenue. Industry studios, unions and guilds are jockeying for position. By example, in 2001 the Writers Guild made DVD, Internet and video compensation an issue in their contract negotiations. The Directors Guild has also been monitoring the Internet's growth and potential. They have approved a highly flexible budgetary agreement for their members to work on direct-to-Internet productions. And the Screen Actors Guild made the direct-to-Internet product one of its issues at the 2001 contract negotiations.

The Internet is offering independent producers the possibility of new revenue as people can pay a fee to watch product on their personal computer. Although the quality is not yet up to theater or television standards, and the technology to show quality video is still not installed on the majority of home computers, it is just a matter of time before material can land at the local theater, a flat-screen monitor or a television set in any room in your home. In a few years you will be able to watch a cooking show from the Internet on a television set in your kitchen. And there is no doubt that the marriage of interactive television and the Internet is around the corner.

Projects are now being specifically created for the Internet, as demonstrated by IFILM.com, a leading online film portal. Sundance's Online Film Festival runs short projects ranging from documentaries to dramas to comedy and cartoons, all using either flash animation or other digital media technologies.

Production companies that produce for film and television have mandated producing product for the Internet. The issue of copyright and piracy in cyberspace, long a major problem, is being technologically resolved through revolutionary licensing services that allow distribution of digital content while maintaining continual downstream control over the use rights of the content to wherever it is accessed. So it is only a matter of time before the Internet becomes its own major market with a requirement for original educational, informational and entertainment product. Most importantly, you can be your own distributor on the Internet. All you need is the product a web presence and a server. It's happening!

Movies personally viewed digitally are here and the demand for original product is around the corner. Once this is part of our daily life, you will be producing volume product specifically for digital viewing. On a recent flight from the East Coast I saw three different passengers watching at three different movies on their laptop computers, while yet a fourth movie was being played on video for the passengers who rented headsets. On that same trip three other people were playing digital games—all of which realize new forms of narrative. It's happening!

Independent filmmakers are enticed by digital video, using Mini-DV cameras capable of swapping out lenses to make very (very) low budget features or to experiment with new techniques. Richard Linklater (*SubUrbia* and *The Newton Boys*) premiered the non-narrative *Waking Life* at the 2001 Sundance Film Festival. It was shot entirely on digital video, edited and then animated using a computer interpolated rotoscoping technique in which colors, lines, characters and objects are continually flowing and moving. Film directors like Wayne Wang and Allison Anders are finding a new and previously unavailable narrative freedom with digital video. But as technology collides with creativity, they also found limitations in staging and scope. There are still unresolved questions about how the image will look if transferred to film or seen on the big screen. Digital video techniques mean that projects can be made more cheaply and more quickly, and this allows films to be made that might not get made through traditional means. But it also imposes limitations or changes in how creativity is employed. The newest 24p digital high definition environment offers resolution running at the rate of 24p frames per second and is fast becoming the standard medium for film mastering and high quality television production. And with the 24p cameras, for original feature work, the end result, although on video, can look like any grain of any film stock manufactured.

There is an enormous explosion taking place, and the outcome is unpredictable. Film may cease to exist as a medium; digital may take over entirely. The End Result Use in distribution will shift as a result. When *Star Wars: Episode - The Phantom Menace* was distributed, it was the first major feature film to be projected digitally in certain theaters. The day may come when everything will originate digitally and be distributed through satellites into a theater, your home or a computer monitor. It is happening!

These technological changes are changing the economics of production and the whole structure of the industry. A producer who only looks to today's marketplace for the End Result Use is a producer who will be behind the curve tomorrow. Technology will forever open horizons, you must have the courage and foresight to be there when it happens.

What does this all mean to you, the producer? It won't change the tenets of producing, but will change the way you go about it. It means that you will make better product for less. With careful thought it is already possible to make a feature film for under $75,000. Both SAG and the DGA already have agreements that permit their members to work for little or deferred payment (or no money at all) at this budget range. Also, you need a contemporary story or project that focuses on character and schedules out over a short time period. Next, digital cameras eliminate the need to purchase and process film stock. They offer new types of mobility, and, while there may be some impact on picture quality, they easily afford enormous ability to adjust for difficult lighting conditions. Relatively inexpensive nonlinear editing equipment is now available, with sound mixing capabilities that permit you to simplify the post-production process and do it in your home. Finally, with the creativity, relationships and passion of the group of people you assemble (following the tenets of producing offered in this book) you can succeed with a very, very, very, low budget feature. It may not be as full in scope as it might be with more resources, as you may be limited with your locations and production values. It may have technical and logistical problems because of the trial and error process of the typically inexperienced crew. And it may present creative restrictions for your director. But if you make the "shoe fit the foot," employ the egos of people to your advantage, and welcome the relationships made during your project, you will be able to accomplish your goal. (However, depending on the end use of the product you might need to find additional resources to transfer to a film negative for distribution. Nevertheless if you think Z-A when you plan, you will know what to do.)

By the time you read this book, there will be new digital wizardry available to you. But the technical and digital wizardry is not what it is about. It is about content, creative vision and a passion to reveal the human condition. It is about dreaming the dream, achieving your goal and telling the story as best you can. The path you take (be it film or digital) is not important. The content is what matters, without it you have nothing—and all the digital wizardry in the world cannot make it better. Now go ahead! Be creative, be courageous, be visionary, be innovative and *Produce!*

INDEX

ABOUT THE AUTHOR

Myrl Schreibman began his career as an actor, and after graduating with his Masters Degree in Theater specializing in Film and Television, he went to work with the legendary filmmaker Jack Arnold, who gave him his on-the-job education in producing and directing. A member of the Directors Guild of America, Myrl Schreibman has produced and directed for feature films, network and cable television, the concert stage, Broadway and regional theater, all to critical acclaim and recognition. His film work has received awards of excellence and his reputation as a producer who is able to "make a quarter look like a dollar onscreen" goes unmatched. For the past fifteen years, Myrl Schreibman has been with the UCLA School of Theater Film and Television and has taught seminars on producing and directing internationally. He consults to several production companies and continues to produce, direct and teach, nurturing new talent along the way.

This book is for everyone, including my fellow actors employed by producers: No film, or for that matter, any form of entertainment would ever see the light of day if the hands of the producer were not holding the reins. The producer's work is not only creative, but also reaches into the areas of financing, gathering people together and playing Mom and Dad to the entire cast and crew. Myrl has played that part so well; for me it was a joy, because I always felt I was not working for him, but with him. As a creative producer (and director), he makes actors feel that it each project is truly a collaborative effort. We actors have to thank Myrl (and producers like him) for the smooth ride over sometimes bumpy roads.

—Eugene Robert Glazer, Actor, *La Femme Nikita*

"Myrl Schreibman empowered me with the tools that enabled me to sell my first project, (The Deal), which is currently in pre-production with a major studio! Myrl's arsenal of knowledge armed me with the ability to negotiate and ultimately receive a co-producer credit, in addition to my screenwriter credit. Without a doubt, Myrl Schreibman's class was one of the most important classes I took while attending U.C.L.A's Graduate School of Film. This book is a must read"

—Joe Lisuzzo, Writer/Producer, Intrepid Entertainment, Inc.

"David (Selby) and I took Myrl Schreibman's course on creative producing at UCLA and we found it an invaluable source for all the ABC's of producing films and television. We soon realized that it was the definitive guide with the theories and nuts and bolts of low-budget production covering the A to Z of successful producing. It provided the knowledge and expertise that we needed to be successful in our production company . . . it is a must-read for anyone before diving into the complicated waters of producing. Everyday we find his theories to be more accurate because of the industry's demand for quality with very little money; especially in television! He is the definitive producer for a project with limited currency."

—Chip Selby, JRA Productions, Inc.